Before Borders

Before Borders

A Legal and Literary History of Naturalization

STEPHANIE DEGOOYER

Johns Hopkins University Press
Baltimore

© 2022 Johns Hopkins University Press
All rights reserved. Published 2022
Printed in the United States of America on acid-free paper
9 8 7 6 5 4 3 2 1

Johns Hopkins University Press
2715 North Charles Street
Baltimore, Maryland 21218
www.press.jhu.edu

Library of Congress Cataloging-in-Publication Data is available.

ISBN 978-1-4214-4391-1 (hardcover)
ISBN 978-1-4214-4392-8 (paperback)
ISBN 978-1-4214-4393-5 (ebook)

A catalog record for this book is available from the British Library.

Special discounts are available for bulk purchases of this book. For more information, please contact Special Sales at specialsales@jh.edu.

For Johan Louis DeGooyer
In memoriam

CONTENTS

Acknowledgments ix

Introduction: Open Country 1

PART I. THEORIES OF NATURALIZATION

1. Naturalization in History 33

2. Ideas of Naturalization 62

PART II. FICTIONS OF NATURALIZATION

3. Law of the Foreign Father 85

4. Open-Door Domestic Fiction 113

PART III. RELATIONS OF NATURALIZATION

5. Unnatural-Born Subjects 145

Coda: The World of Yesterday 169

Notes 175
Index 197

ACKNOWLEDGMENTS

Though I did not know it at the time, the seeds of this book were sown when I worked at an immigration law firm in Toronto, Canada. It was while compiling dossiers on behalf of people wishing to immigrate to the United States and Canada that I first began to understand the relationship between narrative and immigration. Later, at Cornell University, I had the extraordinarily good fortune to expand my thinking with Elizabeth Anker, Rick Bogel, Laura Brown, Jonathan Culler, Isaac Kramnick, and especially Neil Saccamano, who encouraged me to follow my ideas and introduced me to texts that would inspire my thinking for many years. A collaborative project with Alastair Hunt, Lida Maxwell, Samuel Moyn, and Astra Taylor for Verso Books also prompted early thinking for this book. Our cowritten book not only led me to Hannah Arendt's writing on historical naturalization regimes, but it also offered a rigorous model of cross-disciplinary scholarship.

I wrote the first draft of this manuscript in Cambridge, Massachusetts, through a fellowship from the Harvard Radcliffe Institute and a visiting professorship in the Harvard English Department. My deepest gratitude to the Radcliffe Institute staff—Sharon Bromberg-Lim, Tomiko Brown-Nagin, Rebecca Haley, Sean O'Donnell, Meredith Quinn, and Hyun Jin Yoo—for providing every imaginable resource to support my work. Special thanks as well to my exceptional research assistants—Jessica Boutchie, Lani Roberts, Tamara Shamir, and Amanda Wasserman—who brought comradery and organization to archival labor. My first year in Cambridge was intellectually richened, and made considerably more fun, by the fellowship of Jessica Bardsley, Hernan de Valle, Moon Duchin, Malick Galchem, Francisco Goldman, Lauren Groff, Sam Klug, Min Jin Lee, David Levine, Nicole Nelson, Dana Sadji, Katie Turk, and Javier Zamora. When I moved across campus to the English Department, James Engell, Deidre Lynch, and Nicholas Watson made me feel at home and saw me through the early days of the pandemic. This book would also not have been possible without a generous, and flexible, Burkhardt fellowship from the American Council of Learned Societies, which allowed me time to complete the manuscript remotely at the University of California, Los Angeles. My new academic home, the University of North Carolina at Chapel Hill, provided pivotal financial support for the final stages.

This book was sharpened along the way by several invitations to talk and write about the ideas presented within. I was especially glad to deliver public lectures hosted by the Radcliffe Institute and the Mahindra Humanities

Center. At Harvard, I was also lucky to be asked by the organizers of the Tanner Lectures to converse with Masha Gessen in a seminar about migration. I am also thankful to have been an invitee of the "Exodus and Exile" conference, hosted by Jonathan Sachs and Josephine McDonagh at the Clark Memorial Library; feedback from this event made a substantial difference. A timely invitation from Hector Hoyos to present material from this book at Stanford University led to fruitful exchanges with Karan Barad and Bernadette Meyler, which strengthened several sections. I am also grateful for invitations from Johns Hopkins University (courtesy of Bécquer Seguín) and the University of Melbourne (courtesy of Marc Mierowsky) to speak about material from Chapters 1 and 3. Chapter 2 benefited tremendously from the thoughtful commentary of the Southern California Eighteenth-Century Working Group; special thanks to Bethany Johnson and Sarah Kareem for arranging this meeting. Various friends and colleagues have helped me at various stages, and I wish to thank, Heather Furnas, Roland Greene, Thomas Keenan, Samuel Moyn, Anne Schult, Dustin Stewart, Joshua Swidzinski, Dennis Todd, and Eugenia Zuroski.

As this book came to be, it profited enormously from the generous feedback of several readers. My eternal thanks to David Alff, Ala Alryyes, David Armitage, Ian Balfour, Andrew Bricker, Rose Casey, Ashley Cohen, Jenny Davidson, Matthew Hart, John Havard, Ryan Heuser, Allison Hobgood, Alastair Hunt, Collin Jennings, Rachael Scarborough King, Jonathan Kramnick, Deidre Lynch, Bernadette Meyler, Marc Mierowsky, Jason Pearl, Forest Pyle, Corey Robins, Simon Stern, Charlotte Sussman, Christopher Trigg, Susan Wolfson, and especially Stefanos Geroulanos and Marisa Pagano. I owe a significant and unpayable debt to Bécquer Seguín, whose marginal comments and phone calls not only made me a better thinker and writer but also kept my spirits up during bleak moments. Your friendship means the world to me, Bécquer. This book would not exist without you.

The global pandemic, during which this book was completed, produced many personal and professional setbacks, and there are many who helped me continue my work. That I was able to access crucial books and archival material is entirely due to the kindness and creative thinking of librarians at Harvard's Hollis Library and UNC-Chapel Hill's Davis Library. Thanks are also due to the editorial team at Johns Hopkins University Press—Catherine Goldstead, Kait Howard, Kristina Lykke, Kathryn Marguy, and Helen Wheeler—for ushering this book into publication despite several setbacks. Some of the chapters in this book appeared previously in different form in *English Liter-*

ary History, and an earlier version of Chapter 4 was originally published as "The Poetics of the Passport in A Sentimental Journey," in *Sterne, Tristram, Yorick: Tercentenary Essays on Laurence Sterne*, ed. Melvyn New, Peter de Voogd, and Judith Hawley (Newark: University of Delaware Press, 2015), 201–18. All Rights Reserved.

Most of all, I would like to thank the friends and colleagues in my life who continually remind me that immigration is not merely a topic of academic study. For opportunities to talk, write, and think about the lived reality of immigration in our present moment, I thank Jenny Allsopp, Atossa Araxia Abrahamian, Deborah Chasman, Daniel Denvir, Hernan de Valle, Sarah Fan, Masha Gessen, Roberto Gonzoles, Yogita Goyal, Sharon Marcus, Jesús Rodríguez, Javier Zamora, UndocuCarolina, the Immigration Initiative at Harvard, the Rosa Luxembourg Foundation, and my students past and present.

This book is dedicated to my family, who have nourished me and sustained me across several countries: to my sister Genevieve, whose care packages, both material and immaterial, arrived in the United States at critical moments in my life, and above all to Kelly and Josephine, who moved many times to make my work possible. Home is wherever the both of you are. I love you immeasurably.

Before Borders

INTRODUCTION

Open Country

In 1952 Hannah Arendt, living in the United States as a newly naturalized citizen, identified the advent of the modern immigration regime. The year 1914, she argued in *The Origins of Totalitarianism*, was "like the day before and the day after an explosion."[1] In a matter of days, immigration law in Britain was dramatically altered. A day after Great Britain declared war on Germany on August 4, Parliament legalized the Aliens Restriction Act, which allowed the home secretary to deport aliens from the United Kingdom. Two days later, it passed the British Nationality and Status of Aliens Act, which codified nationality law for the first time—replacing centuries of unwritten common law and haphazardly interpreted statutes—and introduced the statutory power to deprive a naturalized subject of their citizenship. These new laws were a response to a wider movement across Europe to rid nations of newly classed enemy aliens. Their more far-reaching effect was to make citizenship, previously thought to be irrevocable, something that could be taken away. For the first time in modern history, people could be legally stateless on a mass scale.[2]

Statelessness was an extreme and unprecedented outcome of twentieth-century nationality law. Before a regime of mass denaturalization came to replace it, an older system of naturalization had long been used by European countries to integrate foreigners into their communities. During the interwar period, this system began to be viewed as inadequate for handling the large number of individuals seeking refuge across the continent. Rather than find paths of integration for refugees and stateless people, European countries found it preferable to expel or neglect them. To underscore the extremity of this treatment, Arendt drew a historical contrast with an earlier period in which states used naturalization to solve a refugee crisis. "Unlike their happier predecessors in the religious wars," she noted, modern refugees were "welcome nowhere and could be assimilated nowhere."[3]

The "happier predecessors" of the expelled interwar migrants were the French Huguenots. In 1685 Louis XIV revoked the Edict of Nantes, which had granted religious tolerance for Protestants in France, forcing hundreds of thousands of Huguenots to flee for hospitable European countries. The Huguenots emigrated during a time when nationality mattered little for immigration and was not yet a status that could be given or taken away by the state. Before the nineteenth century, nations in Europe imposed few residence, employment, or language requirements for naturalization; England in particular required no visa applications or work permits, established only a selective need for passports, and did not have the ability to revoke citizenship or deprive a citizen of nationality within their state of birth.[4] Millions of migrants were able to make their way across Europe and to the New World without need of identity documents. Thus, the Huguenots would have encountered few legal barriers to their flourishing outside France. Unlike refugees in the interwar era, they were seen as skilled workers, and naturalization was a tool many countries used to attract these laborers to their territories.

Arendt, like many of her contemporaries, chose not to elaborate on why naturalization was once easier for individuals such as the Huguenots. She did not wonder aloud, as this book will do at length, what naturalization was intended to make possible. To this day, naturalization is the only means by which a foreigner can become a citizen of a nation that is not theirs by birth or descent. The idea that someone deemed *foreign, unnatural,* or *strange* could, through the administrative alchemy of naturalization, become someone *familiar, common,* and *similar* is a fundamentally transformative procedure, not only for law but also for culture and politics more broadly. Naturalization emerged in the seventeenth century at a time when legal and cultural understandings of national belonging were witnessing the same larger transformation: the eclipse of, on the one hand, a medieval outlook of belonging as hierarchical and cemented by allegiance to the sovereign by, on the other, the concept of the voluntarism of contract, whereby individuals could choose their own allegiance.

This book will make two general claims about the history of early naturalization. The first is that naturalization in general is a far more radical procedure than we have realized. Long before nationality became something that could be stripped, it had to be conceived of as something that could be given. Naturalization was especially controversial because it bucked an older protocol of perpetual allegiance, which had long ruled that an individual's loyalty to a particular sovereign could never be broken or transferred. This had the knock-on effect of shifting sovereign authority over who could be an English subject from the Crown to Parliament and introducing the possibility that a person could have two or more allegiances. The second claim of this book is that naturalization is a more profoundly generative and creative act than we have previously understood. Today, it is often described as a negative form of cultural integration: a means of coercing individuals to adopt certain social and political characteristics. Yet naturalization was once imagined as a process for turning outsiders into subjects against the powerful natural logics of blood and soil. Through naturalization, national status became something that could be created for a new cast of individuals who, like the French Huguenots, lacked the right to be subjects by birth.

Naturalization created subjects. It was an inherently inventive procedure. Just as the effects of devices such as passports and border walls are never strictly administrative, naturalization has never been a strictly legal maneuver. Early debates about naturalization involved jurists as well as political philosophers and prose fiction writers. Novelists, in particular, explored new civic ideas of voluntary nationality and national expansion in the emergent genre of prose fiction. Several decades after writing political pamphlets in support of the 1709 Naturalization Act, the writer Daniel Defoe imagined the possibilities and risks of eighteenth-century naturalization in several of his novels. In *Robinson Crusoe* (1719), Defoe's titular character undergoes naturalization as a Catholic Portuguese subject in Bahia, the capital of Portugal's colonies in the Americas, to secure a lucrative sugarcane plantation. In *Roxana, the Fortunate Mistress* (1724), the protagonist is a French Huguenot who immigrates with her family to England because of its reputation for welcoming refugees with "open arms," before relocating to Holland to buy herself the title of countess.[5] Defoe depicts his migrants as free agents who travel and temporarily settle their persons and wealth according to self-interest, rather than governmental permission. Alongside jurists, economists, and political writers, novelists such as Defoe took to a new and undefined genre to explore the erosion of long-established protocols of birth and belonging that had hitherto bolstered the idea of nationality and the transformation of national allegiance into an artificial and elected status that could be exchanged or abandoned by individuals according to their self-interest.

The early system of naturalization in England was very different from our modern one, and the break with the old order Arendt noted was real. But the nuances of the shift, which were not as sudden as she observed, deserve closer scrutiny. As this book will elaborate, early practices and ideas of naturalization laid the groundwork for a vision of how subjects and citizens could be produced independent of the soil on which they were born or the blood from which they were descendants. This vision was energized by a distinct, but historically connected, new literary genre that simultaneously worked to undo centuries of classical conventions about which subjects could be dominantly represented in the space of literature. In seeking to understand the uniqueness of this idea in both legal and literary texts, we not only uncover a period of immigration history that proves naturalization's transformative power but also come to newly appreciate naturalization as a creative and fictional idea with a wide range of critical possibilities.

Legal Fiction

In early English common law, naturalization was a legal procedure akin to what we might today call immigration law. But unlike what is meant by the term today, early naturalization was thought to be a fictional procedure that manufactured allegiance for individual and national benefits. Over the course of the seventeenth and eighteenth centuries, naturalization emerged in the English Parliament as a new form of natural subject creation. In 1664, after the restoration of Charles II, a bill was presented to Parliament proposing to grant "universal naturalization" to "all Persons of all Nations, of all Religions, Protestants, Papists, Jews, Mohametans, Turks, Moors, [and] Pagans."[6] The chief advantage of an open-door naturalization policy, proponents argued, was that it would address a depopulation crisis propelled by migration to the New World while also growing England's trade by allowing foreign merchants easy access to English markets. Though the bill did not pass, it inspired other attempts at a general naturalization bill across the seventeenth century and generated a flurry of debate among thinkers including John Locke.[7] In 1709, as England's population was believed to be precipitously in decline, the Whig-dominated English Parliament resurrected the idea of a general naturalization bill to encourage the immigration of new merchants and craftspeople to Britain—specifically the French Protestant Huguenots. As skilled weavers, the Huguenots were especially sought-after foreigners, and England, alongside other European countries, was keen to attract their settlement by offering rights and privileges typically denied to foreigners, such as the right to inherit and to pass down real property and exemption from duties typically levied on aliens. On March 23, 1709, Parliament passed the Foreign Protestants Naturalization Act (10 Anne c. 5). By producing a certificate from a judge (signed by two witnesses) testifying they had taken sacrament in an English church, aliens could take oaths of allegiance and have their names entered into an oath's roll, giving them henceforth the same status "as if they had been born in England."[8]

For all its ingenuity, general naturalization was a relatively short-lived legal possibility. In 1709, the same year as the passage of the Naturalization Act, more than thirteen thousand German refugees known as the "Poor Palatines" arrived in England to seek shelter from French invasion and famine in their homeland. Perceived as poor farmers with little to offer England, the German refugees were abandoned in an encampment outside London. In 1711 (10 Anne c. 9) the 1709 act was repealed by the Tories, leaving the Palatines to be shipped to Ireland and then the American colonies rather than settle in England.[9] In 1753 a proposed bill for a Jewish naturalization act, which would allow Jews to become naturalized by application to Parliament, barely passed the House of Commons before being repealed following an anti-Semitic outcry involving hundreds of newspaper columns, pamphlets, and satirical and political cartoons. While naturalization, in its most radical expression in the late seventeenth century, was proposed for "all Persons of all Nations, of all Religions," by the end of eighteenth century, the idea of universal naturalization had failed in law.[10]

In fact, by the end of the Revolutionary War, when thousands of Black loyalists and enslaved persons migrated to England from America, the idea of universal naturalization had all but disappeared. In 1771 the abolitionist Granville Sharpe tried to persuade his countrymen that skin color should not impede the naturalization of Black enslaved persons and servants as British subjects because "every person who, in any respect, is in subjection to the laws, must undoubtedly be a subject."[11] The British had offered freedom to enslaved African Americans if they fought on behalf of Britain during the American Revolution. But by 1786, the question of what to do with the hundreds of Black migrants who now walked the streets of London resulted in the Sierra Leone Resettlement Scheme: the "Black Poor" were granted citizenship in Britain's new colony in Sierra Leone in exchange for their emigration *from* England.[12] Rather than lean on naturalization as a means of providing rights and privileges to the Black loyalists, as it had done for the French Huguenots, the British government chose to export the loyalists elsewhere, bringing into view an end to an era of liberal naturalization that had already begun to falter with the bid for Jewish naturalization at midcentury. America was no exception to these restrictions. Though one of the grievances that ignited the American Revolution was British control over naturalization policies,

America would lead the way on racialized naturalization. In 1790, despite a perceived need in the United States to attract more settlers to its new republic, Congress nevertheless added a clause to its own naturalization act restricting American citizenship to only "free white person[s] . . . of good character."[13]

Despite its legislative failures—or because of them—the idea of naturalization rose to prominence across the eighteenth and early nineteenth centuries. Its influence, moreover, extended well beyond the legal sphere. Philosophical and literary proponents of the procedure argued that giving foreigners full political and civil rights, such as the right to own property and hold public office, would not only attract newcomers, it would better attach them to English soil. These newcomers might then settle and develop England's land and spur its trade, leading to an overall increase in the general wealth of the nation.[14] In 1693 John Locke made the case in an unpublished article that "Naturalization is the safest & easiest way of increasing y[ou]r people, w[hi]ch all wise govern[men]ts have encouraged by privileges granted to the fathers of children as the Justinium liberorum amongst the Romans."[15] In a series of pamphlets and later in the *Review*, Defoe promoted naturalization for similar reasons, arguing that the settlement of foreigners benefited England economically because it increased the size of its population, the volume of its trade, and its self-sufficiency in industry.[16]

Alongside this liberalizing outlook, fears that naturalized foreigners might upset England's natural order quickly spread. Tory critics of naturalization, such as Sir John Knight, lambasted general naturalization, arguing that foreigners would drain resources that, by natural right, belonged to English individuals. In 1694 Knight, an English merchant and politician, delivered an influential speech in opposition to a bill to naturalize Protestants in England. In his speech, of which tens of thousands of copies were printed and circulated, Knight insisted Parliament should "first kick the bill out of the House; and then let us kick the foreigners out of the kingdom."[17] A century later, Jonathan Swift, anticipating his satirical proposition of eating impoverished children to lessen their burden on society, griped that the 1709 Naturalization Act only succeeded in attracting poor refugees without means to sustain themselves. "To invite helpless families, by thousands," he wrote, "is a wrong application of the maxim, and the same thing, in great, as infants dropped at the doors, which are only a burden and charge to the parish."[18]

Beyond economics, the deeper issue for critics was how naturalization made foreigners into natural subjects without the rite of natural birth on which the early modern idea of allegiance had been understood. In a debate about whether England should have a standing army, the political pamphleteer Samuel Johnson (known as "the Whig" to distinguish him from Dr. Samuel Johnson) indicted the "modern policy" of general naturalization by calling it a "Fetch" that placed trust in foreigners whose allegiance could never be certain.[19] Compared to the English, foreigners were enemies who should not be regarded as "friends." "Who can vouch for inhabitants unknown?" Johnson asked.[20] Even Protestant refugees from France, whose plight Johnson pitied, or neighboring Dutchmen, whom he admired, should not be naturalized in England. The liberties of Englishmen should never be awarded "lightly" or errantly transferred to a foreigner.[21] To naturalize, in his opinion, was to *not* be natural and yet, unjustly, have the same rights as a natural-born subject. For Johnson and others, it was unclear in whose interest naturalization operated: Did the English nation receive advantages for the legal settlement of migrants, or did naturalization merely open England up to the individual benefit of foreign merchants, depressing the wages and livelihood of England-born subjects?

These same issues are at play in today's debates over immigration. However, unlike now, in the eighteenth century there was no general legal way to deny or prohibit the residence of aliens in England.[22] As Johnson admitted, England was an "open Country."[23] Foreigners were free to enter at any time; there was no military guard or standing army to thwart entry or escort removal, though there were other, less direct ways of policing migration in the form of the Poor Laws, penal transportation, and vagrancy laws.[24] Naturalization was a legal procedure designed to lift legal hardships by providing rights such as the right to pass down real property to children or to hold public office, both of which had historically been denied to foreigners. Naturalization was thus a positive freedom: the freedom to have the same rights as native subjects. It was the positive aspect of this freedom that critics objected to when they argued that naturalization would lead to the deterioration of a long-standing, unwritten practice of balancing out the rights of natural subjects and aliens. What disturbed them most was the erosion of a distinction they held to be naturally rather than positively given. To those who considered themselves true-born Englishmen, naturalization sounded a clarion call for a law that clearly defined who counted as an English subject and who was an alien. It allowed individuals with unverifiable births to purchase and pass down property horizontally (across national lines) rather than vertically through primogeniture. In the early seventeenth century, the landmark *Calvin's Case* (1608) sought to resolve questions concerning whether a Scottish toddler could inherit property in England, a kingdom in which he was not born. Before the case, there had been no written law determining who could be a subject of England; subjects were those born under the allegiance of the Crown. After the Union of the Crowns, which united Scotland and England under the same monarch, questions multiplied about whether Scots had rights as subjects in England. The justices in the case ruled that Scottish individuals born after the Union of the Crowns in 1603 were the natural subjects of King James, who inherited both the English and Scottish thrones. What we see in the reports on this case is that nationality law was first adjudicated through the question of how foreigners born outside the nation could be subjects *within* it. The ruling of *Calvin's Case*—that a Scot born outside England could still be, if born in relationship to the English Crown, a natural-born English subject—would set down the first common-law definition of the English subject and would later shape the rule of citizenship in the United States.

Calvin's Case would not stabilize questions about nationality, however. Fears about foreigners becoming natural subjects continued to proliferate, especially when a Dutch foreigner, William of Orange, inherited the English throne in 1689. A culmination of these concerns can be seen in a clause added to the 1701 Act of Settlement, which was passed to secure indefinite Protestant succession to the English throne. All people "born out of the Kingdoms of England, Scotland, or Ireland," the clause held, were barred from receiving a grant of land from the Crown and holding public office as a privy councillor or as a member of either house of Parliament.[25] In 1705, seemingly against this rule, Parliament passed a naturalization act to allow the accession of Princess Sophia, Electress and Duchess Dowager of Hanover, to the English throne. Clearly, the power of naturalization to produce a Protestant heir was deemed greater at this moment than the procedure's alleged threats to the stability of the realm. Even so, the clause to the Act of Settlement targeting those "naturalized or made a Denizen" reveals the extent to which naturalization preoccupied political and legal discourse in the period.

One way of understanding the general reactions to early naturalization is to examine them through what we would today call subject formation. Many scholars have written about the growth of the subject in the eighteenth century. They have, for the most part, been interested in the psychological sense of the subject: the subject as an individual who is perceived to have depth, privacy, and interiority.[26] This book tracks subject formation in the political sense—a sense that, importantly, works against the notion of interiorization. In his *Dictionary*, Dr. Samuel Johnson recognized that the idea of nationality was "publick, general; not private, not particular."[27] As we shall see, the alignment of law with the ostensibly natural act of subject production called attention to nationality as a public *and* perfunctory status. Far from surreptitiously working to secure national sovereignty as naturalization is thought to do today, naturalization in the eighteenth century created a voluntary, topical, and immediate form of belonging. It forged bonds of allegiance for foreigners who, according to interpretations of common law, were not naturally born into the "ligeance" of the English Crown. The idea that sacrosanct and unbreakable bonds of allegiance, given to individuals by the sovereign and through God, could be invented by a civil process of law was considered heretical in the extreme by many. As contemporaries of the naturalization debates claimed, naturalization was "but a *fiction of law*."[28] The procedure proposed to separate a fictive legal persona from an individual's natural self, thus allowing a foreigner to pass as natural under the law without being born as a natural subject.[29]

According to Lon Fuller, a legal fiction is that which is "adopted by its author with knowledge of its falsity." That is, it is an "expedient, but consciously false assumption."[30] Classic examples of legal fiction include the concept of corporate personhood, which artificially vests corporations with the distinctions of persons, such as residence and nationality, in order to provide them with legal rights. Another is the doctrine of survival, which uses age to fictionalize an account of who died first in the case of simultaneous death. As Simon Stern has argued, all law is shaped by legal fiction, but some legal fictions are more overt about their fictionality, laying bare the legal fiction's "own fashioning [as] . . . a means of exploring its attitude toward its imaginative status."[31] This is the case with naturalization. To become a rights-bearing person in the eyes of the law, foreigners had to assume an obviously artificial persona in law. In effect, through naturalization the natural, flesh-and-blood individual was replaced with a legal persona, or "persona ficta."[32] In Latin, *persona* originally referred to a theatrical mask, and this sense survives in the idea of a legal persona, an artificially designed identity meant to obscure personal and material facts of life.

Naturalization not only covered a person's interior with an exterior mask, it also replaced or overlooked that person's history. When a person naturalized, their past was changed to align the circumstances of their birth with those required for the purpose of the law. Unlike the modern practice of listing place of birth on official citizenship documents, early naturalization was a powerful legal mechanism that overlooked the material facts of an individual's birth to rewrite a foreigner's past for their new country. For the purposes of administering the law, especially property rights, a foreigner seeking to become a subject needed to be "reborn" in England. The notion that a foreigner could simply change their native allegiance proved unsettling to many. If a person could administratively become a subject of a sovereign under whom they were not born, then natural birth was no longer the decisive factor for national belonging. Most worrisome, naturalization meant that subjects could change their allegiance multiple times, undermining the once-unbreakable relation between sovereign and subject, the common-law principle of *ne exuere ligeantian*, or perpetual allegiance. Natural ties could be dissolved by a civil act of legislature.

Yet critics of naturalization remained blind to how messy and unclear the allegiances of natural-born subjects actually were. There were no definitive legal precedents or statutes for handling such subjects. The difference between subjects and aliens, before the seventeenth century, had been understood, mythologized even, rather than legally expressed. After King John seized the English lands of individuals loyal to the French king Philip II in 1206, a general deduction held that "aliens" were those who were not permitted to own land in England. This was an assumption that would be tested by *Calvin's Case* in 1608. The question of whether foreigners could be made into subjects, beyond the accident of a king assuming two thrones, would occupy cases linked to a Scottish-born earl, John Ramsey. But these cases opened as many questions about allegiance as they settled.

To try to set these relations straight, writers from across the fields of philosophy, literature, and politics argued vigorously about the function of naturalization law and the language it used to create England's newest subjects. While, for its opponents, naturalization was a practice that would effectively lead to England's downfall, thanks to the introduction of spies who lacked an inborn sense of allegiance, for supporters such as Locke and Defoe, the ability to exit the obligations of a prior allegiance was viewed as an important liberalization that allowed subjects to act, for better and for worse, on their own will. Justices and political and economic writers did their best to explain the workings of what was heralded as a new form of *civil* or *political birth* in their legal reports. But, by design, legal fictions are not engineered to provide satisfying, much less exploratory, narratives. Exploratory narratives were instead supplied by the emergent genre of prose fiction. In a genre thought to be producing its own powerful fictions, authors dramatized for broader audiences the lived experience of naturalization's new frontiers, further clarifying what was at stake in these debates. As we will see, authors themselves pushed the novel into expanded territory, introducing characters whose liminality continue to provoke critical debate.

Generative Fiction

Today, scholars speak of naturalization as a negative kind of making, especially in the realm of culture. Outside law, naturalization is often seen as an ideological process: assimilation, acculturation, simplification. In literary and cultural theory, it is an act of manufacturing: the way a text, for example, tries to pass off as natural and God-given what are in fact political and social conventions. The word *naturalization* in this context implies a covert operation. It is, as Friedrich Engels described social Darwinism, the "sleight of hand" that transposes social theories onto living nature, or vice versa.[33] In order to be witnessed, naturalization requires the special services of the denaturalizing critic, who patiently separates the artificial from the natural, the strange from the familiar, and the fictive subject from the living person. *Naturalization*, in literature and culture, is the name for an operation that obfuscates the difference between the fictive and the natural.

The term *naturalization* conjures the modern immigration procedure for granting national rights and privilege to foreigners, ensuring their political and legal acquiescence to a new state. But while legal and cultural-ideological senses of the term are today linked to projects of assimilating or obfuscating difference, historically, naturalization was viewed in law as an overtly fictional procedure. In the early modern period, understandings of naturalization hewed closer to the word's etymological meaning. The English word *naturalization*, which derives from the French word *naturaliser* and is rooted in the Latin word *natio*, means, at its simplest, "to make born." Significantly, early naturalization was not yet understood as passing off as God-given what was in fact political or social. In the late seventeenth and eighteenth centuries, naturalization appeared precisely as a fictional conception of nationality—what Johnson called a "Fetch"—invested in the expedient creation of new subjects rather than drawing lines between them. To opponents, it was naturalization's brazen creativity, the fact that the process was engineered by Parliament rather than based in natural law, that made it dangerously liberalizing. We are so used to thinking of naturalization as a process of controlling national membership and covering over fictionality that we have forgotten the centuries of history in which naturalization was a creative process for expanding who could be classified as a subject of a country. If today naturalization is denigrated for faking the appearance of naturalness, in early modernity it was disparaged for not appearing natural enough.

To understand the essential difference between historical naturalization regimes, it helps to understand the history of naturalization alongside concurrent developments in narrative fiction. While the English government was developing legal instruments to recognize new national subjects, prose fiction writers such as Daniel Defoe, Tobias Smollett, Samuel Richardson, Laurence Sterne, Frances Burney, Maria Edgeworth, and Mary Shelley were also experimenting with naturalization. On one level, this engagement was topical and contextual. Many of these authors mention some historical version of naturalization directly in the plot of their novels. Defoe's protagonists, Roxana and Robinson Crusoe, undertake a version of the procedure; Sterne's traveling Englishman in *A Sentimental Journey* pursues naturalization in France using *Hamlet* as a passport; and Smollett and Edgeworth, mention, in rare sympathetic portrayals, the bid in 1753 for Jewish naturalization in their novels *The Adventures of Ferdinand Count Fathom* (1753) and *Harrington* (1817), respectively. But the novelistic engagement with naturalization in the eighteenth century extends beyond contextual reference to debates about the law. Early novelists wrote alongside overtly political writers such as Locke, Sir Edward Coke, and Josiah Tucker to imagine the creation of new forms of national and international allegiance. As they populated their novels with foreigners, merchants, servant girls, and other subjects who had not featured significantly in Western art before, novelists broke the conventions of classical poetics—what Erich Auerbach calls "the rule of the separation of styles"—and created the possibility of boundless and formless imaginative space.[34] They were able to create this space because, in Hanoverian Britain, the novel, too, was "open Country." Just as there were no laws prohibiting foreigners from crossing national territories, the novel, unlike the epic or tragedy, had no formal rules or system of generic governance for who or what could enter its pages. The novel could indiscriminately admit all sorts of human experience.[35]

While lawyers, jurists, economists, and political writers were making sense of the legal development of naturalization, literary writers began to experiment with ideas about naturalization to sort out the reception, acculturation, and legal protection of foreigners in England. Alongside legal naturalization, which was being used by lawmakers to secure rights and privileges for foreigners who had never remotely been considered subjects before, the novel began to imagine new and previously unnatural forms of belonging in order to produce new subjects. In addition to exposing the arbitrariness of ancient aesthetic rules, novelists erased the conditions of birth that had previously been important to classical literary genres. As critics have noted, many of the period's signal generic innovations in prose fiction (the family romance, gothic, sentimental, and epistolary novels) feature plots based on a character's uncertain parentage or place of birth. Few scholars, however, have paid attention to how many of these plots concern the dynamics of foreign birth. Defoe's *Robinson Crusoe*, for example, tells the story of the son of a German father who ends up in Brazil, where he naturalizes as a Catholic Portuguese subject before being shipwrecked on an island for twenty-six years. Smollett's *Adventures of Ferdinand Count Fathom* revolves around the escapades of a proclaimed English protagonist who is born in a wagon with his head coming out in Holland and his feet in Flanders. Richardson's longest, and by some accounts most popular, novel, *The History of Sir Charles Grandison* (1753), concerns a protagonist who proposes marriage to a Catholic Italian woman and contemplates raising their future daughters in her faith. Burney's *The Wanderer* (1814) features a refugee protagonist who arrives in England from France to claim asylum from several society-minded families. Released the same year as the publication of Burney's novel, Shelley's *Frankenstein* tells the harrowing tale of an unnaturally born creature who, like Robinson Crusoe, has a naturalized father but, unlike him, cannot be received as a subject in any national territory. All of these novels will be discussed at greater length in the chapters that follow.

It is worth noting how many other novels not discussed in this book also take up the plights of characters who are not born in England. Aphra Behn's *Oroonoko* (1688), considered by many to be ground zero for the novel in England, tells the tale of an African prince tricked into slavery in the West Indies. *The Woman of Colour* (1808), an anonymously written novel that has lately garnered much attention, concerns a Black heiress born in Jamaica, while *The Female American* (1767), also written anonymously, traces the adventures of a half–Native American, half-English woman. Charlotte Smith's third novel, *Celestina* (1791), narrates the story of a secretly adopted French orphan raised in Scotland. Indeed, many "English" novels pursue the perspective of people born in Scotland, Wales, and Ireland, places that for a large chunk of history were considered entirely foreign to England.[36] Most of Walter Scott's novels are set outside England and feature characters who seem far from English; in fact, most of early nineteenth-century fiction is set outside England entirely, in the colonies or British peripheries, and a significant portion is interested in the figure of the "white creole," a colonial subject living in the West Indies and perceived to be less than a "true born Briton."[37] I will have more to say, especially in Chapters 2 and 4, about how labels such as *domestic* and *English* have steered literary critics away from seeing foreign birth and naturalization as fundamental concerns of much of the literature of the long eighteenth century.

It is certainly true that the new civil bonds of allegiance proposed by naturalization were also the subject of poetry—Oliver Goldsmith's *The Traveller* (1764), for example, speaks gloomily of an independence unique to England that leads to "nature's ties decay" and the rise of "fictitious bonds, the bonds of wealth and law," while Charles Churchill's *The Farewell* (1764) lampoons the "liberty of choice" that some men feel to make "ev'ry Country as the same."[38] Meanwhile, Defoe's arguably most famous work, the satirical poem *The True-born Englishman* (1701), was understood by many of its earliest readers in relation to Defoe's support for the general naturalization of the Huguenot and Palatine refugees.[39] But prose fiction of the period saw an extended and more positive engagement with naturalization. Like the legal fictions of naturalization, many novels facilitated and mobilized narratives that led to the production of new subjects. They too worked against the sacrosanct principles of perpetual allegiance that legal naturalization was also seeking to thwart. Going further than legal practitioners, however, novelists devised fictions that more fully comprehended and imagined a universe where nationality could be exchanged or abandoned. They designed plots and engineered characters that put the implications of naturalization in wider social and political contexts, and they used narrative to integrate characters who could not, at the time, be considered political subjects. Shelley's *Frankenstein*, perhaps the most extreme and yet simultaneously fabulous example, integrates the story and history of a stateless creature into its narrative of a monomaniac, naturalized Swiss scientist, making it possible for readers to see the homeless creature as just as much a member of the society depicted in the novel as its legally entitled citizens. To this day, the integration of new and more diverse subjects into fiction remains one of the primary ways of conceiving the ethics of literature. The creation of subjects who are seen and read as individuals is one of literature's most important ethical and political functions.

By bringing together the history of naturalization, the importance of legal fictions, and the experiments and effects of prose fiction, this book makes naturalization visible again for modern scholarship. Or rather, it restores naturalization to the visibility it once enjoyed in the long eighteenth century in both law and literature. Before naturalization was a means to limit and control entry into the nation-state, it was, for jurists, philosophers, and fiction writers of the long eighteenth century, a creative mechanism of national expansion. At heart, naturalization was a bold effort to create new subjects as older, narrower protocols limiting subjecthood to birth and bloodline succumbed to new pressures. Yet through its experimental fictions, naturalization produced a fundamental friction between the traditional feudal understanding of the nation, which privileged the allegiance assigned at birth, and an emergent voluntarist model that saw allegiance as something that could be abandoned or changed. If we pay attention to the fictional process of making subjects, in both law and literature, we develop a more positive and generative conception of the relationship between fiction and the state while narrating a new fictional conception of nationality. Naturalization thus emerges in this book as both a legal and a literary theory of fictional subject-making.

Nationality and Individualism

Given its importance to an array of eighteenth-century writers across economics, literature, law, and politics, it is surprising that scholars have largely overlooked the history of naturalization.[40] One reason for this neglect may be that naturalization intersects two major developments that scholars of the period tend to consider separately: the development of individualism and the rapid expansion of trade, both within England and across emerging global markets. The Enlightenment era is thought to have inaugurated, according to C. B. Macpherson, a new vision of the individual as a self-possessed, self-governing person: an individual who, later in the nineteenth century, would become the rights-bearing bourgeois, liberal subject.[41] This individual, as Ian Watt comprehended, was so fully saturated by a new economic order that they no longer had any collective ties, not to family, church, village, guild, or nationality.[42] In Franco Moretti's account of the eighteenth-century individual, by contrast, national ties were not weakened; they had not yet fully formed. In the eighteenth century, Moretti argues, "the strictly *national* element had not yet affected everyday existence."[43] It was not until the nineteenth century, according to Moretti, that fiction accomplished the "great symbolic achievement" of contracting cosmopolitan space into the domestic interior and inventing the middle ground of the nation.[44] Only when people were properly estranged from one another could the fiction of belonging to the same nation be born. Until that time, the eighteenth-century subject was primarily a domestic or bourgeois subject, with little thought given to its national status.

If cultural and literary historians have neglected the evolution of naturalization, several historians have indispensably documented its economic rationales and the parliamentary history of the bills themselves.[45] For the most part, even the small amount of scholarly interest in the naturalization debates has remained narrowly focused on economic tracts and pamphlets, almost entirely neglecting naturalization's appearance in literary culture. The exacting contextualization of these parliamentary histories, using mainly archival sources, has produced an initial sketch of naturalization's power in the seventeenth and eighteenth centuries. Yet the drive to focus on naturalization as a matter of economic history has occluded a cultural realm that also participated in and extended this debate. To think of naturalization as only an economic matter is to overlook the larger orbit of what was a complex form of subject creation—a matter that was worked out in varying ways by legal form and prose fiction in the period.

At the same time, historians who have paid attention to the cultural development of nationality in the eighteenth century—most prominently Linda Colley in *Britons: Forging the Nation, 1707–1837*—have, like literary and cultural historians, passed over the naturalization debates of the period. Colley maintains that English nationality came to be felt and imagined in relationship to "others" outside England, particularly the French.[46] But to see nationality as the result of aggressive relations among nationalities disregards the many legal and cultural attempts to settle foreigners *within* the nation. As E. P. Thompson points out in his review of Colley's book, historians cannot be certain that the average Briton was staunchly loyalist.[47] And Benedict Anderson, in an important shift away from the enormously influential concept of imagined communities that made him famous and continues to endure for its explanation of nationalism among historians, political theorists, and literary critics, eventually abandoned the idea that culture could settle the borders of national communities. As he admitted in his 2006 memoir, *A Life beyond Boundaries*, research on nationalism tends to disregard compelling contrary evidence. "Using the nation and nation-states as the basic units of analysis," he noted, "fatally ignored the obvious fact that in reality these units were tied together and crosscut by 'global' political-intellectual currents.... Very few people have ever been 'solely' nationalist."[48] Despite his later-life realization of the "serious flaw" guiding his earlier research and the "obvious fact" of the coexistence of internationalism and nationalism, the idea of the imagined community has settled into received wisdom.[49]

Just as Anderson did not consider earlier in his career how imagined communities could be intersected by international and national issues, he also did not think through the legal dimensions of national membership. If he had, the legal side of nationality would have no doubt troubled his account of nationalism. Legal naturalization does not impose a uniform culture or convince people that they are members of the same nation, as cultural nationalism was thought to do. It generates belonging precisely by overlooking language and place of birth, and instead creating an equivalency between foreign-born subjects and natural-born ones through a trick of law. Dilating on this fact, this book seeks to recover earlier legal and literary endeavors to invite the world into the nation, endeavors that rendered national allegiance relatively porous for the sake of individual and national self-interest. It also takes seriously the paradoxical and creative proposition that naturalization was intended to *make* foreigners into so-called natural subjects, and it rigorously unpacks the fictional structure of naturalization in relation to traditional English conceptions of allegiance. The fictions I explore are ones that openly expose, and then consolidate, the fiction on which nationality depends.

The novel, too, has always been an international development.[50] As Guido Mazzoni shows, before the nineteenth century, European nations had different terminologies and particular genealogies for the novel. Yet all of these nations emphasized a shared origin for what they variously called *le roman, der Roman, il romanzo, la novela, la novella,* and *the novel.* The geographical boundaries and origins of the novel were contingent. European traditions of the novel witnessed a lexical shift from narrow in 1550, when European literatures rediscovered the Greek novel; to embodied in 1670, when the word *roman* was meant to invoke the medieval tradition of romance; to general in the nineteenth century, when the novel was characterized, in the words of Mazzoni, as "a polymorphic space providing a home for stories of a certain length that do not fall within the confines of more rigidly codified narrative genres (epic poems, works of history, and the chanson de geste)."[51] While the word *novel* itself is etymologically linked to eighteenth-century Britain, before the nineteenth century, the word, and its Continental counterparts, did not have a stable definition. In other words, the identity of the novel in the eighteenth century, like the concept of nationality itself, was in flux.

Scholars who have searched for the origins of the novel by focusing on the conceits of its narrative form—the way novels tell ordinary stories of everyday life—have generally done so within nineteenth-century paradigms that rely on the unacknowledged backdrop of the nation-state. These paradigms, according to Étienne Balibar, produce a "retrospective illusion," the perspective that events in the eighteenth century are part of a teleological story that sees the novel as reaching its fullest expression in the nineteenth-century nation-state.⁵² Read as part of a teleology, the subject in the eighteenth-century novel is only a more limited and private version of the full-fledged citizen who only emerges in the nineteenth century. This account of subject formation in the novel thus aligns with the modern school of nation-state development theorized in the work of political scientists and historians such as Ernest Gellner, Charles Tilly, Carlton Hayes, Benedict Anderson, and Eric Hobsbawm.⁵³ According to the modernist interpretation, it was only in the nineteenth century, when developments in print combined with industrialization, mass education, historical awareness, and political participation, that loosely connected and rural populations could be integrated into a nation-state. In sync with this school of thought, and directly citing Tilly, Moretti heralds the nineteenth century for bringing "a number of processes . . . into being (the final surge in rural enclosures; the industrial take-off; vastly improved communications; the unification of the national market; mass conscription) that literally drag human beings out of the local dimension, and throw them into a much larger one."⁵⁴ Moretti applies this developmental schema to a thesis about the development of the novel: "The novel found the nation-state. And being the only symbolic form that could represent it, it became an essential component of our modern culture."⁵⁵

This is not to say that there has been no scholarly discussion of the relation between the nation and eighteenth-century fiction. According to Nancy Armstrong's highly schematic narrative, in the eighteenth century, "being British" referred to "one's place of birth, native language, or home."⁵⁶ By the late eighteenth century, however, "the novel had to refigure the social body so that readers could imagine it remaining English while taking in foreigners and foreign objects and extending itself onto foreigner soil."⁵⁷ Yet from the perspective of legal and cultural narratives of naturalization, the question that Armstrong sees as arriving only at the end of the century emerged earlier, in the seventeenth century, and not as a threat to the coherence of the nation. The question of how the English could take in foreigners and remain English was the very foundation of the naturalized identity and legal fiction of *Britishness* and of Great Britain, the multinational entity constituted by the nations of England, Wales, and Scotland (with Ireland, especially after the formation of the United Kingdom of Great Britain and Ireland in 1800, being its own complex case). "Being British," as opposed to being English, was from the outset a naturalized identity that was furnished, first, in legal cases after the Union of the Crowns in 1603, and then settled by law by the Acts of Union in 1706 and 1707. Britain was a legal and administrative identity that had very little to do with language, birthplace, or where one called home.[58]

Another important study of nationality and fiction, Ning Ma's *Age of Silver*, seeks to displace the assumption that novelistic modernity was invented in Europe by introducing a new, East–West theory of the rise of the novel, one that considers the form in China, Spain, and Japan.[59] Yet as I discuss more fully in Chapter 3, Ma's global account proceeds from a nativized understanding of the English novel, one that requires a work such as *Robinson Crusoe* to be decidedly English for the purposes of transcultural comparison. Srinivas Aravamudan has also investigated the status of the nation and the eighteenth-century novel in *Enlightenment Orientalism*, in which he reads an array of oriental tales, spy fictions, scientific speculations, it-narratives, beast fables, and satirical fictions to advocate for "a new taleology."[60] I join Aravamudan in resisting teleological accounts of the novel as nation-bound. Yet this book will push that resistance further by arguing that even canonical novels cannot be construed as explicitly bound by the nation. Like Ma, Aravamudan confirms the general teleology that puts the novel and the nation together—if only, and importantly, through alternative forms and traditions. Instead, I outline how even the most canonical novelists, those whose novels have come to define the canon of *English* novelists—Defoe, Smollett, Richardson, Sterne, Burney, and Shelley—wrote long-form prose fictions that opened beyond the English nation, decentering nativity as a principle of national inclusion and exposing and testing the permeable boundaries of the nation rather than settling those boundaries' existence.

The Paranational and the Global

As I have argued, since the late eighteenth century, we have gradually lost sight of an earlier view of nationality as porous, malleable, and linked to the emergence of global markets and the colonialist ambitions of empire. In our myopia, we have come to view nationalism and the novel through the lens of the cultural formation of the nineteenth-century nation-state, adopting what Andreas Wimmer and Nina Glick Schiller term "methodological nationalism."[61] Rather than adopt this conservative and nation-bound lens, this book returns to an alternative account of national belonging that was forged in the legal and literary developments of the eighteenth and early nineteenth centuries, showing that the development of prose fiction was not as domestic and interior-facing as has been hitherto understood and that the law itself had yet to harden into an insider-outsider binary. Writers of the long eighteenth century were, in fact, invested in questions about the status of the individual in a world of increasing mobility and expanding trade. As the case studies in this book make clear, prose fiction directly and indirectly experimented with fictional forms of national inclusion. That is to say, the novel was concerned with legal questions about nationality and placed its naturalized subjects in worlds and situations heretofore unconsidered by law.

Throughout this book, I use the word *paranational* to describe the early context in which these literary experiments took place. *Paranational* is distinct from two similar terms that prevail in scholarship on immigration. The first is *international*, whose legal meaning as the relationship between nations was coined by the English jurist and philosopher Jeremy Bentham in 1780.[62] The second is *transnational*, which refers to the movement of people and trade across nations. *Paranationality*, by contrast to both terms, signals both the internal and external movements of individuals at a time of porous territorial borders and in an age when religious affiliations were often more important than national ones, and when the modern conception of state borders as "closable" was nonexistent.[63] Indeed, nationality is a profoundly modern idea. Following the French and American revolutions, nationality replaced the concept of allegiance, but it only became a meaningful term in nineteenth-century international law.[64]

The concept of the paranational is also distinct from the bordered conception of the nineteenth-century nation-state and novel, as well as from the older view of nationality as being a natural and perpetual allegiance.[65] The prefix *para-* registers how naturalization, as a procedure for subject creation, introduced uncertainty about the location of national allegiance. It underlines objects that are auxiliary or derivative in a manner that is parodied or considered defective. The prefix also has a different sense. It can mean, according to the *Oxford English Dictionary*, "analogous or parallel to, yet separate from or going beyond, what is denoted by the root word."[66] *Paranationality* therefore registers nationality as it was worked out in a complex of undefined boundaries in space, inside and outside the nation and on and between territorial and imperial borders. It is important, however, to distinguish the paranational form of the novel from theories of cosmopolitanism. Naturalization was not about embracing or overlooking nationalities for the sake of a greater humanity but rather about encountering them in collision and connection. Paranationality is not a utopic extension of love to all in the world; rather, it frames the understanding of nationality through a limitrophe as an identity that can be exchanged and contracted through civil procedure. Paranational individualism recognizes national boundaries—it does not see past them or deem them irrelevant but rather sees them as voluntary, not sacrosanct.

Whereas historians of law and literature have tended to concentrate on the state as a domestic or municipal entity, this study presents naturalization as, at once, a domestic, municipal, and transnational issue. Moreover, it does not distinguish between domestic and international, seeking instead to examine the internal, external, domestic and foreign, and municipal and international viewpoints of the era. The story I tell in this book is therefore not a "rise" narrative. It is not an origin story that explains the progressive development of literary and legal thinking about naturalization. If anything, it is the story of a "fall," one that casts our current thinking about naturalization as regressive when compared with the view of it as a general procedure in the eighteenth century. In other words, I follow a narrative that shuts down as restrictions to block the entry of immigrants into England began to formalize at the eighteenth century's end. In doing so, it upends key narratives that depict the early novel as more domestic and limited in scope in comparison with novels of the later nineteenth century. In the novels and legal narratives examined here, grand narratives that scholars have used to partition the eighteenth and nineteenth centuries into a narrative of domesticity and nationalism are undone. Long before scholars could claim that the novel was interested in harnessing the boundaries of the nation, novelists were working to expand and ultimately nullify the idea of natural bonds of allegiance.

By recovering and explicating the legally and textually mediated ideas of naturalization in prose fiction, we begin to properly understand early modernity's evolving views on liberalized allegiance. Moreover, we realize how profoundly our reading of early eighteenth-century law and literature has been hobbled by homogenizing narratives that describe the period's engagement with individualism as exclusively concerned with depth rather than breadth, or the story of the novel as one of the progressive closing off of the private from the foreign, leading to a "cramp[ing] into domesticity," as Margaret Doody has described it.[67] Once we are prepared to abandon this narrow and anachronistic view of legal and literary history, we can begin to understand how the individualism of prose fiction in the eighteenth century functioned as an alternative rather than embryonic precursor to the cultural and identity-based forms of *Volk* nationality of the nineteenth century.

This leads me to a note about the title of this book. *Before Borders* harks back to a time before borders in two distinct but related senses. The first has to do with physical, territorial borders. Before the nineteenth and twentieth centuries, geographical borders were not used to control the passage of goods and people. As Luca Scholz clarifies of mobility in early modern Europe, "The image of closable pre-modern state borders is a backward projection to the benefit of the nation-state."[68] This does not mean that borders were open in ways called for by contemporary theorists of "open borders"—indeed, such an idea requires and presupposes, as a point of resistance, the existence of closed political borders. It means that the long eighteenth century was a period of *paranational* slippage, when movement and mobility was controlled at the gates of the city or by parish authorities rather than at the supranational level, and when a territorially inscribed understanding of aliens and subjects had yet to develop. Second, the title refers to a time before disciplinary borders, a time when the novel was not yet a thing called "a novel" but rather prose fiction, a nascent genre of writing undoing the rules attached to classical literature and art. To return to this period before borders, in legal and literary senses, requires that we ourselves check our modern assumptions about law and art.

Before Borders concerns how fictional acts of subject creation, whether in law or literature, experimented with a conception of open-ended national belonging. This conception has more in common with modern studies of global and international networks than with the portrait of dowdy domesticity that literary scholars, conscripting one era in the service of another, have drawn of the novel before the advance of nineteenth-century nationalism. Indeed, because of the early novel's failure to conform to the nineteenth-century nation-state framework and its interest in the nascent legal infrastructure for immigration, this book offers a rich archive for thinking through modern ideas about the "global" and "world literature." If we hope to denationalize literature under the auspices of something like the borderless ideal of world literature or global fiction, then we must also attend to the actual experiences of how nationality travels in law—and how literature of the period, particularly the novel, engaged that experience. Modern scholars of global Anglophone literature such as Aamir Mufti, Ragini Srinivasan, Matthew Hart, and Pheng Cheah, to mention only a few, caution against the celebration of a borderless category of literature without thinking about the territorial borders of the state and the borderless category of capital, which have only grown more pernicious in recent decades.[69] The search for global literature and histories in earlier periods must be equally attentive to the legal fictions of nationality. The aim of a globalized literary history cannot simply be achieved through the study of counterarchives or by expanding coverage to consider novels in translation. It is not only by widening the canon with the addition of new or undervalued texts, or by paying attention to the geography depicted therein, that we are able to understand the period's paranational resonances. We must understand how nationality traveled as an idea—how nationality itself was becoming something that could be legislated by and through fiction.

Finally, *Before Borders* does not propose that the eighteenth century was a more progressive period for immigrants than our current era or that its literature did not manifest racist and colonial ideologies about subject formation. I do not dispute the insights of those who have written accounts of the relationship between the novel and the colonies, nor do I wish to suggest that a procedure designed to attract a clutch of European migrants did anything to alleviate the suffering of millions of Africans, Indigenous populations in colonial America, and indentured white servants. As Charlotte Sussman's insightful study of mobility in the eighteenth century reminds us, "Liberty most often meant the freedom to stay put—to be protected from the various kinds of 'removal' prevalent during the period—not just the strictures of the Poor Laws, but also impressment into the army or navy, penal transportation (offered as an alternative to the death penalty), the displacement of land enclosures, the late-century Scottish clearances, or, in the form that marked the limit of the 'unfree,' capture into slavery in Africa."[70] I turn to naturalization to bring together legal, economic, and literary discourses to reconceptualize a rhetorical operation that was meant to apply only to a select elite white minority of rich merchants and skilled Protestants but that nonetheless had wide implications that were tested by a variety of people. Naturalization, when looked at contiguously with the novel, expands to include more than the integration of Protestant refugees or the promotion of English trade. It becomes a heuristic to make sense of the novel's political and aesthetic project, which endures to today. Recovering the legal, economic, and literary contexts in which writers worked through the problem of naturalization is imperative for understanding how legal and cultural ideas about immigration evolved from the early modern to the modern period. What we see in this book's case studies is that the novel engaged the ideas of naturalization in fiction against the grain of nativist ideologies. And long after the legal naturalization acts themselves were repealed, novels persisted as spaces in which the legal implications of naturalization law were brought to their fullest expression, opening up exhilarating investigations that continued an experiment begun in law.

A New Framework for Law and Literature

Beyond reevaluating the role of nationality in the novel, this study of naturalization offers a new paradigm for the examination of law and literature. In the seventeenth and eighteenth centuries, legal and literary scholarship shared a fictional process that can only be appreciated through the exploratory veins of interdisciplinary scholarship. My way of combining legal and literary scholarship in the chapters that follow might strike readers of each discipline as peculiar. The approach to examining law, for example, appears decidedly more literary than that of legal theorists. Unlike in standard approaches to legal history, I read against the progressive narrative of a judgment and instead examine all parts of a judge's report, especially the obiter dictum. I also seek to understand the rhetorical complexity of naturalization by drawing attention to the creative process for making subjects and, latterly, citizens. For literary scholars, my way of prioritizing legal form to analogically understand and contextualize literature might seem to soften literature's celebrated power over legal analysis. However, I emphasize that law and literature contiguously worked on the same problem of subject production.[71] Understanding this shared concern yields exciting new understandings for the history of both immigration and literature.

Of course, the analogy pursued here between naturalization as law and naturalization as literature is not exact. These processes are not, and need not be, causally related. In making this point, I draw inspiration from David Hume, who, although he is mainly remembered for his theory of cause and effect, in *A Treatise of Human Nature* also argues for the existence of other, less direct forms of connection between general ideas. For Hume, a causal relation is structured by a relationship wherein one object has the physical influence to effect change or movement in another. To illustrate the force of causation, Hume turns to an example from law. A judge, he says, "is one, who in all disputed cases can fix by his opinion the possession or property of any thing betwixt any members of the society."[72] That is, a judge has the enactive power to turn words into actions through his judgments and sentences. But it is in two other bonds of association—resemblance and contiguity—that this study wishes to find a conceptual resource for understanding the relationship of naturalization in law and literature. These bonds are comparatively weaker in Hume's analysis, as evidenced by the references to art and architecture he uses in *An Enquiry concerning Human Understanding* to illustrate their relationships. In resemblance, "a picture naturally leads our thoughts to the original," while a contiguous relationship occurs through proximity in space: "The mention of one apartment in a building naturally introduces an enquiry or discourse concerning the others."[73] In resemblance, one object conjures the appearance of the other; in contiguity, coexistence in space determines an association: a building naturally produces discussion of the building next to it. These two weaker associations are premised on an aesthetic connection—whether appearance or spatial proximity—rather than performative force. The analogy between law and the novel is premised on the idea that they both share a similar connection in space and time. They both share a distinctive narrative mode.

The bonds of unity that Hume sees as weaker are precisely the ones I want to use to align naturalization and the novel in the eighteenth century. This might seem like a surprising proposition to make at a moment when law and literature, as an interdisciplinary field of study, is reckoning with precisely the problem of literature's material force and the relationality between legal and literary discourses.[74] But there will be no claims here for a causal relevance of the novel to the law. Members of Parliament were not reading novels when they drafted general naturalization bills, or, if they were, they left no record of their reading. And while many of the early novels produced in England directly reference naturalization procedures (often in the opening sentence), the legal context of naturalization cannot solely account for the power of naturalization in prose fiction.

The relationship between naturalization and the novel is, by contrast, more imaginative. In the seventeenth and eighteenth centuries, naturalization law and the novel were both used as instruments to convert strangers into fellow subjects in a period with ill-defined rules about who could be a subject. Lawyers and jurists experimented with ways to determine who could be a national subject in England and, through naturalization, how a person could be made a subject, while prose fiction writers actively broke ties with older, classical rules of representation to develop the openness that would later characterize the modern and contemporary novel. The novel, as we know, would continue to thrive as a genre defined by unruliness and openness to any subject or object under the sun, while the law of nationality and naturalization would move in the opposite direction, growing more constricted with the advance of the modern immigration regime. But in the long eighteenth century, two processes that today are very distinct were convergent.

By looking at the contiguous relationship between law and literature, this study of naturalization moves away from questions of enactment and causation—how literature produces law or how law directly produces literature—to questions of cultural interference: What can we learn about naturalization from considering law and literature together? Rather than examining the eighteenth-century novel as a way of practicing law (what is known as the "literature as law" approach), or as merely an illustration of legal naturalization (the "law in literature" approach), this study of the adjacency of naturalization and the development of long-form prose fiction is a means to understand the liberalization of nationality: how nationality was required to be a tokenistic status before it could be imagined as an affectively deep relationship.[75] By studying law and literature together, we are able to gain new perspectives. When legal history is approached as a series of precedents that define cases in a causal sequence, we ignore the fact that notable axioms of modern statutory interpretation, such as a later precedent trumping the earlier, are anachronistic to the eighteenth century. In fact, careful statutory drafting and sophisticated statutory interpretation were not common practice until the mid-nineteenth century.[76] How a culture made sense of naturalization as a legal fiction lives instead in the dicta, where metaphors, similes, and narratives of history offer various theories. We can continue to use nineteenth- and twentieth-century knowledge claims about nationality to guide readings of older literature, but we do better to see law as equally unsettled and ongoing as the literature we seek to understand. By bringing legal ideas of naturalization to bear on the early novel, and vice versa, I am aligning two processes that were already working side by side in their own time.

Another word to describe what I am calling contiguous history is what Lisa Lowe calls "intimacy." In *The Intimacies of Four Continents*, Lowe connects the ideology of the possessive liberal individual—the theory of the individual as the sole agent of their own liberty—to its vast colonial outsides through "the dynamic relationship between the always present but differently manifest and available histories and social forces."[77] Bringing together histories that are often held apart, Lowe untethers the liberal individual from its domestic, bourgeois, and nationalist paradigms, mapping it more widely onto capital, empire, and colonialism and disrupting the interiority of the liberal individual with the horizontal scales of geography: the vast shores that separate enslaved persons and bring them together in laboring conditions in colonial America, for example. Lowe writes that it is "necessary to conceive settler colonialism, slavery, indenture, imperial war, and trade together, as braided parts of a world process."[78] I am also interested in examining connections that have been lost to nationalist disciplinary protocols. I seek to use naturalization—the remaking of the national subject in seventeenth- and eighteenth-century England—as a heuristic to bring together an array of discourses about individualism that have often been held apart. The individual, I contend, did not emerge in a domestic sphere ideologically sealed from the outside world but in relation to open questions and ideas about national limits and the freedom to migrate and emigrate. The possessive individual has been seen as one of the main links between literature, politics, and philosophy in the eighteenth century. However, the possessive individual was also produced by fictional forms that legibly inscribed its movement across counties, countries, colonies, and empires. What happens to the individual's allegiances and self-identity when it travels? This question was central to the thinking of many philosophers and writers of the time, from Locke to Shelley. Yet novelists had their own, unique way of rendering the fictionality of national membership intelligible in their art. Often, it is these aesthetic experiments that have been the most enduring.

Theories, Fictions, and Relations

This book is divided into three parts: theories of naturalization, fictions of naturalization, and relations of naturalization. The first part, comprising two chapters, is devoted to historical and aesthetic theories of naturalization as they have been articulated in legal and literary histories. Chapter 1, "Naturalization in History," examines several legal cases related to naturalization—namely, *Calvin's Case*—as well as a series of cases relating to the estate of John Ramsey. These cases, which ostensibly turned on inheritance of real property, informed the basis of early immigration law. I then turn to Locke's underconsidered argument about naturalization, which he lays out in his *Two Treatises on Government* and in an unpublished paper. From these cases and political arguments, the formal and temporal qualities of naturalization—its fictional and paranational qualities—emerge. Chapter 2, "Ideas of Naturalization," critically explores naturalization in the style of Raymond Williams's book *Keywords* (which surprisingly does not feature the word *naturalization*) and turns to various aesthetic theories, especially those drawn from Marxist critique and poststructuralism, to argue that naturalization not only provides a legal context for understanding the novel but also offers a heuristic for understanding how novels introduce new subjects into literature. Here, I speak to an idea of naturalization as a model of positive creation rather than ideological subterfuge.

Chapter 1, on the history of naturalization in law, and Chapter 2, on the cultural idea of naturalization, can be read alone or as primers for the case studies to follow. The case studies in the following chapters reveal how jurists and novelists share a similar aim: the production of new subjects without natural grounding. The various technical characteristics of legal naturalization are energized by novelists in the departures they take from traditional conceptions of literature grounded by classical rules and the scenarios they invent for their subjects. The idea submitted in Chapter 2 is that cultural critics and legal scholars might be energized in turn to think differently about the creative powers of law and literature.

Most of the legal cases discussed at length in this book arose in the 1600s, after the Union of the Crowns in 1603 but before general naturalization became a topic of public outrage in the early eighteenth century. It was at this moment of public examination that the literary experiments I cover began to extend the ideas first concentrated in law. Part II, accordingly, offers two chapters that examine how naturalization features as a contextual and aesthetic component of several prose narratives across the long eighteenth century. Chapter 3, "Law of the Foreign Father," offers a dramatically new reading of Defoe's *Robinson Crusoe* that draws on the history of the "Poor Palatine" refugees. *Crusoe* has long been thought of as quintessentially English, exemplifying both the English novel and the English subject. I challenge this critical consensus by contextualizing *Crusoe* in debates about early nationality legislation, such as the Aliens Act (1698), which prevented aliens from bequeathing property to heirs in England. This law is globalized with Crusoe's naturalization in Brazil, which he undertakes in order to buy a lucrative slave plantation. Defoe, I argue, was interested in the plasticity of nationality as presented by the legal fiction of naturalization.

Chapter 4, "Open-Door Domestic Fiction," takes issue with a prevalent thesis about the eighteenth century: that in its second half, genres of romance and the picaresque were suppressed and surpassed by domestic realism before becoming nationalized in the nineteenth century. This claim, which has been useful for political and literary theorists alike, neglects the way in which so-called domestic fiction engaged questions about the transfer of nationality and personal identity across national territory. To make this evident, I consider the *last* novels written by several major authors who have been considered to be primarily domestic writers—Smollett, Richardson, Sterne, and Burney—as examples of "paranational fiction": formal experiments that leave open the possibility of membership, rather than advancing a singular national formation.

The book's final part attends to what I call *relations of naturalization*. It is in this section that I resume the discussion begun in this introduction on new models for law and literature. Chapter 5, "Unnatural-Born Subjects," charts two ways of conceiving the relationship between legal and literary naturalization in the eighteenth century. The first examines how the writer Maria Edgeworth sought to adapt her fiction to the Jewish Naturalization Act in 1753. While Edgeworth's novel and the context of its writing suggest a causal relationship between legal and literary engagement with naturalization, I propose a second, better way of contemplating the contiguity of law and literature in a reading of the famous epistolary frame narrative of Shelley's *Frankenstein*. When Shelley revised the novel in 1831, she made two changes that underline the importance of viewing the Creature's position from the perspective of naturalization. If we juxtapose the Creature's exclusion from Geneva and Switzerland to the integration of other foreigners, we can begin to understand *Frankenstein* as a project in which Shelley exposes the hypocrisy of national exclusions and ultimately reveals how the Creature might be "naturalized" into a nonnational community by means of narrative rather than law or nature. This narrative naturalization, I suggest, occurs not through the powers of human sympathy, or through the processes of law, as it does for Victor Frankenstein and Elizabeth, who naturalize in Geneva shortly after their birth. Instead, Shelley makes naturalization operative for the Creature at the level of the novel's narrative form.

Before Borders challenges readers to consider the long eighteenth century outside the frameworks of the nineteenth and twentieth centuries, so that they can take stock of an important idea that was concerned with the very opposite of cultural nationalism. In the coda, I make an additional move and consider the implications of natality and nationalism as a legal and literary fiction into the current era. While English law and literature were once invested in breaking down what was perceived to be an archaic notion of perpetual allegiance, that very breakdown also allowed citizens of Britain to have their nationality expunged. Denaturalization, I argue, is the dark downturn of naturalization's liberalization in the eighteenth century. If, however, the full liberalization of citizenship is denaturalization, naturalization nonetheless can still be relearned as a powerful form of invention from which we can, and must, rethink subject and citizen formation. Whether positive or negative, understanding the Enlightenment background of this powerful procedure proves crucial.

PART I

THEORIES OF NATURALIZATION

CHAPTER 1

Naturalization in History

One of the great misunderstandings of immigration history is the idea that, before the nineteenth century, America and Europe were lands of open borders and few restrictions, welcoming all who dared to cross rough seas and ragged roads. This is not so much an idea that is actively defended by historians and legal scholars of immigration as it is a suggestion that comes into view amid an outsize focus on the immigration policies of the late eighteenth, nineteenth, and twentieth centuries. Detailed and necessary narrations of the rise of exclusionary immigration policies and enforced border control engendered by the 1882 Chinese Exclusion Act, the 1914 British Nationality and Status of Aliens Act, and the 1924 Johnson-Reed Immigration Act have had the effect of making immigration before the nineteenth century seem freer and unregulated by comparison.[1]

It is true that before the nineteenth century, there were few impediments to prevent migrants from immigrating to other nations. National borders in the modern sense did not yet exist to inhibit individual travelers, and the restrictive devices that regulate immigration today—visas, work permits, passports, and employment and language requirements for naturalization—only came into being during or after the nineteenth century. Deportation was not a full-fledged legal possibility until the twentieth century.[2] It is a mistake, though, to assume that the legal architecture of immigration did not exist in earlier times; it did, but it served a fundamentally different purpose from the "probationary model" of the modern era.[3] In the seventeenth and eighteenth centuries, naturalization—the main statutory policy for immigration—had not yet systematically attached to a project of cultural and affective nationalism or to an idea of national security. Instead, in an opposite framework, naturalization disconnected immigration from personal and communal identities. Rather than shore up the boundaries of the nation, as it is thought to do today, it created a bureaucratic and mercantile path for individuals to exercise their liberty to migrate regardless of country of birth, and it simplified and cheapened national privileges for desirable alien merchants, sailors, and tradespeople. In this crucial period, the legal procedure of naturalization came to support the idea of what I call "paranational" liberty: the right of the private individual to roam and settle anywhere they chose. It opened England to foreign settlement at a moment when the country's population was thought to be declining, and when there was pronounced interest in bolstering Protestantism across Europe and providing people to the colonies. While Jews and Catholics would, with few exceptions, be restricted from naturalization and, on the whole, naturalization policy targeted a relatively select and wealthy group of white and male individuals, the idea that new national subjects could be created by statute, rather than godly and sovereign will, gave rise to an architecture of immigration that opened up the nation rather than sealed it in hermetic defense.

The politics of the Jacobean and Stuart eras had a profound impact on this earlier development of immigration, as has been widely acknowledged. The common view, famously touted by Hannah Arendt, casts naturalization as an "appendage" of the nation-state—a means of exerting sovereign control over national membership. I chart the emergence of another form of naturalization in the schism between Parliament and the king over the control of naturalization after the Union of the Crowns.[4] Of this earlier history I make three claims. The first is that during this schism, naturalization became attached to what I call "voluntary" or "paranational" allegiance: the idea that an individual's natural allegiance—the relationship to a king in whose territory they were born—can be suspended or overridden, allowing that individual to transfer their allegiance to a new country. As a procedure that takes its name from the idea of being a secondary ("para") status, seventeenth- and eighteenth-century naturalization engenders nature and returns individuals to liberties that afford them the opportunity to stay or leave.

The second point is that naturalization in this early period offered a fundamentally different form of subject creation from the legal pathways to citizenship that came to be designed in the twentieth century. Rather than assimilate foreigners to the cultural narratives of the nation-state, naturalization sought to fictionally re-create natural allegiance for foreigners through a dispassionately bureaucratic process that had nothing yet to do with interiority or felt belonging.[5] To become a naturalized subject was to be given the barest plot of a new life story. The hallmarks of realism later associated with the development of the novel in the period are notably absent from this history. Instead, what I call the *naturalization imaginary*—the slapdash use of various legal fictions and creative metaphors to explain how the law could create new subjects—became a major component of naturalization narratives. And in my third and final claim, I argue that naturalization before the nineteenth century occupied a now forgotten major place in liberal and Enlightenment philosophy. The idea of voluntary allegiance and a concomitant "right to leave" were debated and discussed by a wide variety of seventeenth- and eighteenth-century jurists and writers, including Sir Edward Coke, John Locke, Immanuel Kant, and Emer de Vattel.

That the pre-nineteenth-century history of naturalization has gone relatively unexamined is largely due to its confinement to a small and rarely read archive of statutory reports and economic pamphlets. In 1868 a Royal Commission was appointed, headed by Sir Alexander Cockburn, lord chief justice of the Queen's Bench, to examine the history of British allegiance and naturalization and make recommendations for the alternations to nationality law as part of an effort to reduce tensions between the United States and Britain over the doctrine of indelible or perpetual allegiance.[6] The commissioners had little legal guidance or precedent on which to reconstruct this history. Allegiance had long been steeped in tradition rather than written in law. According to the eighteenth-century jurist William Blackstone, the doctrine of perpetual allegiance was a rule derived from ancient Gothic custom and could not be abandoned even when a person no longer resided in England:

> An Englishman who removes to France, or to China, owes the same allegiance to the king of England there as at home, and twenty years hence as well as now. For it is a principle of universal law, that the natural-born subject of one prince cannot by any act of his own, no, not by swearing allegiance to another, put off or discharge his natural allegiance to the former: for this natural allegiance was intrinsic, and primitive, and antecedent to the other; and cannot be devested without the concurrent act of that prince to whom it was first due.[7]

Following the dictates of custom and tradition, an English subject could not forsake their bond to the English Crown even if they had spent most of their life in another country. Allegiance was not a voluntary act; it was founded in natural law rather than a chosen, contractual relationship. To refute this customary understanding of allegiance, and argue for the release of Britain from its responsibilities toward subjects in America, the commissioners thus turned to the history of naturalization, where they discovered that they were not alone in puzzling over the problems posed by the unwritten law of allegiance; statutes from as far back as the 1300s had sought to deal with questions about how natural allegiance was to be understood in relation to children of natural-born subjects and aliens born outside the realm of the kingdom.

The Royal Commission sought to locate the legal history of naturalization by examining how the law developed longitudinally through a series of interconnected precedents. Yet the history they were ultimately looking for, the history of how naturalization allowed for the severing of bonds between subjects and their kings, required attention to microscopic details that often have little to do with particular rulings. It is by reading beyond the rulings of these cases—in the superfluous, incidental, and nonbinding statements of lawyers and judges, what are known as the obiter dicta—that we encounter the legal fictions about naturalization that enacted a new model of subject creation that would eventually extend beyond law itself. Legal history examined only through holdings or precedents, as the commissioners chose to do, not only anachronistically applies a system of legal interpretation to early modernity, it also neglects the many metaphorical conceits that were used to make sense of both natural and nonnatural allegiance in the early modern era, as well as Parliament's ability to wrest the power of naturalization away from the sovereign.[8] In this new age, Parliament sought to expand the power of this fiction by conceiving of naturalization as a civic source of nationality that vied conceptually with the allegiance attached to the king under natural law. As a civic foundation, naturalization invented natural subjects against the traditional idea that allegiance was simply a declaration of the existence of the law of nature as the law of God. However easily this novel act of subject-making has come to be overlooked or forgotten, reconsidering its origins allows us to recover an alternative tradition of nationality in the eighteenth century, one bound to an overtly artificial fiction.

This chapter proceeds in three sections, each of which outlines a different stage of naturalization's development as it advanced a powerful new form of subject creation. The first section argues that a dispute between the king and Parliament over the status of Scots in England after the Union of the Crowns led to the first inquiry into naturalization, which had until this point been assumed to be the king's royal prerogative and was seldom understood as a parliamentary power. When it became apparent that Coke, chief justice of common pleas, and other jurists could not explain naturalization within the framework of natural law, a series of obscure cases attached to the estate of a Scottish earl in the middle of the seventeenth century concocted bizarre legal fictions—ones that invented a rudimentary new life history for aliens—to try to explain the power of Parliament to invent natural subjects. By turning naturalization overtly into a fictional conceit, these legal cases, which are considered in the second section, then paved the way for a view of naturalization as the steward of individual liberty, maneuvering entrepreneurial individuals across national boundaries without the burdens of perpetual allegiance. In the final section, I show how naturalization transformed from a legal fiction—an idea largely confined to legal cases concerning the rights of Scots in England—to a general economic policy idea. At this time, fictions of naturalization were delinked from law and attached to seventeenth-century political and economic ideas about individual liberty, most significantly in the writing of John Locke. Overall, this chapter seeks to establish the historical and political ideas about naturalization as they intersected with the idea of legal fiction. As we shall see, naturalization became attached to a progressive liberal project to free individuals and capital from the trappings of allegiance.

A Tale of Two Allegiances

The story of naturalization begins with the story of two kings. In 1603, following the death of his imperiously heirless cousin Elizabeth, King James VI of Scotland became the next ruler of England and Ireland. The Union of the Crowns was a remarkable event—two quarrelsome kingdoms suddenly joined under the protection of a single monarch—but as James VI traveled south to assume the English Crown, the majesty of the moment quickly turned to unease. A band of loyal companions joined the Scottish king on his journey, and their arrival at court sent a question rumbling through the English Parliament: If the new king were to grant land to these Scottish followers, would they have the right to pass it down to their heirs? The question, in what it demanded of the concept of allegiance, proved to be much larger than a claim about property.

Before the Union of the Crowns, the distinction between subjects and aliens had been understood rather than legally expressed. England had long drawn foreign traders and middlemen to London to trade and settle among its subjects. In general, rich alien merchants were free to travel in and out of the realm, but the king reserved the right to restrict the movement on anyone.[9] No legal distinction between aliens and English subjects existed in law before the thirteenth century. In 1206, however, when England lost Normandy to France and, in retaliation, King John seized the English lands belonging to those loyal to the French king Philip II, a general deduction arose that "aliens" were those who were not permitted to own land in England.[10] Without holding property, aliens could not sue in court or hold public office. It is from this seizure of land that the first common-law rule about aliens can be traced. From the Middle Ages onward, English subjects came to be identified not through positive expression of their status but in terms of their capacity to own or inherit land.[11]

Thus the question about whether James VI could grant English land to his Scottish followers was also a question about whether they could become Englishmen, since no other distinction existed to sort the differences between Scots and English subjects. In the past, Scots had been treated the same as English subjects. When they faced criminal charges in England, for instance, they had been denied the privilege, typically accorded to aliens, of a jury that spoke the same language.[12] Yet now, with the ascension of a dual king, James VI of Scotland and also James I of England, the taken-for-granted boundaries between subjects and aliens were destined to change. James VI was a stalwart supporter of a further united England and Scotland, not just at the head but also in law. He even styled himself, after his coronation, "the King of Great Britain," despite opposition from Parliament, and he made no secret of his desire to see all Scots looked on as subjects of England. With one monarch now ruling both England and Scotland, the parliament of each nation had to rethink the sources of national belonging under common law. On what basis were English subjects *subjects*? The answer to this question would advance dramatically new, contradictory, and, most importantly, creative ideas about nationality.

A first attempt at resolving the status of Scots in England took place in 1606. That year, high commissioners from both England and Scotland, who included Francis Bacon, Thomas Craig, and Lord Chancellor Ellesmere, held simultaneous joint sessions of Parliament to craft two bills in line with the king's sentiments. The first bill granted Scots born after the union (the postnati) the status of subjects of England, understanding them as natural-born subjects in natural law, while the second bill proposed a statute to remedy the status of Scots born before the union (the antenati).[13] The Scottish Parliament quickly accepted both bills, while the English House of Commons refused to pass them. The Commons, dominated by members of the gentry who were keen to limit the power of the king, feared the bills would enable him to take the next logical step and use his royal prerogative to naturalize Scots unilaterally. "In the remote past," they argued, "naturalisation might have depended on allegiance, but in modern times it should rest upon an Act of Parliament."[14] English sovereigns had considered it their right to decide which foreigners could be accepted as subjects of England through naturalization. The king and

Parliament worked together to naturalize foreigners, with the king making the ultimate determination through his royal prerogative. After the union, however, the House of Commons began to challenge the king's right to confer English subjecthood and suspend alien disabilities. They viewed the king's desire to naturalize Scots as part of an effort to create a consolidated Great Britain and therefore sought to limit the power of naturalization to its own jurisdiction.[15]

Beyond concern about the king's desire to unify the kingdoms unilaterally, the House of Commons also feared that turning Scots into subjects of England would set a "dangerous example" for inhabitants of other and future nations under English subjection.[16] If aliens from other countries could gain subject status in England, they might establish a majority in the English Parliament and plot to undermine the Reformation. Though many parliamentarians favored English expansion, they also remained committed to maintaining the jurisdictional boundaries between the English subject and any people residing in, or arriving from, future dominions. Their primary concern was to protect the privileges of English subjects in England, rather than, as in the age of empire, clarify the English liberties of the Crown's subjects who emigrated or were conquered people abroad.[17] That is to say, politicians and jurists were not yet articulating the "problem of imperial subjecthood," though they were certainly anxious about it.[18] They were thinking in terms of time—when a person was born—not in terms of space.[19] At this moment, English parliamentarians were bent on limiting the rights of Englishmen to the territory of England itself.

After the parliamentary sessions broke down, the problem of the status of the postnati and antenati Scots was then taken up by a collusive case brought before the Court of the King's Bench, an English court of common law, in 1606. Ostensibly, this case involved the property of a young child named James Colville, who was born in Edinburgh, Scotland, after the Union of the Crowns. When Colville was three years old, his guardians, John and William Parkinson, initiated the first of two civil suits in the King's Bench alleging young Colville had been unlawfully blocked from inheriting two freehold estates in the Shoreditch and Holdsworth areas of London. The child's guardians lodged this complaint on his behalf because of the peculiar hereditary situation produced by the union. Overnight, England and Scotland, which had for centuries been fractious, warring enemies, were now united at the head.[20] On the basis of these unique circumstances, the Parkinsons argued, their Scottish charge was now a subject of England entitled to inherit these properties. In fact, they had purchased the properties in Shoreditch and Holdsworth to test the case.

The suit, which would come to be known in English legal records as *Robert Calvin's Case* (Calvin being a mysteriously corrupted version of the surname Colville, and Robert being a replacement of the child's name with that of his father), gave rise to Britain's first theory of nationality. This theory, which set the parameters of the natural-born subject, would guide nationality law until the twentieth century. It exerted a significant influence on the legal architecture of the British Empire—and, through Coke's written opinion, on the development of citizenship in the United States.[21] Beyond establishing the rules that determined the relationship between subject and king, in England and its colonial conquests, *Calvin's Case*, which was also known as the *Case of the Post-nati*, set in motion an alternative idea about naturalized allegiance—"voluntary" or "positive" allegiance—that selectively opened English property and trade to foreign ownership and involvement.

The central question in *Calvin's Case* was not whether the young charge, a liege subject of James VI in Scotland (crowned James I of England), could inherit a land title in England; it was whether it was possible for *all* Scots born after the ascension to become subjects under English law. Colville, now referred to as Calvin, was represented by the king's solicitor general, Francis Bacon, and the attorney general, Henry Hobart, who argued that Calvin was entitled to claim the liberties of an Englishman because his birth in Scotland after the accession made him a subject of James I. The defense countered that Calvin's claim was inadmissible; the child could not be considered a subject of law in England for the purposes of inheriting a land title, because allegiance to the king of Scotland was separate from allegiance to the king of England. While Calvin was born in Edinburgh and a subject of the king of Scotland, who through historical accident happened to share the body of the king of England, that allegiance did not extend to the king of England. The two parties in the case could agree on only one thing: that people born in Scotland before the accession of James were aliens.

Because it raised questions about the fundamental status of all subjects under English common law, *Calvin's Case* was adjourned to the Court of the Exchequer Chamber, where twelve of fourteen justices ruled in favor of Calvin. Scots born after the union were natural-born subjects in England, they decided, entitled to hold and inherit English land. In the opinion of Coke, as it appears in the jurist John Cowell's account of the case summarized by Herbert Broom, the commonsense reasoning could not be clearer: though the laws and legislatures of the two kingdoms were separate, only one allegiance could exist. "Every one born within the dominions of the King of England, whether here or in his colonies or dependencies, being under the protection of—therefore, according to our common law, owes allegiance to—the King," Coke held, "and is subject to all the duties and entitled to enjoy all the rights and liberties of an Englishman."[22] The sovereign's body could not be divided into two crowns, Coke argued. A native subject was one who was born under the protection of the king; the allegiance owed at birth, and the protection owed upon that birth by the sovereign, was perpetual and could not be rescinded. In other words, allegiance was naturally embodied: the limits of sovereignty were conterminous with the limits of the king's body.

To frame the rights of Scots born under James's crown, Coke turned to unwritten natural law. In his influential conclusion, allegiance derived from nature rather than from a relationship forged by law. Birthright nationality was characterized as a natural and indelible relationship between individual subjects and their sovereign. Yet Coke also sought to temper the king's prerogative, which, since the Middle Ages, had been understood as a general power that belonged to him by way of natural law. It was on the basis of natural law, rather than royal prerogative, he argued, that Calvin and all those born under the allegiance of James I were found to be subjects of England.[23] Natural law turned the allegiance of subjects to the king into a new hierarchy that only mimicked the structure of a natural family, with the two separate kingdoms claiming the same paternity as if they were brothers and sisters.

Calvin's Case spurred a period of clarification for the doctrine of allegiance and associated ideas of subjecthood in England. Before the suit, allegiance was a murky concept, in part because England lacked a written constitution and, arguably, a defined sense of national consciousness.[24] In the feudal era, an English peasant's allegiance to the Crown could be traced through a hierarchical chain of commitments—peasants showed allegiance to feudal lords, who, in turn, genuflected to the monarch. Subjecthood derived from this system, but it was understood through obligation rather than rights. The only inherent privilege afforded to the subject, as mentioned, was the ability to hold property.[25] Thus, holding property, or having the ability to hold property, was key to understanding who a subject was and why someone would want to be one. It is important to note, especially for understanding later histories of immigration in the early eighteenth century, that social rank and religious affiliation were far more important status markers than nation of birth. This was one reason why England, for instance, was interested in the naturalization of the propertied French Huguenot refugees in the 1680s and refused the naturalization of suspected Catholic German refugees in the early eighteenth century.[26] Over time, allegiance evolved into something that all British lords and peasants demonstrated to the Crown, and English common law, after the ruling of *Calvin's Case*, began to view "subjects" as those born within the territories and with the protection of the Crown.[27]

In addition to resolving the nature of Calvin's allegiance, counsel on both sides of the case also had to consider how the postnati might become members of the English nation. Toward this end, the plaintiff and the defendant each cited in their arguments an obscure statute from the fourteenth century, *De natis ultra mare* (1350), to address the issue of the status of children born abroad. The statute read in part, "All children inheritors whose fathers and mothers, at the time of their birth, be, and shall be, at the faith and ligancy of the King of England, shall have, and shall enjoy, the same benefits and advantages . . . as other inheritors aforesaid in time to come."[28] The statute defined children born outside England as existing within the boundaries of the ligeance of the king. Therefore, though Coke and others predicated Calvin's allegiance on the conditions of his birth, the invocation of *De natis* revealed the historical willingness of Parliament to devise and seek legal solutions to what we would call today the principle of jus sanguinis, in which the ethnicity and nationality of the parent extends to the child. While the natural law at work in *Calvin's Case* held that children of natural subjects born outside the territory of the English Crown could not be considered natural subjects, Parliament, through this historical statute, rendered such children the "same" as natural-born individuals for the purpose of according them basic rights and privileges, such as the right to inherit property and, thus, stand for parliamentary office.

Nevertheless, though it provided a unique opportunity for the court to examine hitherto undiscussed aspects of allegiance and subjecthood, in the end, *Calvin's Case* only settled the status of the postnati—Scots born after the king's accession. The case clarified that a subject could expect protection, and vicariously the privilege of holding real property, in exchange for obedience to the king; but it did not lead to a written understanding of subjects and foreigners in law. As a result, the status of antenati Scots—those born before the union—was left unresolved. The court did not recognize an antenatus who was an alien to James I in England (but a subject to James IV in Scotland) as having a tie of descent to England in the manner determined by *De natis*.[29]

As to why the antenati were excluded from the ruling of *Calvin's Case*, some legal theorists postulate the English Parliament feared that granting subject status to the antenati would result in a deluge of new Scots entering England. Parliamentarians felt more comfortable extending status to postnati because, three years into King James's reign, there were few people born in Scotland during that time and fewer still who resided in the country and held property claims in England.[30] Others suggest that even though King James was sympathetic to the antenati and wanted them to be regarded as subjects of the English Crown, he lacked confidence that they could make a persuasive collusive case under common law.[31] A significant reason—one that led the English Parliament to initially reject the two bills on the status of Scots devised in the joint session—was that Parliament wanted to keep the power of subject-making out of the king's hands and within their court. As Coke would state, only Parliament had the power of naturalization: its jurisdiction "was so transcendent and absolute, as it cannot be confined either for causes or persons without any bounds."[32]

Indeed, on the whole, *Calvin's Case* can be viewed as an inquiry into the power of Parliament to place the origins of allegiance within the scope of human, rather than natural, law. While the justices in *Calvin's Case* ruled, much to Parliament's chagrin, that the postnati were natural subjects as determined by natural law, those subjects had not, in the end, been *made* subjects by a royal grant. King James had hoped to use his royal prerogative to naturalize the antenati, but Coke and others thwarted his plans, arguing in their decision that the king had only the power to render the antenati a more limited form of denizens.[33] Denizens were not complete subjects. They could inherit, hold, and pass on property, but they could not retroactively become subjects or bequeath property to children born before their denizenship. *Calvin's Case* followed this latter rule. While the difference may seem slight, and in practice it often was, it formed the basis of a conceptual difference—which would soon become a conceptual chasm—in legal power. A denizen by royal patent did not have pure legal blood and lacked the retroactivity that would change the conditions of an alien's birth for the purpose of their recognition under law. Only naturalization via Parliament could purify a foreigner's legal blood, rendering an alien effectively the same as a natural-born subject in law.

This parliamentary understanding of naturalization was a by-product of the resolution of *Calvin's Case*, which left the fates of Scots born before the accession not only unresolved but misunderstood within common law. According to Coke, natural allegiance could never be changed. An individual's subjection to the Crown began at birth, and this subjection lasted for life. The king, Coke declared, could not make an individual inheritable who was not inheritable by way of common law. Parliament, though, could make aliens into subjects: "There is another kind [of subject] that is an alien naturalized," Coke is reported as saying in "Commentary upon Littleton," "and that must be by Act of Parliament."[34] *Calvin's Case*, therefore, was not only an examination of the status of Scots born after the Union of the Crowns. It was also, perhaps more radically, an inquiry into Parliament's power to create new English subjects and, crucially, a test of the boundaries between Crown and Parliament. In Scotland, the king was an estate represented within Parliament; James had become used to playing a much more active role in legislation and other parliamentary business than the English Parliament could stomach.

Yet, interestingly, and confusingly, Coke also held that "this alien, naturalized to all intents and purposes is a natural-born subject."[35] Consequently, because of the rigid and unchanging nature of naturalized allegiance, a subject who came to be naturalized in the wake of the *Calvin's Case* decision was essentially identical to a natural-born subject: "One cannot be naturalized," Coke maintained, "even with limitation for life or in tail or upon condition: for that is against the Absoluteness, Purity and indelibility of natural allegiance."[36] *Calvin's Case*, therefore, produced two opposing ideas about nationality. The first defined nationality as an indelible allegiance of the natural-born subject to their Crown—that is, to the "natural" association between birth and allegiance as articulated by Coke. The second, a bare-faced challenge to the king's sovereign right, introduced the possibility that nationality could be created or engineered by parliamentary statute. At the time, these two ideas were hardly regarded as opposites. Neither Coke nor Parliament seemed concerned that laws regarding naturalization, whether made by Parliament or the king, went against established principles of divine or natural law. They were only interested in which body had the jurisdiction to instigate naturalization.

Possibly the greatest outcome of *Calvin's Case*, then, was unintended: a naturalized subject could now *become* a natural subject as if they *had always been one*. What, precisely, was the alchemy of this transformation, and how could it be re-created? Coke and the courts did not provide an answer. Decades would pass before the English courts took up this question and turned to fiction to resolve it.

The Fictions of Naturalization

The Union of the Crowns led to the creation of new identities in old communities. After *Calvin's Case* and with its unresolved tensions, Scots born before the union and living in England suddenly had to defend and express their property entitlements. Between 1656 and 1670, in three cases relating to the property holdings of John Ramsey, an earl and naturalized Scot, lawyers and justices began to consider arguments about how it might be possible for a naturalized subject to transmit land to a natural-born nephew through a relative.[37] Just as *Calvin's Case* had functioned as a trial balloon to advance the rights of postnati Scots in England, the suits relating to Ramsey's property were widely viewed as tests to settle the status of antenati Scots in England and determine the precise way in which naturalization worked. The Ramsey cases are significant for two reasons. First, it is in these cases that we find an attempt to resolve the question of how foreigners (the antenati) could be integrated into the nation through legal fictions. Going further than *Calvin's Case*, the Ramsey litigation attempted to explain more precisely how, in relation to natural law, a legal statute could create subjects. Second, the cases, especially the final case, *Craw v. Ramsey*, led to a reflection on the jurisdictional limits of naturalization and the rights of colonies to pass laws that have effect within England's territorial borders. The Ramsey cases show how the argument over whether natural allegiance could be created was also a debate about whether natural rights inhered in the individual or in the state.

Ramsey was naturalized in England in 1603, the same year as the union. (He had come to England as a member of King James VI's retinue and as a favorite of the king, having rescued James from an attempted kidnapping in Scotland three years prior.) Becoming an English subject enabled Ramsey to purchase a large manor with eighty acres in Kingston-upon-Thames in Surrey. Upon the earl's death in 1626, the question of who would inherit Ramsey's estate seemed, at first, to be a mundane matter. Ramsey himself never seemed to doubt that he was anything but a subject of England when he drafted a will bequeathing his property to the heir of his brother Nicholas, an alien Scot. Yet after the earl died, a royal inquisition intervened to declare that Ramsey had, in fact, passed without an heir. To challenge the escheat, two cases launched by the earl's nephews, John II and Patrick, were brought before the court in 1656. Even though the Crown had reverted the earl's property, each of the earl's nephews believed he had a claim to it. Such was their belief that John II leased Ramsey's manor in 1642 to one J. Foster, on the understanding that his claim to the land was valid; Patrick, in turn, made a similar lease. The question brought before the courts concerned which cousin, vis-à-vis their lessor, could hold the title to the earl's estate. Yet their claims were complicated by the fact that all three of the earl's brothers, as well as the earl's father, Robert Ramsey, were antenati Scots (Fig. 1).

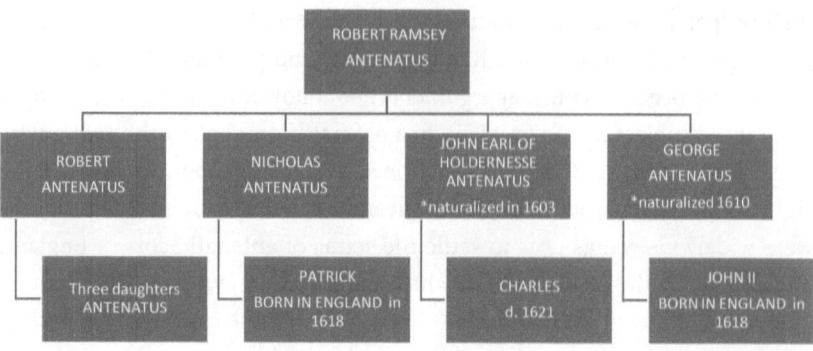

Figure 1.

Only one of John Ramsey's brothers, George, had been naturalized in 1610 by an act of the English Parliament. The ruling of *Calvin's Case* precluded aliens from inheriting English property, so now the court had to decide whether the naturalized son of an alien father was even capable of devising and deposing his property to an alien brother. Ultimately, *Foster v. Ramsey* was resolved in favor of the earl's nephew, John II, on the grounds that his father, George, was a naturalized subject capable of inheriting from a naturalized brother.

That, however, was not the end of the story. Because the case, like the suit involving young James Colville's holdings, extended to matters beyond property—with implications for all subjects living under common law—it was adjourned to the Exchequer Chamber, where seven justices presiding upheld a critical rule for the earl's brother George, affirming that naturalization made the brothers only inheritable to one another. Much like the English properties belonging to Colville in *Calvin's Case*, Ramsey's estate had become the locus of a charged debate about the foundations and jurisdiction of nationality. The court's efforts to rule on the issue directly took up the schismatic ideas about natural allegiance bequeathed by Coke, but this time, they felt the need to explain them more fully.

The reports written by the lawyers and justices involved in the Ramsey cases treat naturalization as a peculiar legal fiction designed to integrate the antenati into the national community of the crowns. In trying to ascertain whether one of Ramsey's relatives could inherit the earl's estate, lawyers and justices had to interpret the meaning of naturalization and the process by which it nullified the conditions of foreign birth and allegiance. This was no ordinary endeavor. The effort drew in and on a philosophical dispute about legal mimesis that explored to what extent a naturalized subject could be a *real* subject. How did a foreigner become, through naturalization, as if they had always been a natural subject? Naturalization had existed as an option for Scots living in England in the middle of the seventeenth century, but many questions about the precise nature of the metamorphosis remained open, as the idea of becoming or being made a natural English subject proved as much a source of fear for natural subjects as a source of lucrative interest for their country.

The first two of the Ramsey cases ruled that naturalization could allow John Ramsey to pass along his estate to his naturalized brother. But within these cases, complicated ideas emerged in the arguments advanced by the three justices of the Exchequer Chamber that further shaped the idea of naturalization. These judges opined that Parliament's power of naturalization, what was termed by Chief Justice Orlando Bridgman a "civil birth," should be more limited.[38] A liberal view of naturalization, Bridgman insisted, would permit enemies of England to live as subjects in the realm without any sense of loyalty to the Crown. An act of naturalization that read, "as if he were born in England," meant no less, in Bridgman's opinion, than one that read, "as if he were born in England *of foreign parents*."[39] According to Bridgman, naturalization did not erase an individual's foreign lineage; that lineage always lingered. Bridgman clearly favored the French royal model of naturalization, in which naturalized citizens remained forever tainted by their foreign origins. In sixteenth-century France, a naturalized citizen was bound by legal disability; the identity between citizen and alien never fused in the conjoining manner of English naturalization.[40] In Bridgman's estimation, *Calvin's Case* had affirmed that allegiance was *ad fidem regis*. An alien Scot could never change the allegiance they were born into despite having changed their "legal blood." Parliament did not have—and should not have—the fundamental power to alter nature. It, in other words, could "make a woman mayor or justice of peace, for they are creatures of men, but it cannot alter the course of nature" and make a woman into a man.[41] Naturalization was a procedural shortcut, not an act of God.

Behind the dissenting judges' opinion lurked the fear that an act of Parliament could, in the words of Bridgman, ipso facto overrule the "obligation of nature" and create new subjects in the past and the future.[42] This is a specter I call the *naturalization imaginary*. Because Coke had not articulated precisely how a naturalized subject's allegiance could be understood as perpetual and indelible under common law, the ruling in favor of John II's inheritance appeared, to the dissenting judges, to give Parliament wide-ranging authority to erase the distinction between the status of aliens and the status of natural-born subjects. To them, Coke had supposed that a naturalized subject was the same as a natural-born subject to preserve the integrity of the doctrine of perpetual allegiance, yet he had either overlooked or ignored what might happen to that subject's original allegiance when subjected to the rule of another crown. Thus, to the dissenting judges, naturalization appeared to annul the very natural-law principle on which the status of the natural-born subject rested. They resented the use of a fiction to obscure the fact of alien birth, fearing, among other things, that this original allegiance could never be overridden and could therefore lead to disloyal behavior in a newly adopted realm.

Further suspicion about the integrity of naturalization's transformative work can be found in Justice Heneage Finch's dissenting opinion in *Craw v. Ramsey*. Finch, echoing the French position, argued that naturalization could do no more than produce an inferior imitation of a natural subject: "The copy cannot exceed its original," Finch claimed, "[and] neither [can] the stream be purer than the foundation."[43] In other words, the child of a foreigner cannot be natural when the father is not. Alienage, in this view, is a form of permanent corruption that cannot be "cured," thus, defected, the naturalized subject is forever bent toward a different class from the natural-born subject. This view of naturalization ultimately came to be enshrined in a 1682 legal primer drafted by the Irish lawyer Charles Molloy, who appears to have drawn on the language of the Ramsey reports to formulate an entry on naturalization, describing it as a "cloathe" covering an alien's "natural Consanguity with a Civil hereditary quality."[44] Naturalized foreigners, in Molloy's view, could be regarded as subjects within England, but their original allegiance to the king or queen of their natal country could never be issued away, and indeed should always be feared. For Molloy and others, such as Justice Bridgman, a person's original allegiance always remained a source of potential treason. Not until the late nineteenth century would dual allegiance be accepted as legally permissible. At this time, a person's "true" allegiance could not be altered by law, and hence a newly ascribed naturalized status was viewed by many as limited, superficial, and not actually a form of allegiance at all.

Proponents of a liberal approach to the problem of subject creation, meanwhile, proposed within the Ramsey cases a competing explanation of naturalization as a process of restoration. In *Foster v. Ramsey*, the lawyer John Maynard imagined naturalization as a "restitution" of an alien's "capacities" as a natural-born subject: "Naturalizations are acts of grace, and so to be taken liberally, being but a restitution to those capacities which [in aliens] are restrained for reasons of state.... That they shall, to all purposes be made natural liege people, are operative words to this purpose, and [the earl and George Ramsey] may do anything that two brothers in England might."[45] For Maynard, naturalization triggered a latent property that allowed the individual to fashion a new self. Through a kind of temporal acrobatics, naturalization returned or restored an alien to their original status as liege subject. Justice Hale, in a concurring explanation, also conceptualized naturalization as a restorative act. Naturalization "cures" the disease of alienage, he suggested, using a medicinal metaphor that implied an alien could return to a healthy state.[46] In these conceits, Maynard and Hale followed Bacon's argument in *Calvin's Case* that "by the law of nature all men in the world are naturalized one towards another. . . . It was civil and national laws that brought in these words, and differences, of civis and exterus, alien and native."[47] Before the restrictive boundaries of the state, all people, Bacon contended, were natural subjects living in a state of communal nature. Consequently, from his perspective, which Maynard and Hale echoed, the retroactive aspect of naturalization restored aliens to their original state as natural subjects, activating the natural capacities of the individual that had long lain dormant. Upon an act of naturalization, unlike the denizen whose conversion into a subject could only be propulsive, the naturalized subject acquired a new life history in which they had always been a natural subject of England. In this way, naturalization was both a natural process—a return to the state of nature—and a civil process that fictionalized the belonging of alien outsiders. Naturalization now lent a temporal narrative through which individuals could erase their pasts.

We can see that the English legal system inherited the basic framework of this temporal loophole from Roman law. According to Clifford Ando, legal fictions that rewrite the past to shape the future were fairly common in ancient Roman law. Because legal identities were porous—"slaves were freed; aliens became citizens; citizens were 'diminished'; Roman citizens who emigrated as colonists to a Latin colony underwent voluntary denaturalization"—jurisprudential discourse had to imagine how status boundaries could be crossed in a manner that was consistent with the legal fact that it was the very project of the legal fiction to affirm.[48] Often these acts of imagination could be quite complex, as in cases seeking to grant citizenship to enslaved persons or to allow aliens to serve in military legions (a service typically reserved for citizens). "In both cases," says Ando, "a non-normative situation in the present is rectified by an enactment that operates in two directions: the present and future are brought into conformity with the law via a grant of citizenship, even as a new past is created that is continuous with the future now being enacted."⁴⁹ As to how the Romans made sense of this rectification, Ando writes, "the legitimacy of the legal system seems to have trumped any concern over the ideological consequences of redescribing the prior life of slaves."⁵⁰ This seems to be the case with the legal fiction of naturalization in seventeenth-century England as well.

For the justices involved in the Ramsey cases, the legal fiction of naturalization voids—or avoids—the unerasable evidence of an earlier natural birth under a foreign power. Such a narrative, outlandish as it may seem, was necessary in order to reconcile a seventeenth-century law that failed to anticipate how nationality could be eradicated or renounced, or how one person could simultaneously hold two national allegiances. To resolve the status of naturalized subjects, judges sought to override the foreign conditions of their birth, either by subscribing to a view that, in natural law, they were originally natural subjects of England or, more simply, by overlooking the conditions of their birth altogether. In the former, the civil birth of naturalization was treated, through a retroactive fictional rewriting of history, as if it were the natural birth of the subject. In the latter, naturalization was thought to produce a second-class copy. In neither of these explanations, though, did what was called naturalization's "civil birth" involve the total eradication of the subject's birth culture through assimilation, as it would in the nineteenth century. In the seventeenth and eighteenth centuries, naturalization either returned an alien to their original state in natural law, which existed before any civil process, or, more expediently, occluded that earlier natural birth from view for the purposes of property inheritance.

With the Ramsey cases, naturalization was viewed, as it was in Roman law, overtly as a "fiction." Justice John Vaughan and others proposed naturalization as "a fiction of law," affecting only those who consented to it. "It hath the like effect that a man's birth has, where the lawmakers have power, but not in other places they have not."⁵¹ Modern readers might misread *fiction* in these instances as meaning something imaginative, in the manner invoked by the early modern English philosopher Jeremy Bentham, who, despite having claimed the utility of "fictitious entities" for describing the world, derided legal fiction as "a willful falsehood, having for its object the stealing of legislative power by and for hands, which could not, or durst not, openly claim it."⁵² Bentham's meaning of *fiction* is not shared, however, by those involved in the Ramsey cases. In the 1650s these invocations would have derived exclusively from the idea of *fictio legis*, a creation without precedent. What these lawyers and judges meant by *fiction* was a necessary and obvious legal construction to achieve an intended result (indeed, the word *fiction* is derived from the word *fingere*, meaning "form" or "construction"). In ancient Roman law, this kind of fiction is evident in the extension of citizenship to a person who either lost it or did not have it before. If, for example, a Roman citizen became enslaved and their status as a free citizen was suspended, they could no longer testify in court or pass down property. To remedy this point of the law, the Romans established a rule in which any citizen who testified after falling into slavery would be treated as if "he had not been made a prisoner"—as if the law prohibiting their testimony had not, in fact, existed.[53] This legal fiction annulled a legal provision without contesting or arguing against its rule—without, that is, convincingly overriding it. For Romans, the legal fiction helped sidestep a legal rule but did not facilitate a phantasmagoric rebirth.

For those drafting the Ramsey court case reports, however, the principle of *fictio legis* did not provide enough clarification at a moment of intense political and economic debate about naturalization. To shore up their explanations, the justices and lawyers involved in the cases embraced analogies of disease and clothing (naturalization as a cure for a defect, or a "cloathe" cloaking an alien birth) to justify their fiction in relation to naturalization. The visions of naturalization offered in the Ramsey cases also make repeated use of reproductive language to explain how this temporal process might work. Naturalization is described as a "second," "civic," or "political" birth. For some justices, naturalization presided over a return to a formative natural state—a clean slate or tabula rasa—from which a former alien could reclaim their status as a natural person. Naturalization, from this point of view, returns subjects, through a legal fiction, to what they always were and, in doing so, provides them with a new, but not invented, life history.

These efforts fell short of fully explaining how one erased or rendered nonexistent a stranger's original allegiance, but they provided elements of plot and narrative to illustrate how the alien subject might transition to the status of natural subject. The fiction these reports deployed was more practical than imaginative, but it was not entirely without explanation. The artificial construction of naturalization was paramount; it did not need to be enjoyable or literally convincing to have an effect. Overall, the Ramsey cases reveal how legal writers thought of allegiance: that becoming a subject was a matter of procedure and paperwork, saying the right things at the right time to the right people. Nevertheless, they still wrestled with how to separate the fiction of allegiance from its natural counterpart. Even if naturalization was procedural, it still had to be construed as somehow natural to remain consistent, in appearance, with natural law. This is why the judges went to elaborate lengths to explain how it worked.

The legal fiction of naturalization all seemed to hang together until the court contended with the thorny matter of jurisdiction in *Craw v. Ramsey*, which exposed its obviously arbitrary hierarchy. This case was the last brought before the King's Bench concerning John Ramsey's estate, issued on behalf of the earl's other nephew, Patrick. The case focused on a creative claim concocted by the lawyer John Maynard, who argued Patrick had a right to inherit the earl's property because his father had been naturalized in Ireland and died in England. The Irish Parliament had naturalized all Scottish antenati in 1634, and though Patrick's father had never lived in or traveled to Ireland, in Maynard's brilliant design, a naturalization statute for Scots in Ireland—a country conquered and colonized by England—should extend to Scots in England. What this meant, sensationally if it succeeded, was a new legal fiction recognizing people whom England had refused to countenance as natural subjects of England by way of a general naturalization bill in Ireland, a dominion over which England held sovereignty. "Your Highness' loving subjects of these your Highness' realms of England, Scotland, and Ireland," began the Irish statute, "are now growing into one nation, without all mark of difference or distinction."[54]

The judges in *Craw v. Ramsey* swiftly shut down this argument, ruling against the inconceivable fiction that Patrick's father, Nicholas, could inherit land in England by way of Irish naturalization. The stakes of the idea were too high, as a ruling in the argument's favor implied any colony or plantation might be able to pass laws with jurisdictional effect in England. Justice Vaughan held that "no laws made in any other dominion acquired by conquest, or new plantation, by the King's lieutenants, substitutes, governours, or people there, by virtue of the King's letters patent, can make a man inherit in England."[55] Referencing the situation in Ireland, Vaughan made clear that naturalization could only make a person into a natural-born subject in places where the lawmakers who passed such laws had jurisdiction. Naturalization could invent new liege subjects through a legal fiction, but the act of invention itself could not be universal. Or, in another framing, naturalization could produce a subject only if that subject had the consent of the nation, and naturalization was a legal fiction that affected only those who consented to it. For Vaughan, "no fiction of law" could make a natural subject in England via the jurisdiction of Ireland—such an idea outlandishly proposed that colonized countries had the power to determine British subjecthood. Moreover, the conceit undermined

England's sovereign authority over Ireland. Leaning on the feudal concept of homage, Vaughan argued all allegiance was hierarchical: as an act of power administered by Parliament, naturalization would threaten the stability of English rule if colonies were allowed to make English subjects. If *Calvin's Case* introduced the fear that alien Scots might become treasonous to England, *Craw v. Ramsey* intensified that concern with its discussion of naturalization as a legal fiction that could give foreigners entering the nation a new life history, while also allowing foreigners elsewhere to imagine that laws passed locally could have effect in England.

What stands out in the Ramsey reports, with their various arguments about devising property and inheritance, is, on the one hand, a sense of the total free license afforded by naturalization, and, on the other, an awareness of its hierarchical complications. All of the judges agreed on the threshold question, which was whether naturalization could grant foreigners the privileges of a natural-born Englishmen. Yet many, like a number of parliamentarians, remained wary of or hostile toward the idea of introducing new subjects into England, especially some who may come to enjoy a higher status than those naturally born there. Essentially, they viewed naturalization as an affront to the natural hierarchy and the power invested in the English nation to determine its subjects. Nevertheless, by articulating the complex substitutional and restorative properties of naturalization, the Ramsey reports unwittingly identified a powerful dual mode of subject creation, one that compensated for the law's inability to jettison natural allegiance. In their framing, naturalization *created* by converting an unnatural subject into a natural one and *restored* to the alien a right they never formally had at birth. That meant the justices, through their arguments, cast naturalization as an act of creation that heretically rivaled the natural creation of subjects by God—the very origins postulated by Coke as the foundation of natural allegiance. As James Kettner summarizes, "Naturalization was a legal act, but it equated a man's status in the eyes of the law with that of a manmade subject by God and nature."[56] The practice endowed foreigners with rights the English received at birth, perversely rebirthing them as natural subjects.

At heart, this complex and obviously contradictory process had to be narrated this way because there was no existent legal framing that could explain how nationality converted aliens to subjects. The Ramsey cases often resorted to clunky metaphors involving clothing, birth, and disease because the law of nature and the law of nations were indistinguishable.[57] To explain the immigration of foreigners required explaining their transformation in natural law.

Naturalization for early modern aliens was, in my framing, a "paranational" issue: it brought foreigners from outside the nation inside without recognizing the outside world in which they existed. The ideas forged in the Ramsey cases formulated, sometimes unknowingly or without full reflection, an alternative conception of allegiance that would come to occupy, to great consternation, political and cultural thinking at the dawn of the eighteenth century.

Locke and the Paranational

If the seventeenth century was a period for exploring the limits of the doctrine of allegiance, then the late seventeenth and early eighteenth centuries would be the period that entertained a new imaginative range for the concept of allegiance. Although the terms of the discussion had shifted from the early days of *Calvin's Case* and the Ramsey cases, when naturalization was a legal fiction used to solve matters concerning the issue of Scots in England, certain continuities remained between the early legal concerns over the question of artificial allegiance and the influential pamphlets later published by William Petty, Andrew Marvel, John Locke, and Daniel Defoe. These authors, writing on economic and political matters in the seventeenth and eighteenth centuries, continued to frame their interest in naturalization around the status of aliens in England rather than the status of colonists and colonized abroad—a large distinction, in addition to the sovereign nation-state system, between proto-immigration law in the Stuart period and the immigration policies of the nineteenth century. But one major difference between the early legal cases concerned with naturalization and the intellectual debates that would follow in the late seventeenth century is that naturalization became a right unto itself. In the intellectual debates that picked up in the later seventeenth century, legal and economic fictions about naturalization became evermore connected to individual liberty: the right of the enterprising individual to travel between national identities without burden.

After a bill was presented to Parliament in 1664 seeking the passage of a general naturalization act, a debate over general naturalization took shape among a set of English economic and political writers, including Thomas Sheridan, Nicholas Barbon, Josiah Child, John Pollexfen, John Bellers, Charles Davenant, and William Temple, who all encouraged reduced fees for immigration.[58] A number of political pamphlets and tracts made the justifications for naturalized allegiance known to a wider audience. These texts, which drew on the fictional conceits of the Ramsey cases, sought to explain to the public the broader repercussions of naturalization beyond the niceties of legal nomenclature. Acquiring a private naturalization act, such as the one undertaken by John Ramsey, was expensive, costing 50 to 60 pounds, or approximately 24,000 pounds in today's currency. To expand access to the act, advocates of general naturalization proposed a price of less than three shillings.[59] More radically, proponents of a "universal naturalization" also advocated for the benefit of naturalization to "extend to all Persons of all Nations, of all Religions, Protestants, Papists, Jews, Mohametans, Turks, Moors, [and] Pagans."[60] The chief advantage of an open-door naturalization policy was to help England become "the commune and nobile Emporium of the world."[61] To make England a leader in trade, Parliament, they argued, had to suspend any boundaries between subjects and aliens, including religious boundaries.

Many economists and political writers bolstered the idea of a liberal and even universal naturalization policy, because they feared emigration to the American colonies would drain England of its population. To them, general naturalization was an appealing way to encourage Europe's Protestants to immigrate to England. In their debates, naturalization appears not as a fictional workaround for alien property holders, as it did in earlier legal cases, but as a full-scale economic and political policy idea. The plan especially gained prominence after October 17, 1685, when King Louis XIV of France revoked the Edict of Nantes, which had offered French Protestants a measure of toleration to practice their religion without persecution. The edict restored Catholicism as the official religion of France and suppressed all nonconforming religions. Protestant churches and schools were destroyed to wide enthusiasm and under official sanction, and French Protestants lost key civil and religious liberties. As hundreds of thousands of Huguenot refugees searched Europe for sanctuary, English parliamentarians weighed, again, a general naturalization act. Many Huguenots had chosen to settle in England in the late seventeenth century, in the east of London, but just as many had found refuge elsewhere, especially in Holland. These skilled artificers, proponents of naturalization believed, would lift the economic prospects of England while strengthening the country's Protestant population at a time when many feared a Catholic heir to the English throne.

The cause of general naturalization did not find legislative success until 1709, and then only briefly. Too many influential men, such as Sir John Knight the Younger, feared that the immigration of other "races" would blot out the "English breed."[62] A majority of Anglicans did not support general naturalization, though proponents tried to promote its advantages for Protestantism.

Others, such as the economist William Petty and political pamphleteer Samuel Johnson, argued against the policy idea, convinced it would send poor foreigners to feed off of England. Johnson went further, arguing beyond economics to decry the problem an artificial allegiance would create: mainly, the potential for spies to infiltrate the realm and steal its national secrets.

Although he was not the most obvious or vociferous of its advocates, Locke also took part in the debate about naturalization. In December 1693, more than twenty years after the rulings of the Ramsey cases, Locke wrote a short essay to influence parliamentary debate on a proposed naturalization bill entitled "For a General Naturalization" in which he presented an argument in favor of increasing the population in England for the benefit of its trade. Just as Rome had granted its citizens privileges in exchange for having children, Locke believed England could increase its population through naturalization. While the core of Locke's argument rests on the economic value of trade over land and the trade of people as goods, the philosopher also argues against a common perception that foreigners, by coming to England, would act as drains on private charity. Even if, Locke surmises, poor, unskilled people arrived in England, they would soon become industrious. "Nobody," he writes, "can transport himself into another country with hopes to live upon mens labour."[63] Unlike the English poor, who are entitled to parish maintenance by law, aliens will receive no social handouts. For Locke, England need not fear the act would lead to a flood of impoverished people. Naturalization would only solicit the rich, who, upon arrival, would immediately begin contributing to the prosperity of the nation. For this reason, Locke judged it was safe for England to open its doors and allow free settlement. Profit would reign over inconvenience, in his view.

Perhaps because Locke's pamphlet on general naturalization was an unpublished occasional piece, scholars have not paid much attention to its relevance to the philosopher's empirical study of the individual and political writings on consenting citizenship.[64] When Locke wrote about naturalization, he was tapping into the newly born legal fiction that the conditions of a person's birth could be overlooked in law for the sake of national trade.[65] But Locke's engagement with naturalization, brief as it was, suggests his theories have a wider purview than national sovereignty or empirical individualism, and that they are bound up with the paranational concept of voluntary allegiance I have identified. In recent years, the historian David Armitage has taken up the question of whether Locke can be identified as an early international thinker. Armitage notes that Locke, like Thomas Hobbes, believed that after the development of civil society, in which individuals contract themselves to the state, nations themselves remain in a state of nature with no larger body or head to guide relations between them.[66] "The whole Community," Locke wrote in 1690 in the *Two Treatises*, "is one Body in the State of Nature, in respect of all other States or Persons outside of its Community."[67] Yet individuals in Locke's schema may break their covenant and return to the state of nature. For the most part, an individual's right to break a contract with the sovereign has been read as the right of rebellion against a tyrannical ruler: the right of revolution *within* the nation; but in the *Two Treatises*, Locke also speaks of the individual who leaves the territorial jurisdiction of the sovereign. When a migrant leaves the commonwealth, the commonwealth no longer has any power over them. A migrant is a free agent, in Locke's account, with the right to "go and incorporate himself into any other Commonwealth, or to agree with others to begin a new one, *in vacuis locis*, in any part of the World, they can find free and unpossessed."[68] In the *Second Treatise*, Locke qualifies this right, however, in line with arguments about perpetual allegiance. He argues that while "*a Child is born a subject of no Country, or Government*," they forfeit their right to leave at the "Age of Discretion," when they must give tacit or express consent to be a member of the political society they find themselves in.[69] Thereafter, the only time this individual has the right to emigrate from their country is in the event of a catastrophe, such as a military invasion or an earthquake. Three years later, in 1693, Locke, when writing about naturalization, had apparently changed his opinion. Now he endorsed the idea of an individual leaving a former allegiance to take up business or trade as a naturalized subject in England. In this way, Locke gave voice to an idea of paranationality that had been churning through the courts and in pamphlets: the question of how individuals were to change allegiances, to move to new territories, and to covenant anew.

Locke and other general naturalization proponents articulate a picture of a political world that is both interconnected and self-interested—a picture that today, three centuries later, some scholars might venture to call globalist but that I have recast as paranational to underline the primitive nature of immigration law in the early modern period. Lacking law and norms for the handling of immigration, naturalization was the only legal vessel, so to speak, that could cross between foreigner and subject. At this time, the idea of being blocked from a country's borders, or restricted from immigration by laws, was not a feature of law or political life. For Locke, individuals retained a fundamental freedom to absolve a social contract merely by leaving its jurisdiction, a right Locke and others readily accepted because it was a right effectively unavailable to most people in the less mobile seventeenth century, and because it authorized their economic and political ideals. The same holds true for his theory of naturalization. Locke understood naturalization as a form of interest conversion: once foreigners leave their native countries and settle in England, their self-interest becomes England's interest. In this way, his argument for naturalization resembles the standard liberal justification, as employed by Defoe on behalf of the Palatine refugees (a case that I outline more fully in Chapter 3), that foreigners will be good for the economic prospects of England. Locke's view of naturalization is also compatible with the outline of the autonomous, consenting individual put forward in his political and philosophical writings. Locke himself, it may be recalled, fled to Holland to avoid charges of sedition from the Crown. In Holland, he fraternized with Protestant French refugees whose plight after the Revocation of the Edict of Nantes would have affected his thinking. Through his pamphlet on naturalization, it is possible to see Locke, in flagrant disavowal of the interpretation of perpetual allegiance offered by *Calvin's Case*, as offering a novel view of nationality more in line with the discussion of naturalization in the reports attached to the Ramsey cases: the idea that naturalization can override the natural fact of birth through a secularized legal form separating the legal from the empirical individual. The justices in the Ramsey cases conceived of all subjects as originally "natural" until made unnatural. In a like vein, Locke theorizes individuals as in a state of nature until they consent to enter a contract between an individual and a sovereign. Unlike the jurists of *Calvin's Case*, Locke considered territorial jurisdiction.

Locke, like Coke, did not expressly think through the internationalism of his theory of government. As John Dunn writes, "The political liberty that Locke had sought to vindicate in the *Two Treatises* was a liberty for Protestants within the British State."[70] In the later stages of his roles as secretary to Lord Shaftesbury, secretary of the Lord Proprietors of Carolina (1668–71), secretary to the Council of Trade and Plantations (1673–74), and member of the Board of Trade (1696–1700), Locke developed policies in the self-interest of England.[71] While it is difficult to construe Locke as an expressly international thinker, he is a paranational one: his ideas about the self-owned liberty of individual rights advance from his thinking about the right to leave or to enter other national territories. Under this conception, naturalization is the formal device that allows natural individuals to transgress the limits of natural allegiance.[72]

It is worth noting that the individual Locke sees becoming malleable as they absolve a covenant with a community is not quite the same conception of the individual emphasized by literary scholars of the period. Ian Watt, Nancy Armstrong, and Jonathan Kramnick have all contextualized individualism from the perspective of Locke's account of personal identity in the *Essay concerning Human Understanding*. According to Armstrong, Locke's theorization of the individual as self-enclosed and self-governed underlines the development of prose fiction in the period: the novel, she writes, "perform[s] what the Lockeans could only theorize: the possibility that a new form of literacy could provide something on the order of a supplement capable of turning an early modern subject into a self-governing individual."[73] Yet I stress the relation between Locke and the Ramsey cases because these accounts understand naturalization as creatively generative and uniquely volitional. Naturalization relies on a retrospective structure: an unnatural subject is returned, through legal artifice, to an original state of liberty paradoxically by undoing the unnatural distinctions created by the mechanism of political language. Rather than producing domesticated, self-governing individuals, naturalization instead legislated the individual's right to move autonomously between nations and governments—a more republican idea of citizenship, not tied specifically or necessarily to any conception of monarchial allegiance. Moreover, naturalization does all this not by showing a fully realized interior individual but by narrating a life absent of subjectivity and interiority.

The Ramsey cases and Locke's writing on naturalization therefore set the precedent for the full-blown engagement with naturalization that would occur with the passage of the General Naturalization Act in 1709. The justices in the Ramsey cases, and later Locke, conjure individuals who have no natural or national allegiances and individuals whose natural rights can absolve their contract with a national sovereign. What becomes evident from these portrayals is that the individual subject, in their imagining, was far from a domestic or passive subject. As Clive Parry summarizes in one of the few histories of naturalization, "In a time when ingress to the country was free and when little or no inquiry was made as to circumstances or intents, what was before and afterwards a matter of grace and favor must have approximated very closely to a matter of right."[74] Undoubtedly, naturalization, as I have historicized it, will appear hypocritical to many readers from the retrospective lens of history: dissenters, Catholics, Jews, Africans, and Indigenous people were all excluded at various points from the vision of settlement propagated by naturalization schemes. In the short term, naturalization was a temporary project to induce the migration of foreigners for the sake of national development, and it is limited to periods in immigration history when labor was in short supply. The elasticity of naturalized national identity occurred across identitarian lines—religious affiliation and, later, racial categorization were very much particulars of exclusion for naturalization, though not exclusively for Locke.[75] Yet naturalization bent the feudal idea of natural allegiance by imagining a world in which allegiance could change or be overlooked. The idea that foreigners had a right to leave the country of their birth and contract with a new crown or republic fundamentally rearranged the understanding of subjection in the seventeenth and eighteenth centuries, making way for a civil notion of national belonging—a voluntary allegiance—that premised belonging on relationships and equivalencies forged by civil law.

In the seventeenth century, naturalization was understood by lawyers and justices as an ad hoc parliamentary procedure for settling specific foreigners in the absence of laws guiding the formal reception of strangers. At the beginning of the eighteenth century, the practice of naturalization was a political sweetener dangled before foreign craftsmen and Protestants in the hope that they might take up residence in England, swelling the population and growing its trade. Under this scheme of naturalization, foreigners were transformed or "reborn" as natural subjects through the artificial pathways of law. This was done not to assimilate them to the national community but to make them correspond to natural-born subjects for the sake of the internationalization of property. It is the paranational component that originally made naturalization so unsettling for writers and politicians in the seventeenth and eighteenth centuries. Naturalization was thought to transform—in the past and in the present—the natural life of a foreigner. It brought foreigners into a relationship of allegiance with the English Crown, allowing them to become natural in a local and domestic context while suspending from view their unbreakable allegiance to another crown, an allegiance that formed the cornerstone of protection for all subjects and that, if allowed to be easily jettisoned, could lead to a breakdown of natural hierarchies. A foreigner could be domestically natural for the sake of England's growth and trade, yet still a natural subject somewhere else. There simply was no coherent immigration law established to make sense of how allegiance traveled in an international context.

Naturalization produced through its fictions a fundamental friction between an older understanding of the nation and an emergent contractual model. In England, a naturalized Scot was now perfectly equal to a natural-born English subject, yet that equality resided in legal language rather than the divine right of kings. Natural allegiance became something that could be created artificially according to the whims and willpower of Parliament. What was so troublesome about naturalization in the seventeenth century, then, was that it exposed how the natural rights of the individual had no national preference; they were free to roam—and did in an obvious and overt manner. Naturalization emerged as an engineered process, a legal fiction to fast-track or short-circuit a foreigner through human and natural laws. It did not hide its manner of artificial creation, nor did it make cultural demands. If you knew where to look, naturalization was all plain to see.

CHAPTER 2

Ideas of Naturalization

To naturalize is to blend nature with history. Raymond Williams advanced this idea in his seminal essay "Ideas of Nature," which examines how humans project their own ideas onto nature while fantasizing their separation from it. For Williams, as for many scholars, the crucial task of the social critic is to denaturalize the world, to reveal how things we think of as natural are, in fact, social and political creations. "We have to look at all our products and activities, good and bad . . . to see the relationships between them which are our own relationships," he writes.[1] Hedgerows may seem like time-weathered features of the English countryside, for example ("little lines / Of sportive wood run wild," as William Wordsworth styles them in "Tintern Abbey"), but they were first introduced as field boundaries to carve up the land for agricultural and aristocratic interests. Analogously, writers hark back to a primordial "state of nature," an invented primitive condition before the introduction of civil society, to rationalize the inevitability of certain political conventions and laws. Naturalization, according to Williams, is not the supernatural process of making nature; it is the human practice of faking it.

Given Williams's interest in naturalization as an important process in human history, it is surprising that he does not take up the word in his influential *Keywords: A Vocabulary of Culture and Society*, which offers critical etymologies for derivative terms such as *native* and *nation*.[2] Perhaps naturalization was what Williams saw himself as exposing in his analysis and he saw no need for a second definition. He would not have been the only person of his generation to make this assumption. In 1977 Fredric Jameson used *naturalization* in the title of his review essay on Louis Marin's *Utopiques: Jeux d'espaces* ("Of Islands and Trenches: Naturalization and the Production of Utopian Discourse") without once using the word in the body of the review.[3] One gets the sense that the word *naturalization* is, somewhat ironically, for Marxist critics like Williams and Jameson, the self-evident process by which humans make nature.

But what happens when we excavate the word *naturalization* with the same historical contextualism and etymological consideration that Williams extended to other terms in *Keywords*? This is precisely what I do in this chapter. In particular, I show that *naturalization* in seventeenth- and eighteenth-century legal and literary history has a very different meaning from the modern idea to which we have grown accustomed. In the eighteenth century, the dominant meaning of *naturalization* was that of a legal fiction that finagled an equivalence between a foreigner and natural-born subject in civic law. Much modern literary and cultural theory, by contrast, understands naturalization as the ideological process of passing off political and social constructions as if they had always been with us. Naturalization is a form that *mimics* biological (and therefore natural) modes of reproduction. Naturalization, in early modernity, was an overtly fictional process invented by law, while our received definition of naturalization in literary studies and history today, in the work of Roland Barthes, Fredric Jameson, Jonathan Culler, and Lauren Berlant (to name only the few I will engage with here), derives from cultural understandings of the interplay between language, reading, and larger social and political ideologies. There is obviously no causal connection between these ideas of naturalization, yet the grip of these modern ideological notions has prevented us from understanding a different use of the term. In early modernity, writers did not fear naturalization as a projection of biology but rather the opposite: they feared naturalization as a *nonbiological* process.

What disconcerted eighteenth-century jurists and critics about naturalization was that it proposed to alter a foreigner's life history in the past and rebirth a new story as if they had always been a subject of the British Crown. It was a procedural rather than a biological process. As we have seen in the historical narrative charted in the previous chapter, legal naturalization in the seventeenth and eighteenth centuries brought new subjects into being in defiance of traditional and tacit understandings of English subjecthood. Those new subjects were hardly oppressed, and the legal introduction of rich merchants and other entrepreneurs into England was hardly an egalitarian operation. Nonetheless, the process of naturalization, in its defiance of the strictures of an understanding of perpetual allegiance, prepared the way for a civic interpretation of national belonging that persists today. To this day, naturalization remains the only way a noncitizen can obtain citizenship in a nation-state outside of the biological protocols of birthright and descent. Before the rise of strong forms of nationalism and the codification of nationality law in the nineteenth and twentieth centuries, naturalization ushered new subjects into the national community despite assumptions of their unnaturalness under a monarchial model of allegiance.

As I argue in the second half of this chapter, this earlier legal understanding of naturalization can inspire us to consider a new way of thinking about naturalization as a process that creates new subjects. And in holding up naturalization rather than denaturalization, I emphasize how categories that critics elsewhere might chide for being artificial also prove to be sheltering and sustaining; they can bring new subjects not only into view but also into recognition. Such is the line of argument I pursue at the end of this chapter in a reading of Samuel Richardson's *Pamela*. *Naturalization* becomes a new critical term for understanding the cultural work of making subjects appear in public in ways that stymie a reader's ability to reason their lack of belonging. As the three case studies that make up the second part of this book will show, early naturalization was an open fiction that sought to reengineer allegiance and subjecthood, allowing for the appearance of new subjects in national life. In anticipation of these studies, this chapter enlivens the imaginative aspects of naturalization, treating the operation as much more than a historical idea limited to the field of immigration.

Ideas of Naturalization

The English word *naturalization* derives from the French word *naturaliser* and the Latin word *natura*. In Latin, *naturificatus* means "brought into being." Yet in its earliest usage in English, naturalization had a decidedly more civic function: "the action of admitting a foreigner or immigrant to the position and rights of citizenship, or of investing with the privileges of a native-born subject." The civic demeanor of this definition points directly to how it entered the English language. According to the *Oxford English Dictionary*, the English source of the word is a discussion in the Scottish Parliament in 1558, which concerned "Franchemen" living in Scotland.[4] The noun has been in use slightly longer than the verb. In both cases, however, the first English use is in a legal context, and in both cases, the word denotes an activity or process that *does* something rather than *is* something.

The earliest meaning of naturalization was in a legal context ("to make native"). In the Jacobean and Stuart periods, this meant that naturalization was thought to showcase the association between nature and the civil order. In law, naturalization underscored, at each step, the labor of rendering, making, and converting at the heart of its procedure. Historians, cultural critics, lawyers, judges, economists, and politicians did not need to work very hard to see how naturalization intermixed human labor and nature. The civic and the natural, the past and the present, the lawyer and the womb—each of these pairings clanged awkwardly together in the seventeenth- and eighteenth-century legal fiction of naturalization. Indeed, the word *naturalization* itself showcased the mixture. The addition of the suffix *-ization* or *-ize* (to make) to the word *natural* denotes the *process* by which someone or something is made natural. It emphasizes that nature is something made rather than something latent or passive. Early legal naturalization was not a process that presumed a cover-up, as modern cultural ideas about naturalization have held.

In addition to externalizing its techne, the early legal procedure of naturalization challenged an onlooker's ability to differentiate between a subject born naturally and a subject born in law. A critical question emerged: What did it mean that a subject born in law was "as if" they were a natural-born subject? The "as if," on the one hand, signaled that a foreign-born person was to be the same as a native-born subject, but it also called attention to a difference between these individuals. Legal naturalization did not present human law as if it were timelessly natural. In fact, it did the opposite. It revealed the constructedness of human law—yet, as legal fiction, it made a national subject all the same. Once a foreigner elected to be viewed as if they were a natural-born subject, the idea of an allegiance that was determined by blood was thrown into disarray. Justices and other writers devised two ways to sort out this confusion: On the one hand, naturalization might be explained as a magical process that restored a foreigner to their natural state as subject, as one justice in the Ramsey cases theorized in the previous chapter. This meant reworking the past of naturalization to shape the future of allegiance. On the other, naturalization might be regarded as a technique of equivalence, putting a naturalized subject on the same footing as a natural subject. The first explanation was considered heretical, the second more expedient. But both ideas challenged the sanctity of natural law and proposed new ideas about subject creation.

The legal meaning of naturalization was only dominant for twenty years or so, however. From the middle of the fifteenth century to the late sixteenth, the word *naturalization* expanded from its original legal meaning, "to make native," to include the linguistic idea of "adopting into a language," and then finally to refer to "acclimatization," in its looser, cultural sense. All three of these meanings—the legal act of giving a foreigner the rights of a native, the linguistic act of adopting a word into a language, and the social act of making something appear natural—are usefully brought together in the opening passage of Daniel Defoe's novel *Robinson Crusoe*:

> I was born in the Year 1632, in the City of *York*, of a good Family, tho' not of that country, my father being a foreigner of *Bremen*, who settled first at *Hull*. He got a good estate by merchandise, and leaving off his trade, lived afterwards at *York*, from whence he had married my mother, whose relations were named *Robinson*, a very good family in that country, and from whom I was call'd *Robinson Kreutznaer*; but, by the usual corruption of words in England, we are now call'd—nay we call our selves, and write our name—Crusoe, and so my companions always call'd me.[5]

In the very first lines of the novel, Crusoe informs his reader that his father was born in present-day Germany before settling in England. This detail introduces us first and foremost to the politics and economics of naturalization. To trade in merchandise and purchase an estate, Crusoe's father would have had to naturalize in England (otherwise he would have owed alien custom fees and had trouble purchasing and passing down his estate to any of his three sons). While we cannot know whether Crusoe's father undertook naturalization, these opening lines, strikingly, appear to mimic the form of an early petition for naturalization. Individual petitions were standard features of the naturalization procedure. An individual, or a group, would make a short petition before Parliament, and if accepted, a bill of naturalization would then be drawn up. (The procedure for general naturalization was different—it naturalized all people under its generic umbrella in one fell swoop—which is partly why it was so controversial.) The individual petitions tended to follow a standard form, offering something of a short life history for the petitioner. For instance:

> THOMAS WENTWORTH, gent, sonnes unto John Wentworth, Esquier, deceased, borne at North Elmseall in the Countie of Yorke within your highness realme of England. That whereas the said John Wentworth, deceased, was according to the lawes of Holie Church married unto a Dutch woman born at Zutphen in the Province of Gilderland by whom afterwards hee had issue your suppliants the said John Wentworth and Thomas Wentworth, both born at Zutphen aforesaid in the province of Gelderland....[6]
>
> JOSEPH BATAILHEY, born at Bordeaux, for the last 16 years a factor in London for Mr. Leachland, the King's wine merchant, since whose death he has served

wines to the King by order of the Committee for the Revenue: was bred a Protestant, has spent most of his time here and married an English woman.[7]

CHRIS RIDDELL, *alias* ROSHE, jeweler to the Protector. Being a German, and brought up a Protestant, the troubles in my own country preventing the exercise of my religion or trade. I came here 13 years ago, and have lived peaceably, and married Elizabeth, daughter of Mich. Pudsey, of Ellisfield, county Oxon, and have 3 children, who might, on their mother's death, inherit part of their grandfather's estate, if I were naturalized.[8]

Naturalization petitions, despite the variance of style, feature a similar set of particulars: the petitioner's place of birth, place of settlement in England, occupation, marriage, and evidence (if any) of Protestant faith. Together, these details formed a truncated version of the life history of the person pursuing naturalization, a narrative that, if the petition was successful, would be replaced with one describing the foreigner, in past and future, as if they had always been an English subject. As I examine at length in the next chapter, Crusoe's father's petition for naturalization into England has been so successful, both inside and outside the world of the novel, that later generations of readers and reviewers unfamiliar with the legal forms of naturalization have overlooked the Crusoe family's German ancestry, even though this ancestry is rendered as clear as day in the first sentences of the novel. This oversight has allowed Robinson Crusoe to be seen by many readers as an English subject par excellence.

Following the more dominant legal meaning of *naturalization*, cultural and creative understandings of the term also inform the opening passage of *Robinson Crusoe*. Beyond the legal action of giving a foreigner the rights of a native, the passage accentuates the linguistic notion of naturalization as adopting a foreign word into a language, signaled here by the corruption of Robinson's German last name, Kreutznaer—an invention meaning "follower of the cross"—into bastardized English. Yet the pivot from the legal notion of naturalization (as forecast in the details about the national status of Crusoe's father) to the idea of linguistic interchange ultimately works to further liberalize legal ideas about naturalization. It implies that naturalization is a bureaucratic veneer. Notably, the passage focalizes Crusoe from the perspective of a foreigner who decries the English language's "corruption" of foreign words. The line thus contrasts with the opinion of Dr. Samuel Johnson, who understood linguistic naturalization as a foreign language's taking over native English: "This naturalization," he writes in the preface to his *Dictionary* about the introduction of foreign words into English, "is produced ... by an admission into common speech in some metaphorical signification, which is the acquisition of a kind of property among us."[9] The legal idea of naturalization provides the model for the linguistic understanding of the term so resolutely that Johnson's opinions on naturalized words in the English language are essentially indistinguishable from political opinions on general naturalization. He frames the rejection of linguistic naturalization as a matter of injury, decrying, when it comes to the words in the *Dictionary*, "the folly of naturalizing useless foreigners to the injury of the natives."[10]

For literary scholars such as Ian Watt, the circumstantial details about Crusoe's lineage in the opening passage of *Robinson Crusoe*—his father's place of birth and the exact year of his own birth—signal that the novel is written in a realist mode. The entire opening passage of Defoe's novel is most often read by critics as evidence of the definition of naturalization as "bringing one's work closer to a realistic representation." This understanding was far from the dominant understanding of naturalization at the time Defoe composed his novel, however. Instead, the *Oxford English Dictionary* cites another passage from *Robinson Crusoe* to demonstrate this secondary figurative sense of *naturalization*. Crusoe says he "was so naturaliz'd to the Place" of the island on which he has long been shipwrecked.[11] Crusoe is not legally naturalized to the island—though, importantly, as we will see in the next chapter, he does naturalize as a Catholic subject of the Portuguese king in order to purchase a slave plantation in Brazil. Crusoe uses the word "naturaliz'd" here to mean that he has grown accustomed or acclimated to his life on the island.

This usage can be found widely in writing across the late sixteenth century. Drawing on the political and legal categories of denizen, naturalization, and alien to explain the transmigration of the soul, John Donne, for instance, writes in a sermon of a "Spirit" who "in an instant can denizen and naturalize that soule that was an alien to the Covenant."[12] The more general idea of naturalization as "making natural" is also famously used by Michel de Montaigne in his *Essays*. If he were a scientific writer, Montaigne supposes, he would "naturalise art as much as [scientific writers] artify nature," a statement that heralds Montaigne's early view of the idea of naturalism.[13] Though modern readers might detect evidence of a cultural or ideological meaning of *naturalization* in Montaigne—as having the appearance of the natural—this usage was rare in the seventeenth and eighteenth centuries. By far the more dominant meaning of *naturalization* in this period was the notion derived from law, which referred to making subjects appear "as if" they had always been subjects of a crown.

While newer meanings of *naturalization*, such as Montaigne's, were both obvious and relevant to Defoe and other contemporary writers, in England they shared a common origin in law.

To naturalize, or to undergo naturalization, was a transitive process that changed someone foreign to someone considered familiar. The process, as we know from *Calvin's Case* and the Ramsey cases in the previous chapter, was legally and linguistically innovative: in defiance of the idea of indelible allegiance, naturalization proposed that national allegiance could be voluntary and changed or adapted for political and economic reasons. According to Priscilla Wald, one of the few scholars to have traced its meaning, naturalization "heralds the possibility of adaptation and the promise of transformation. It implies an environment that can accommodate the introduction of a foreign element."[14] Naturalization, that is, transforms the legal identity of an alien in a manner that suggests the natural origins of a natural subject are unnecessary. If a person from, say, Holland, Norway, or Barbados could easily become as if they were a natural-born subject in England by paying a few shillings and saying a few words to the court, then how sacred and natural could natural allegiance and the nation really be? "Naturalization is not an occult process," Wald reminds us. It "is not meant to seem *natural*; it is squarely in the realm of civil law. Rituals and ceremonies—the performing of a prescribed oath, the pledging of allegiance to a flag—characteristically mark the conversion and call attention to the conventionality of the process."[15]

But Wald is only partly right about the historical basis of naturalization. In the seventeenth and eighteenth centuries, naturalization, while not viewed as an occult process, was also neither squarely in the realm of civil law. Instead, naturalization brought civil and natural laws together in ways that were confusing at best and often regarded as heretical in the extreme. The parliamentary process was thought to usurp the Crown's divine power to determine who were the subjects of England. In other words, the theological component of *natura*—the sense of bringing a soul into being—hovered alongside civic interpretations of the idea, the bureaucratic process of making foreigners into natural-born subjects for the purpose of legal privileges. There was not yet a conventional civic sphere that naturalization could be cordoned into. Because its process of making was not hidden from view, naturalization was also felt by many to be a dangerous affront to a natural order of allegiance and subjecthood.

Naturalization was especially confusing in the early modern period because there was not yet a distinct practice of immigration or international law. The procedure occurred through what we might think of as a parliamentary gimmick: since allegiance was understood to be indelible and absolute, naturalization worked to reinvent an alien's past through legal fiction so the alien could gain lucrative political and economic benefits in a new land. Naturalization was both a practical strategy for reaching a goal and a dissatisfying rendition of the natural-born subject. Essentially, it created a fictional equivalency between naturalized and natural-born subjects in the law. It was this legal equivalency, with its notion that subjecthood could be voluntary in addition to derived from the constitution, that proved to be so preposterous to a variety of eighteenth- and seventeenth-century contemporaries. Naturalization did not create or reproduce new natural-born subjects ("Aliens will not have their Affections changed, nor their Alliances extinguished by Naturalization," wrote one contemporary commentator) so much as suggest that naturalized subjects were *equal* to natural ones.[16] In the early modern period, naturalization involved an awareness of the false or failed relationship between the natural and the civic orders, brazenly introducing the interests of trade and capitalism into the sacred rites of the nation.[17] The 1709 General Naturalization Act, or the Naturalization of Foreign Protestants Act, was viewed as a cheap and convenient way of granting subject status, one that did not fully equate the naturalized foreigner with a trueborn subject nor sharpen the distinction between the two identities. Instead, because of the indistinction, the process of early naturalization opened fundamental questions about what it meant to be a subject, natural or otherwise. By the twentieth century, naturalization had become so unmoored from the particulars of its legal roots that it had evolved into a normative and entirely civic process that threatened to collapse the distinctions between nature and the state, as well as between the alien and the citizen.

This collapse was especially apparent to cultural theorists of the late twentieth century. "Something strange has happened to citizenship," wrote Lauren Berlant in 1997 at the beginning of *The Queen of America Goes to Washington City*.[18] Ronald Reagan's presidency, and, along with it, the ascendance of the American Right and free-market economics, dramatically changed the understanding of citizenship in America. Reaganites cultivated a new image of the American citizen as an anxious victim who needed to reassert proper American values. Citizenship became a feeling and a future-oriented practice: a person showed that they were a true citizen by having the proper desire for America, which they performed in private and public acts, from heterosexual sex in the bedroom to lobbying for the rights of fetuses at demonstrations. Becoming a citizen was a process of desire, a process of "Americanization" in which "identifying with an 'American way of life' increasingly involve[d] moral pressure to identity with a small cluster of privatized normal identity."[19] Here we should be less interested in the questionable precision of the historical narrative presented by Berlant's thesis (panics about cultural nationality are by no means particular to 1980s and 1990s America) than in how Berlant situates contemporary legal naturalization in relation to political and cultural anxiety about nationality. In Reagan's America, naturalization moved from being a strictly legal procedure to being a cultural process of "self-erasure, self-transformation and assimilation" designed to cleanse immigrants of their dirty differences.[20] Naturalization became a form of desiring citizenship.

In a 2005 article entitled "Notes toward a Queer History of Naturalization," Siobhan Somerville further historicizes this link between reproduction and citizenship.[21] Somerville argues that in early American history, naturalization has also "been encumbered with assumptions about a heterosexual, reproductive subject, and so tends to reinforce the model of an organic, sexually reproduced citizenry."[22] The 1790 Naturalization Act, for example, which was the first immigration law to set forth who could be a US citizen, promoted a biological and reproductive idea of citizenship because it presumed that a "prospective citizen would be not only white and free but also a (potential) parent."[23] Naturalization as a heterosexual form of reproduction, in Somerville's opinion, is underscored by a meaning in the term's etymology I have not yet covered:

> In definitions regarding the term's usage with plants or animals, the meaning becomes more subtle: to naturalize is "to introduce (a plant or animal) to a place where it is not indigenous, but in which it may survive and reproduce as if it were native; to plant (a bulb, etc.) so that it requires no cultivation and becomes self-propagating, giving the effect of wild growth." The process of naturalization, then, is one in which the difference between the indigenous and the imported becomes effaced.... In other words, biological reproduction becomes a key sign by which the naturalized organism passes as indigenous.[24]

While Somerville recognizes that naturalization is a performative process, she sees it, alongside Berlant, as one that dangerously mimics and reinforces reproductive models of producing citizens. In the previous chapter, I noted how reproductive metaphors about "political birth" or a "second birth" were often used by judges to explain the transformative process of naturalization in the seventeenth century. Yet, significantly, early modern naturalization was not thought to be achieved through sexual reproduction. Contra Somerville's etymological history, it was only in the nineteenth century that the word *naturalization* began to be used to define the cultivation and introduction of plants into nonindigenous places. One of the unnerving things about naturalization for eighteenth-century jurists and critics was that the procedure proposed to alter life history and give birth to a new story about a foreigner, through a garishly technical procedure rather than a reproductive process. Naturalization did not make citizen-subjects through a love and desire for England, as Berlant claims of modern American naturalization. Early naturalization only erased differences between natives and foreigners on paper.

Although it shares language with sexual reproduction, the kind of civil or political birth proposed by early naturalization was viewed by many commentators as frighteningly nonbiological. We see these fears, for instance, in the adjudication of the status of postnati Scots in *Calvin's Case*; and in the judges' reports attached to the Ramsey cases; and, indeed, in the political and legal status of the unnaturally born creature in Mary Shelley's *Frankenstein*. Naturalization perturbed because it made a person's biological origins impossible to decipher and easily turned foreigners into subjects through a flimsy legal and nonbiological fiction. In the seventeenth and eighteenth centuries, the "economies of desire" Somerville describes had little to do with naturalization.[25]

Naturalization and Critique

While cultural theorists maintain different views on when legal naturalization became attached to biological imperatives and cultural nationalism, they overall see the idea as a historical phenomenon. Naturalization is something that *changes* ("Something strange has happened to citizenship," to quote Berlant again). The cultural and literary idea of naturalization, on the other hand, even though it resembles the panicky concerns of legal naturalization, as theorized by Berlant and Somerville, remains strikingly unhistorical: *naturalization* is the word in cultural theory for a general process of ideology—the way a text or convention, for example, aims to treat various political and social functions as if they were biological, thereby concealing, falsifying, and fabricating their constructedness. Naturalization represents, according to Terry Eagleton, the "belief that all ideology, without exception, is crucially concerned to 'naturalize' or organicize social practice."[26] Lorraine Daston and Fernando Vidal write that naturalization acts as a "means to shore up a social convention . . . by asserting that it is dictated by nature and is therefore irrevocable or optimal or both."[27]

The cultural idea of naturalization exists everywhere in cultural criticism if you look for it. But it is especially prevalent in theories of the novel. Michael

McKeon observes, for instance, that Crusoe is "able to naturalize the artificial laboratory of conditions of his utopia because he has learned to internalize divinity," an observation he makes in a chapter titled "*Robinson Crusoe* and the Naturalization of Desire."[28] According to Clifford Siskin, the function of historical development in the novels of Jane Austen and, decades later, in the theory of Karl Marx and Friedrich Engels "is not necessarily to undermine hierarchy, but . . . to naturalize its instability as a sign of maturation."[29] Speaking more directly to themes concerning the foreigner and the native, Laura Brown writes that the narrator in *Oroonoko* employs a strategy by which "the native 'other' is naturalized as a European aristocrat."[30] Meanwhile, the back cover of Joseph Slaughter's book *Human Rights, Inc.* describes the bildungsroman novel as "naturalizing the assumptions and conditions that make human rights appear commonsensical."[31] These statements are a nonrepresentative selection, but they nonetheless show how frequently naturalization is used to describe aesthetic ideology in modern scholarly discourses about the novel. Diverse as the arguments contained in these examples may be, each proposes that the task of the critic is to reveal a function of aesthetics that has been hidden by the work of naturalization.

This critical disposition perhaps received its clearest expression many decades earlier. In his book *Mythologies* (1957), Roland Barthes examines modern myths as what he calls "the naturalization of the concept."[32] Myth, he argues, creates a false causality between signifier and signified through the illusion of nature. Red wine, for example: though it has harmful effects on the health, leads to disorienting intoxication, and is produced for profit in Algeria, a poor Muslim country, red wine is mythologized by the dominant class as a refreshing, healthy, egalitarian, and specifically *French* drink. Algeria's land is used, in this way, to cultivate a product that is of no benefit to its own people (they cannot drink it or profit from its production). Furthermore, the French people are led to revere a civic drink that is corrosive to their individual health. Naturalization for Barthes, as for so many cultural and literary theorists of the twentieth and twenty-first centuries, denotes the process of passing off political or economic modes of production as timeless, natural ideals.

In the twenty-first century, no school of thought or literary methodology has done more to entrench an ideological view of naturalization than Fredric Jameson's blend of Freudian and Marxian/Hegelian theories of history, which drove his analysis of the "political unconscious" of texts. Texts, in his view, have an unconscious that must be interpreted against allegorical master narratives of capitalism. To detect the presence of these master narratives,

Jameson proposes strategies of interpretation that bring to light the real political unconscious dynamics of works and then, in a second step, rewrite this content to connect it to the class conflict of its time. "Our first task as critics," writes Jameson in the review essay mentioned earlier, "is to project a contradiction, or in other words a set of binary terms, a conceptual opposition, such that the literary or figurative text before us may be grasped or reread as the 'resolution' (myth) or the 'neutralization' (Utopia) of the hypothetical opposition thus posited."[33]

In the field of narratology, naturalization is used to describe a strategy of reading. In a chapter in *Structuralist Poetics* entitled "Naturalization and Convention," Jonathan Culler adopts the term *naturalization* to delineate a process by which readers bring unfamiliar texts and scripts "into relation with a type of discourse or model which is already, in some sense, natural and legible."[34] Whereas Barthes uses the term *naturalization* to describe how myths essentialize capitalist commodities, Culler invokes it to specify the process of reading by which weird or strange novels are made sense of through preexistent and normative ideas. Unlike the Russian formalist concepts of estrangement and defamiliarization, which are denaturalizing techniques, in Culler's account naturalization is something that assimilates what seems puzzling or disorienting in a text to match the understanding a reader already has of its existence. For example, confronted with a text that appears to be nonnarrative, such as the Ithaca chapter in James Joyce's *Ulysses*, a reader will lean on familiar generic frames (perhaps a narrative about a drug bender or a hallucination) to make sense of the chapter's run of particulars. These particulars are then etched into the contours of a narrative, helping to make sense of what is supposed to be, as Culler calls it, an "alien" encounter.[35] In this understanding, naturalization is something that readers *do* to a text. Narrative is a matter of interpretation, not an assumption. It is what readers make of a novel, not what they experience passively while reading a novel.

These prominent examples are different in emphasis, but they share a comportment: ideology critics worry that politics can be disguised as nature to an unsuspecting reader, while deconstructionists such as Culler maintain that the truly radical aspects of certain texts risk being co-opted by readers bent on understanding them through corrupting domestic frames. In other words, both articulate a cover-up that is unknowingly conducted by the reader or that happens to the reader if they are not reading a text for its contradictions. Stephen Best and Sharon Marcus summarize the methodological agenda operating in such examples as "symptomatic" and "suspicious," borrowing from Paul

Ricoeur's description of the critical disposition of Friedrich Nietzsche, Marx, and Sigmund Freud as the "hermeneutics of suspicion."[36] More recently, in her reappraisal of critique in the academy, Rita Felski notes how often "nature" (in scare quotes) has been taken up by critics as a deity to be toppled, exposed, and denaturalized. Why, she asks, "have nature, and naturalizing gotten such a bad rap?"[37] Indeed, in a recent response to his decade-old argument about naturalization, Culler admits that his view of naturalization "is not wholly a positive operation."[38] Naturalization, he maintains, is a form of *domestication* that dampens unruly foreign ideas for the sake of making them intelligible. "For many of us of the narratological persuasion, especially those who were active in the days of structuralism," he writes, "the word *natural* is a red flag, a rubric under which various cultural processes and norms are concealed and seek to escape analysis."[39]

Why are naturalization, domestication, and intelligibility negative operations? This question hovers over the entirety of this book. My interest in it, however, is distinct from the engine bells of postcritique and the "weaker" forms of criticism it promotes. This study, for instance, is interested in localizing and particularizing a view of naturalization in the long eighteenth century, in both literary and legal frameworks, against dominant narratives of generational change that have framed much criticism. I do not want to make grand claims about how criticism, on the whole, should be conducted (with or without critique), nor am I, in the end, satisfied to promote naturalization as a methodology for literary criticism writ large. In launching a highly local and particular investigation of naturalization, rather than a broad narrative theory, I want to, first, excavate the complexity of a word that has been seen as self-evident to many and, second, reveal how its modern connotations have been casually alienated from earlier ones. Attending to these differences can help us understand a history of immigration and literature from comparative rather than Whiggish perspectives, and from within different interpretative communities rather than strictly presentist ones. Felski thinks it is better to "direct our criticisms at the specific ideas or issues at stake and dispense with the reproachful charge that something is at fault just because it has been *naturalized*."[40] I think this is right. Yet this can only be accomplished through a more rigorous, critical, and historical account of what naturalization as a specific mode of production meant.

Naturalization, as it has been deployed as a cultural analytic in the twentieth century, fittingly names the work of ideology because legal naturalization itself was essentially, at the same time, a means of controlling and fortifying the state. When we turn to history, modern etymologies of the term become useless to us for uncovering older meanings of naturalization. These accounts risk distorting how past historical actors themselves understood naturalization, what they feared about it, what they perceived to be its benefits, and how they thought it would shape national belonging. And just as our contemporary cultural ideas of naturalization tend to mirror the term's contemporaneous function in law, we can see how early modernity's discourses of naturalization reveal a general comportment and contiguity between law and literature. The legal idea of naturalization and the new cultural genre (the novel) can be meaningfully brought together in early modernity, just as they have been, though tacitly, in the criticism of the twentieth and twenty-first centuries.

New Subjects, New Histories

Many commentators regarded the early novel as heretical and radically heterodox writing that grossly abandoned classical aesthetics. The novel, as Thomas Pavel writes, lacked a "written statute" from which it could derive its rules. "Just as English and American judges do not simply obey statutes, custom, and precedent," Pavel writes, "for a long time novelists took a pragmatic approach, feeling free to imitate forms or to innovate."[41] I would extend Pavel's legal analogy further: like commentators on legal fiction, commentators on the novel had to make sense of its abuse of traditional rules to understand what was emerging. Much of early commentary on the novel was concerned with attempts to make the bewildering newness of the novel conform with older standards and forms. Some, like the Restoration-era English playwright William Congreve, tried to make the novel consistent with older rules. He argued, for example, that his fictional writing merely adapted the rules of drama to narrative.[42] Henry Fielding also likened the novel to the epic in his famous characterization of the novel as a "comic epic in prose."[43] These efforts at accommodation rarely worked, however. Most readers knew that the epic and the novel were not of the same species. Richard Hurd, for example, reprimanded the novel for its failure to subscribe to classical rules. Novels, in his opinion, were "hasty, imperfect, and abortive poems."[44] The writer Elizabeth Griffith appeared to agree: "I know not whether [the novel], like the epopee, has any rules, peculiar to itself."[45] Novelists—though they were not identified as such at the time—were chronically accused of violating the classical dictates of ancient poetics and condemned for indulging in moral obscenities.[46]

Indeed, summarizing the earlier theories of Friedrich Schlegel and Georg Hegel, Guido Mazzoni writes that "few boundary lines are discernable in this apparently formless space."⁴⁷ A novel, for example, can narrate a life from within the consciousness and particularities of a singular person, or it can zoom out and look at a life from an exterior perspective. It can tell a story in prose but not remain limited by that style (consider, for example, Alexander Pushkin's *Eugene Onegin*, a novel in verse). It can tell a story, as Virginia Woolf does in *Mrs. Dalloway*, of a wealthy woman on her way to buy flowers for a party, or the story of a poor servant fending off the advances of her imperious master, as in Richardson's *Pamela*. There were, moreover, no geographical limitations for the novel. While Aristotle held that good tragedy stayed rooted in a single setting, novels traveled wherever their authors chose to roam. Walter Scott could set his novel *Guy Mannering* in Scotland, England, Holland, and India, while Defoe could have several of his protagonists travel to America.

In a sense, then, the generic identity of the novel came into being as a form of rebellion: novels were understood as art forms that did not conform to the rules of the epic poem or classical historiography. Most important for the extended comparison with early legal naturalization proposed by this book, novels disengaged classical rules determining who could be a subject of literature. For Aristotle, tragedy permitted the representation of people "better than we are": the kings and queens, knights, and aristocrats who performed mighty deeds.[48] Comedy, meanwhile, was reserved for lowly people, enslaved persons or clowns, who performed trivial or entertaining actions. This hierarchy organized by subject, style, and genre was still operative in the first half of the eighteenth century to the extent that such writers as Defoe and Richardson were continually measured against its standards. "Up until the second half of the eighteenth century," Mazzoni writes, "it was not obvious that stories about private, common individuals were worthy of public attention and problematic interest."[49] When novels emerged, they ignited controversy and criticism for what we might today call their democratic principles.

I have so far charted a long etymological history of naturalization and argued that the formal affinity between early naturalization and the early novel simply cannot be glimpsed through our modern theories of naturalization. However, to make this point starker, I want to turn to Richardson's *Pamela* to see how naturalization works as a form of fictional subject-making—not through assimilation or privatization but by openly challenging rules that are designed to seem natural.

Naturalization in Samuel Richardson's *Pamela*

Richardson's *Pamela: or, Virtue Rewarded* (1740) is a novel that seeks to naturalize its main character. It tells the story of a poor servant girl and frames her as a suitable subject of literature, and of middle-class and upper-class life, in an age when such figures were not understood as subjects of art or literature. The novel begins, famously, with an elaborate advertising campaign of letters that prepare the reader for a new kind of "natural" literary decorum. Jean Baptiste de Freval, a French Grub Street translator who wrote one of the many opening "puffs" for Richardson, distinguished *Pamela* from older forms of epic and autobiography by insisting that "nature may be traced in [Pamela's] undisguised Inclinations with much more Propriety and Exactness, than can possibly be found in Detail of Actions long past."[50] Perhaps the strongest bid for Pamela's "natural" authenticity came from an anonymous writer, whose observations Richardson included in the preliminary materials for the second edition. The anonymous writer contests the opinion that the "low scenes"—the "uncommon" eloquence of a servant girl, for example—were "out of nature." Triumphantly, he declares the contrary: "Out of nature, do they say? 'Tis my Astonishment how Men of Letters can read with such absent Attention! They are so far from *Out of Nature*, They are absolute *Nature herself*!" (363).

This kind of naturalization—the introduction of new subjects and a new literary mode into narrative space—also happens to be a major component of the novel's plot. Pamela's master and seducer, Mr. B, continually seeks to undermine her professions of natural authority by likening her writing to farfetched fantasies from romance: "the Girl's Head's turn'd by Romances, and such idle Stuff" (93). Whether she makes charges against him in writing or in person, Mr. B repeatedly deflates Pamela as having no clear, logical, or factual intelligence. Mere "scribbling," he calls her writing; "hideous squalling" and "blubbering," he trivializes her rejection (68, 24). And when belittlement is not enough to stay her pen, Mr. B derides everything Pamela speaks and writes as the "noise and nonsense" of a "prating perverse Fool" (34, 33). At least four times, Mr. B accuses Pamela of concocting a story worthy of romance rather than tragedy:

> O my good Girl! Said he, tauntingly, you are well read, I see; and we shall make out between us, before we have done, a pretty story in Romance, I warrant ye! (32)

> I'll tell you, Pamela, why you need not take this Matter in such high Distain!—You have a very pretty romantic Turn for Virtue.... (69)

> She may be turned loose to her evil Destiny, and echo to the Woods and Groves her piteous Lamentations for the loss of her fantastical Innocence, which the romantick Idiot makes such a work about. (163)

> There is such a pretty Air of Romance, as you relate them, in your Plots, and my Plots, that I shall be better directed in what manner to wind up the Catastrophe of the pretty novel. (232)

Mr. B's parody of stubborn self-advocacy also functions as a powerful refusal to recognize Pamela as a credible individual. Her "honest" assertion of herself cannot be heard or understood as honest or natural for fear it gains legitimacy. In response to Pamela's insistence on the "lawlessness" of Mr. B's abduction, Mrs. Jewkes, Mr. B's vile administrator, scoffs, "Is it not Natural for a Gentleman to love a pretty woman?" (110). Downgraded to a romance plot, Pamela's resistance generates no pathos according to the conventional laws of genre. Sexual attraction between a man and a woman is the way of the world, and, in Mrs. Jewkes's estimation, Pamela is a buffoon for thinking that she, a lowly servant, might represent a worthy case of tragedy.

Pamela's "natural" authority is thus not natural enough in the first half of Richardson's epistolary novel. And so it must be naturalized in the second. *Pamela*'s fictional editor and prefatory puff writers serve as important agents of naturalization in this respect. Having read Pamela's letters in their entirety, they can testify to the overall worth of her writing. They can, moreover, prepare readers for how the letters should be read and interpreted according to a new standard of representation. Pamela's associates within the text, however, do not have the benefit of this framing narrative, nor can they, at first, read Pamela's letters as a sustained and continued collection. Instead, Mr. B, Lady Davers, and the landed gentry in Mr. B's neighborhood all regard Pamela's letters as rebellious singularities that breach time-honored standards of public decorum. Mr. B is the first to make specific mention of this conflict when he argues that Pamela's private regard for her "virtue" should not be as important as her outward respect for social hierarchy: "Is it not part of Honesty to be dutiful and grateful to your Master?" (31). Lady Davers upholds an even stricter division between social positions. "Thou knowest nothing, wench," she chastises Pamela, "of what belongs to people of condition; how should'st thou?" (361). Of course, as we all know, Pamela does convince Mr. B and the wider community of her natural worth. By having her individual letters sewn together in a journal, thus narrating Pamela's life history in a format that can be circulated in the community, the heroine becomes naturalized in the eyes of Mr. B and the wider neighborhood.[51]

Pamela thus narrates its own overturning of the rules of representation. For centuries, these rules, in line with the Aristotelian tradition, had set the standards of suitable literary emotional response. This process, as many scholars have written, is not without suspicion of its artfulness. Many of Richardson's earliest readers, importantly Henry Fielding, accused Pamela of boldly employing the arts of a rhetorician for gain in the public sphere.[52] Even today, scholars such as R. F. Brissenden and Terry Eagleton have seen the "turgid idealizing" in *Pamela* as evidence of a larger, historical ideological project. What they overlook, however, is the radical power of a lower-class servant girl using a voice that is not hers by "nature." Equipping a servant girl with a hitherto unknown psychological dimension, Richardson disrupts a system of ordered representation that separates subjects into dichotomies of base and beautiful, comic and tragic, and assigns them relationships appropriate to their character and circumstances. Moreover, Richardson allows a new voice to circulate among the wider public, surpassing the confines of the domestic house that wished to keep its servants silent. Detached from her physical body, Pamela's letters generate new forms of recognition based on the material power of her words rather than the intellectual rules of decorum. *Pamela*, unlike Richardson's final novel, *Sir Charles Grandison*, which features a protagonist considering marriage with a Catholic Italian woman, does not explicitly discuss the implications of legal naturalization. Yet it reveals a parallel structure between aesthetic and legal naturalization as processes of introducing new subjects. The novel exposes—just as legal naturalization had done for Scots and other foreigners centuries earlier—the arbitrariness of a system of social hierarchy. It critiques and exposes the arbitrary rules by which Pamela was denied the ability to be seen as a subject of pathos. When Pamela borrows the language of her superiors, she does not collusively assimilate into their order; rather, she exposes the bias on which the division of the social spheres has been predicated and reveals the process by which an "unnatural being" might be naturalized into an order that is simultaneously natural and unnatural. Her success—conservative as it seems to many modern readers—is her ability to prove that she cannot be excluded from an exclusive social order.

Pamela in this way demonstrates Jacques Rancière's pathbreaking theory of the novel. Rancière rethinks the shift from classical to modern forms of representation as the transition from a hierarchical regime of belles lettres to a "democratic" regime where anything can be represented. He argues that an artform such as the novel is political not because it represents political themes or opinions, or because it has a causal imprint on political life, but because it reconfigures what can be seen and said. Novels such as *Pamela*, for example, bring the viewpoints of the lower classes into the same sensible fabric as those of the upper classes. They introduce their perspective into a continuum of what can be seen and heard. The novel is an art form that renders those who were absent from the classical rules of literature into proper literary subjects. That is, it makes visible subjects who, under older rules, were not thought fit to be subjects. He does not use it, but *naturalization* might be another word for this transition. Indeed, it is telling that, for Rancière, the process of making new subjects in art and politics is "a litigious matter, which opens a space for their testing or verification."[53]

New subjects arrive and settle into narrative space by challenging the classical representative orders that have long excluded or relegated them to the lower position of comedy. This is different, however, from the egalitarian tendency some scholars have identified in sentimental literature. Novels such as Oliver Goldsmith's *Vicar of Wakefield* (1766) or Henry Brooke's *Fool of Quality* (1765–70) have been thought to generate empathy for a newer array of subjects through an arsenal of new narrative devices. The historian Lynn Hunt, for example, locates the advent of human rights in the "explosion of emotions" that Jean-Jacques Rousseau's novel *Julie* produced in readers, which in turn led readers to empathize more widely with others across class, sex, and national boundaries.[54] The empathy fostered by the inner psychology of epistolary novels, Hunt argues, fostered the conditions of a "new political and social order."[55] Empathy and equality are, in this way, coextensive for Hunt. By bringing a reader into the social world of a lowly servant, a novel such as *Pamela* helps them conceive of servants as fully realized humans worthy of equal treatment. Yet Hunt neglects the narrative naturalization process through which this transformation happens, preferring instead to understand sympathy as a physiological process, a form of embodied recognition, produced by texts, which, in turn, can have a causal force in history. Hunt's view of sentimentality is substantially different from Mazzoni's and Rancière's formal emphasis on equality. Hunt makes an argument about narrative influence on social and political change, while for Mazzoni and Rancière, the challenges wrought by the novel are wholly aesthetic: novels expose the arbitrariness of classical rules; they do not expand voting rights or end corporal punishment. Legal naturalization was a process that worked through the ruse of legal fiction, neither substantiating the foreigner as someone deserving English subjecthood nor making them a full-fledged human being. The novel, if we extend the understanding of Mazzoni and Rancière, undertakes a similar maneuver. It undoes a classical model of representation by rendering its hierarchies arbitrary and archaic.

What was so daring about many sentimental novels was not that they made readers weep for subjects who had previously been scoffed at or ignored; it was that they posed a challenge to a representative natural order that insisted a poor servant girl could not be the subject or object of tragic suffering. The challenges introduced by the novel did not occur through the emotional conduits of sympathy, as Hunt narrates in her history of human rights. Instead, they occurred as a revolution against the natural logics that had previously barred certain subjects from representation by exposing them as artificially bordered.

The challenge posed by prose fiction in the long eighteenth century was not a challenge to the idea that "nature" was a social construct, which often appears to linger as the critical issue before scholars today. On the contrary, it was a challenge to the idea that the concept of the natural could not be expanded to include newcomers. The next three chapters in this book expand on this idea, revealing how legal and literary understandings of naturalization were meaningfully intertwined across a spate of eighteenth- and early nineteenth-century novels. These chapters examine the thematic representation of naturalization in eighteenth- and early nineteenth-century prose fiction—the naturalization of Robinson Crusoe as a Portuguese subject in Brazil to purchase a slave plantation, the birth of Tobias Smollett's roguish protagonist in a wagon passing between two national territories, Yorick's search for a new passport in Laurence Sterne's *Sentimental Journey*, and Victor Frankenstein's naturalization from a natural-born Italian to a Genevan subject. In matters of plot, each of the novels emphasizes just how much the debate over legal naturalization resonated with literary writers of the period. Yet the thematic material merely opens a window onto the formal commitment that the novels share: the contiguous process of bringing new subjects into existence through elaborate and obviously fictional procedures. By changing our approach on naturalization, by reconsidering the naturalizing project as a means of introducing and sustaining new subjects, our portrait of how the early novel expanded the nation changes considerably.

PART II

FICTIONS OF NATURALIZATION

CHAPTER 3

Law of the Foreign Father

The eponymous hero of Daniel Defoe's eighteenth-century novel *Robinson Crusoe* has long been regarded as the prototypical Protestant, bourgeois, and colonizing English subject. Looking back from the 1950s, Ian Watt observed that "most English writers . . . have tended to accept Crusoe as the typical Englishman, apparently undeterred by any of his anti-social idiosyncrasies."[1] By "most," Watt was likely referring to three nineteenth-century writers: Walter Scott, who declared in 1837 that Robinson Crusoe "forms no bad specimen of the True-Born Englishman"; Karl Marx, who, while a German émigré in England, framed Crusoe in 1867 as a distinctly English *homo economicus* ("our friend Robinson soon learns by experience . . . like a true-born Briton, to keep a set of books"); and Leslie Stephen, who, in his influential account of Defoe's novel, heralded Crusoe in 1874 as the "typical Englishman of his time . . . the broad-shouldered, beef-eating John Bull, who has been shouldering his way through the world ever since."[2] In the early twentieth century, James Joyce transformed these characterizations into an influential conception of Crusoe as an English colonizer and father of the English novel, which, in turn, became the foundation for many seminal postcolonial readings of the novel in the twenty-first century.[3]

But if post-nineteenth-century writers were secure in their estimation of Crusoe as an English subject, Defoe and his contemporaries were far less certain. As we have seen, in the opening paragraph of *Robinson Crusoe*, Defoe makes two moves—one legal, the other aesthetic—to call attention to his protagonist's muddled relationship to England:

> I was born in the Year 1632, in the city of *York*, of a good family, tho' not of that country, my father being a foreigner of *Bremen*, who settled first at *Hull*: He got a good estate by merchandise, and leaving off his trade, lived afterward at *York*, from whence he had married my mother, whose relations were named *Robinson*, a very good family in that country, and from whom I was call'd *Robinson*

Kreutznaer; but by the usual corruption of words in *England*, we are now call'd, nay we call our selves, and write our Name *Crusoe*, and so my companions always call'd me.⁴

The first move concerns the national status of Crusoe's father, who was born in Bremen, Germany. To his contemporary readers, Crusoe's foreign ancestry would have produced strong doubt and disagreement about his status as a natural-born Englishman. The second one underlines Crusoe's foreignness through his narrative position in relation to England. Strikingly, Crusoe says he was born "of a good family, but not of that country," viewing York ("country" meaning both "county" and "native country") from a foreign and peripheral perspective.⁵ Reading himself through the origins of his foreign father, Crusoe decenters York, and vicariously England, distancing himself with the critical deictic "that country," which he repeats twice.

Why does *Robinson Crusoe*, allegedly the first realist and English novel, openly estrange its titular protagonist? Most scholars have deflected the issue of Crusoe's father, turning to Defoe's 1701 popular poem *The True-Born Englishman*, which swipes at the xenophobic response to Dutch-born William III's ascendency to the English throne, to explain the German ancestry.⁶ Ridiculing the possibility of a pure English heritage, the poem ends with the contention that "scarce one Family is left alive, / Which does not from some Foreigner derive."⁷ But the opening sentences of *Robinson Crusoe* represent more than a passing nod to an earlier poem. Throughout the novel, Crusoe's foreignness is thematized to the extent that Defoe's early poetic interest in mottled nationality appears as a precursor to the more fully realized prose narrative engagement with the issue. In turning for the first time to process fiction, he engages a specific set of contemporary debates about naturalization and negotiates the very property of Englishness, the question of where and under what circumstances it resides, in cultural and legal senses. In addition to beginning the novel with a reference to Crusoe's foreign father—in a passage, as we saw in the previous chapter, resembling a naturalization petition—much of the novel's plot can be tied to a debate about naturalization that had swept through the public imagination in 1709, years after the composition of *The True-born Englishman*.

For the history of nationality law, and for Defoe's contemporary readers, the periodization noted in the first paragraph of Defoe's first novel is distinctive, set as it is at a time that preceded legal provisions for foreigners living in England. Though Crusoe, born in York in 1632, is a natural-born subject of

England, according to the law he could not have inherited real property before 1698 because his father was foreign-born. It was not until the Aliens Act of 1698 that natural-born subjects born to alien parents were permitted incorporeal rights attached to real property.[8] Because seventeenth-century offspring followed the condition of the father in what is known as *partus sequitur patrem*, Crusoe would suffer legal consequences for his father's alienage even though he himself was not an alien. His economic status as an heir—a status he assumes after one brother dies fighting in Flanders and another disappears—is voided by his father's inability to hold and therefore transmit real property.[9]

From the perspective of eighteenth-century legal history, then, Crusoe's mobility, which is one of the novel's pivotal tropes, is intricately tied to the question of whether his father is a naturalized subject. For Crusoe to be a proper heir, his father would have had to pursue a parliamentary act of naturalization after arriving in England from Germany. Readers cannot of course know whether Crusoe's father pursued such an act, but Defoe would have known that such an act would have been expensive and difficult for him to obtain, especially in the early seventeenth century.[10] Yet in many ways this matter is beside the point. Whether we assume Crusoe's father naturalized in England, thus enabling Crusoe to enjoy rights as an heir, or whether we speculate that Crusoe was driven to leave England to secure a more lucrative settlement otherwise unavailable to him (as we see later in this chapter, this is what Charles Gildon, an early reviewer of the novel, argued), the problems of legal naturalization emerge as central to the novel. If Crusoe's father naturalized in England, we can continue speaking—with the law licensing our ability to do so—of Crusoe as the middle-class son who defies his father's advice to remain within the "middle station."[11] If, conversely, Crusoe's father did not naturalize in England—a likely prospect—then a new argument can be made that Crusoe was compelled to leave England by economic incentives, in addition to the mysterious desire many scholars have noted. In either case, Crusoe's rejection of his father's advice to remain in the "middle station" can be reconceived as evidence that Defoe believed, following John Locke and others, that individuals were at liberty to thrive in any environment, domestic or international, and that nationality was the product of a legal and economic contract rather than an organic, natural right.

A fuller picture of nationality and naturalization practices in the early eighteenth century invites a reconsideration of the relationship between Defoe's first novel and England—as well as, indeed, the relationship between the novel and the nation-state in general.[12] But to understand the centrality of naturalization to *Robinson Crusoe*, and how it engaged and emerged contiguously with a new voluntarist conception of nationality, we need to consider the wider orbit of the novel in which Crusoe's nationality proves to be far less important or is actively changed based on his economic interest. As he moves through and across a broad field of territories (not only between the English metropole and its colonies but also across the Republic of Salé and the French, Spanish, Portuguese, and Dutch empires), the national currency of Crusoe's wealth and his legal and religious identity undergo several changes. At times, he is a slave. Other times, he is a foreign merchant, a Catholic planter, a Protestant, and a natural-born subject. Crusoe's national identity and character are legally and figuratively transformed by the global trajectory of his adventures. Defoe was attuned to the instabilities and contingencies of national identities, especially for foreigners and refugees, and his first novel reflects these concerns. Through his global travel and legal settlements, Crusoe substantiates the idea of paranational liberty, embodying the right of the private individual to roam and settle beyond the nation of their birth. His migration amply reflects Locke's maxim that an individual is inherently a "Free-man" at birth, beholden to no country or government except by choice.[13] Far from celebrating this ideal, however, the novel also indexes Defoe's opinion that naturalization would be best used by England to avoid the extra-settlement of wealth in rival empires, as occurs with the profits of Crusoe's Brazilian slave plantation.

In the first section of this chapter, I concentrate on the key legislation pertaining to naturalization in the early eighteenth century and its relationship to Defoe's fiction. Defoe was a prolific commentator on naturalization in his early pamphlet writings and in many ways used *Robinson Crusoe* to advocate for the settlement of refugees in England. He not only positions Crusoe's parentage within a debate about the naturalization of French and German refugees and foreign merchants, but he also has Crusoe undertake legal naturalization in Brazil to purchase a plantation, effectively converting him to Catholicism and making him a legal subject of Portugal. Contrary to nineteenth-century culturalized understandings of nationalism, Defoe engages nationality in these moments as an outward, rather than inward, property that can be exchanged or traded.

In the second section of the chapter, I turn to the pillars of English national identity constructed around Protestantism. Here I show that, although *Robinson Crusoe* has been seen by many modern scholars as a fictional Protestant spiritual autobiography, the novel was, in its own era, regarded as a fiction that dangerously eroded national and religious boundaries. I then turn to the matter of empire and imperialism. *Robinson Crusoe* imagines a world of global capital and trade that runs across national and imperial borders. Read within the context of legal and aesthetic naturalization, it takes on new importance as a novel about the porousness and disposability of national and religious identity in relation to international trade and migration in the eighteenth century. In the final section of the chapter, I build on the earlier discussion of Locke's conception of citizenship, positioning Defoe in relation to the theory of volitional nationality proposed in the previous chapters.

The bulk of this chapter is concerned with events that are external to Crusoe's life on the island—events that bookend a long novel and are remote from the life that has preoccupied generations of commentary. That is to say, I do not focus on Crusoe's life on the island or his relationship to and domination of Friday. If we fixate solely on this location and relationship, we risk feeding the illusion that Defoe was invested in creating an independent and economic modern individual divorced of national community. Nothing could be further from the truth when we consider the way Crusoe's identity easily shifts and benefits from a series of conjunctural relations tied to naturalization. As John Donne famously wrote, "No man is an island entire of himself."[14] Crusoe mobilizes precisely this irony. The more isolated he is, the more English he has appeared—but the larger geographical context of the novel, especially Crusoe's travels to and from Brazil, offers an expanded and reterritorialized "Englishness": a national identity that can be sloughed off as easily as it is donned.

Defoe and Naturalization

Lest it be thought that I am imparting too much importance to a few passing details, it should be noted that Defoe was consistently deliberate in his fiction about the national identities and legal positions of his protagonists. The protagonist of *Moll Flanders* is born in Newgate Prison and assumes a Flemish nickname before departing for America, where, according to colonial naturalization law, she lives long enough to be considered a naturalized subject of the Carolinas. In *Roxana*, a Huguenot refugee from Poitiers comes to marry a Dutch merchant who then pursues a bill of naturalization so he might properly be called an Englishman in his wife's "native" country. The hero of *Colonel Jack* quits London to serve as a member of an Irish army regiment stationed in France, where he then changes his name to Jacques. The titular character of

Captain Singleton is kidnapped and sold to a "gypsy" as a young boy. Raised as a ward of a parish, he is sent to work at sea, where he is captured by Turkish pirates, is rescued by sailors from Portugal, and, after a two-year stay in that country, sets sail for the East Indies. When asked if he will ever return to England, the captain quips, "I came out of England a child, and never was in it but once since I was a man; and then I was cheated and imposed upon, and used so ill that I care not if I never see it more."[15] Even the anonymous protagonist of *Memoirs of a Cavalier* has dubious English origins. He spends most of his early life in the Swedish army, where he learns, as Patrick Parrinder aptly puts it, that nationality and allegiance are but "flags of convenience."[16]

It is certainly true that many of Defoe's characters uphold prejudicial nationalist sentiments. Captain Singleton, for example, explains that "it's natural for an Englishman to hate a coward."[17] Yet in his most famous prose fiction, Defoe shows he is acutely aware of the relationships among immigration, property, and wealth accumulation as well as the more minute particulars of how naturalization works. In addition to being set in a period that lacked legal provisions for the children of foreigners, *Robinson Crusoe* debuted at the tail end of a debate over the origins of Englishness and the relationship of Englishness to religion. This argument had several iterations, the first of which arose at the end of the seventeenth century. In 1685 Louis XIV's Revocation of the Edict of Nantes effectively terminated the right of Huguenots to practice their religion in France without state persecution, causing more than fifty thousand French Protestants to emigrate to England. Britain's 1698 Aliens Act was then passed in response to this wave. The law provided a means to acknowledge the legal existence of alien Protestants who had proved to be beneficial craftsmen and laborers, granting their children a wider array of rights within England, such as the right to inherit. In 1709 almost ten years before the publication of *Robinson Crusoe*, Parliament's Whig majority again legislated on the issue. The 1709 General Naturalization Act granted even more privileges than the 1698 Aliens Act to Protestant workers in England, including the rights to hold property and public office. The act allowed any foreign individual who was willing to swear an oath of allegiance to the Crown, take sacrament in the Church of England, and pay one shilling to exist, in the eyes of the law, as if they were a subject of England.

The 1709 General Naturalization Act marshaled a new sense of Englishness that the 1698 Aliens Act had only partially realized. Indeed, the General Naturalization Act was a fait accompli of Englishness for foreigners, granting them in a generalized act of Parliament the right to be "deemed, adjudged, and taken to be one of Her Majesty's natural born subjects."[18] The radicalness of this act cannot be overstated; it effectively moved the location of nationality from a prior basis in birth to the contractual qualities of loyalty, faith, finance, and language. The act heeded a retrospective temporality to political subject formation, casting "natural born" status on foreigners from the time of their birth. The rhetorical ingenuity of the act produced strong opposition from Tory members of Parliament, who interpreted the law to mean anyone could become an Englishman by language rather than through shared history, culture, and character. What troubled Tories was that naturalization created a fictional category of allegiance and presumed that saying a few words could retrospectively erase the origins of a foreigners, making them as if they were a native subject. The economist Sir William Petty, speaking on the Tory side, argued that "men [should not] be charmed to transplant themselves from their own Native [land], into a Foreign Country merely by words."[19] As we saw in Chapter 1, this retrospective temporality could be construed as heretical, giving the law a function that was reserved for God alone. Unlike the modern conception of naturalization, early naturalization did not require a foreigner's acculturation or assimilation. It simply erased the conditions of a foreigner's birth and made that foreigner correspond to a natural-born subject in law. In a sense, naturalization relaxed the importance of birth and made national allegiance voluntarist. It exposed that under the long-held feudal model of allegiance, differences between subjects and aliens were not that pronounced, except for the right to property, which naturalization easily granted. Naturalization made nationality exchangeable.

There are several reasons why we can feel confident Crusoe's foreign father is tied to controversy about naturalization. The first concerns the second iteration of the naturalization debate, provoked by a wave of German immigration into England. Immediately after the passage of the 1709 Naturalization Act, fifteen thousand immigrants from the Rhine region of northwest Germany entered England, the largest number of people to arrive in the country in a single year to date.[20] Why these refugees fled Germany is not quite clear. Some historians have argued that the Palatines feared religious persecution from a French invasion, while others have suggested these immigrants were lured to England by a "Golden Book" publicizing the riches available to future settlers of the English colonies. A more likely explanation is that a bad harvest followed by an extreme winter had left the Palatines destitute. What is certain is that, unlike the French Huguenots, the Palatines did not receive a warm welcome in England. They were likened to "gypsies," an association that meant they had become, in English eyes, a "race of Vermin" and "an idle profligate people" who were thought to "infest all the countries of Europe."[21]

Crusoe's father, of course, hails from Bremen rather than the Lower Palatinate. Yet foreign merchants born in Bremen frequently migrated to England to access important trade networks in the aftermath of the Thirty Years' War. Margarit Schulte Beerbuhl has shown that up until 1814, Germans constituted the largest group of immigrants to seek naturalization in England; after 1714 (five years before the publication of *Robinson Crusoe*), most foreign merchants came from Bremen.[22] Even though Crusoe's father was not a poor farmer from the Palatinate, both groups of Germans, though belonging to different classes and performing different occupations, were often lumped together as foreigners seeking naturalization and as a danger to security at this time. For example, in a letter published in the *Examiner*, Jonathan Swift, in a characteristically vitriolic (but not satirical) assessment, conflates both groups when he demands that Englishmen "immediately banish, or murder the Palatines; forbid all foreign merchants not only the Exchange but the kingdom; persecute the dissenters with fire and faggot; and make it high treason to speak any other tongue but English."[23]

The second reason it is possible to claim that *Robinson Crusoe* deliberately engages with the early eighteenth-century naturalization debate is that Defoe himself was one of the controversy's most prolific commentators. In June 1709 Defoe devoted three issues of his periodical *Review* to the Palatine refugee migration. On June 23, he mentions certain "discontents" raised against the settlement of the Palatines in England and ventriloquizes this critique as follows: they "will starve our poor, rob the Manufacturers of their bread, and help to impoverish us."[24] In an allusion to the pro-naturalization argument of the economist and politician Josiah Child, Defoe argues that to address the question of how the Palatines might be received in England, readers must speak about "what we mean, when we say, People are a Treasure and that the Strength and Riches of a Nation consist in the number of its inhabitants."[25] Two decades later, testifying to the longevity of his concern with the Palatine refugees, Defoe reflected on a failed proposal to settle the Palatines in New Forest in *A Tour thro' the Whole Island of Britain* (1727).[26]

Defoe's defense of the Palatines is consistent with his economic policies and views on trade. In his tract *Lex Talionis* (1698), written the same year as the passage of the Aliens Act, he argues that "no number of foreigners would be prejudicial to England."[27] In Defoe's opinion, England had more to gain than lose commercially from the integration of outsiders. Too much of England's land had gone untouched, unfarmed, and to waste.[28] The naturalization of foreigners benefited England economically because it increased the size of its population, the volume of its trade, and its self-sufficiency in industry. This view went against the prevailing Tory sentiment that immigrants such as the Palatines were better shipped off as indentured laborers to the colonies. Notably, and uniquely for the time, Defoe argued against the resettlement of the Palatines on the American plantations. He believed foreigners needed to be legally settled and naturalized in England lest they become wandering refugees who did nothing to encourage the fortunes of England. Once legally settled in England, migrants such as the Palatines, and foreign merchants such as those from Bremen, would heap prosperity on English trade by dint of hard work and labor or through the accumulation of wealth. The reality, though, was that most Palatines did not remain in England: one group was directed to Ireland and another was sent to America, where many died during the sea voyage or found themselves sick and starving in settlements in the Carolinas and New York.[29]

Defoe not only wrote about naturalization in pamphlets, he was identified as its most liberal champion. Published in 1709, the anonymous poem *Canary-Birds Naturalized in Utopia* colorfully cataloged in doggerel verse a series of acrimonious objections to legal naturalization, situating Defoe at the center of the controversy. The anonymous author clearly delineates the poem's motive in its preface by invoking Thomas More's satire *Utopia* and its "levelling or laying Things in common."[30] Yet unlike More, who did not set his utopia within a specific period, *Canary-Birds* addressed a palpable and contemporary crisis: the 1709 naturalization bill. The poem's allegorical conceit outlines the complaints of a flock of native birds ruffled by a second set of birds, who, newly settled in Utopia, have begun to demand equal privileges, "As if no Birth-right had been given / to our own Birds from unkind Heaven" (3). The canary birds and their "fond Allies" represent two positions on naturalization (3). There are the native birds for whom the "Condescension is too much" and who believe that "To nat'ralize'em is a Jest" (4) (this intolerable absurdity is later vivified in the couplet, "making Magna Charta / An useless Jest of Magna Fart-a" [9]). This first group identifies a common enemy: "Daniel Foe, that Grand Canary," who wants to relinquish English "liberties and livelihoods," turning Utopia into "Plato's hotch-potch Common-wealth" (9). Then there are the "Dissenting Birds," among whom Defoe belongs, who speak to the "natural freedom" of foreign birds and defend their right to enjoy the same privileges as Utopia's native dwellers (10). The Dissenting Birds trumpet the superiority in craft and trade of the foreign canaries and their potential to "Increase our Commerce to the Indies" (14).

Canary-Birds Naturalized in Utopia acutely illustrates the perceived power of naturalization to lay false and fictional claims to hereditary and natural rights. Utopia's birds deride naturalization as a weak copy of natural rights—twice they employ the word *jest*—but their very outcry, their procession of speeches, each more impassioned than the last, suggests naturalization was anything but a pale copy: the designation proved a powerful rival to native dominion by making it impossible to distinguish between foreigners and natives. Naturalization, as we saw in Chapter 1, not only became the locus of one of the earliest attempts to codify a distinction between aliens and subjects (in an age before settled nationality law), the act undid the traditional understanding of national allegiance as vested in one's place of birth, designing instead a new individual subject, one volitionally attached to the nation through an overtly fictional and self-conscious structure. Defoe, as the "Grand Canary," was viewed by many as the public representative of this new idea of allegiance.

Thus, in 1719, Defoe's choice of a foreign father for Crusoe manifested his concern for an English economy and nation that was not receptive to the legal settlement of foreigners. The most direct expression of this concern in the novel occurs when Crusoe arrives in Brazil around 1655, brought by the captain who saves him from enslavement in Africa. While he is randomly taken to Brazil, Crusoe's decision to settle there is bound up with the controversies of legal naturalization. Crusoe informs readers that in order to legally purchase a sugar plantation in Salvador de Bahia, he must become a naturalized subject. Defoe passes this practice off as common enough in Brazil (Crusoe's plantation neighbor, Wells, is notably hailed as "a *Portuguese of Lisbon*, but born of *English* parents" [29]), but there is no historical evidence that the practice of naturalization ever occurred in the vassal territories of the Portuguese or Iberian empires.[31] The practice is most likely a fictionalization on Defoe's part, a global imagining of the effects of the 1698 Aliens Act that works to reinforce the intimate link between the law and the ability to settle down as established at the beginning of the novel.[32]

Much has been made of Crusoe's industry and economization on the island, yet all of Crusoe's labor—the harvesting, accumulating, building, and fortifying—guarantees him nothing upon his return to England. Even the thirty-six pounds he has stored in his island cave and smuggled onto his rescue ship is not enough to ensure a settlement in England. Thus, after Crusoe leaves the island and finds he does not have enough money to settle in England, he makes an inquiry about the fate of his Brazilian plantation. From the Portuguese captain, Crusoe discovers not only that his plantation partner is still alive but also that the profits of his plantation have grown exponentially in his absence. In this moment he also learns that a portion of these profits have been siphoned off by the Portuguese king and Catholic Church, for the advancement of Catholic religion among aboriginals and for the relief of the Brazilian poor: "One third to the King, and two thirds to the Monastery of St *Augustine*, to be expended for the benefit of the poor, and for the conversion of the *Indians* to the Catholick Faith" (220). After Crusoe takes possession of the remaining profit, he uses the "above 5,000 l. sterling in money, and ... an estate ... in the *Brasils*, of above a thousand pounds a year" (224), to temporarily settle himself in England at the end of the novel before resuming his wanderings, which are portrayed in the sequel volume, *The Farther Adventures of Robinson Crusoe*. Crusoe's partial return reinforces a view of the novel as interested in paranational settlement and migration as well as in nationalism. Not only does Defoe highlight one of England's rival empires as the interim and long-term beneficiary of Crusoe's enormous wealth, he takes pains to show how Crusoe first became interested in settling in Brazil because of its generous naturalization policies, an echo of the same policies that led many refugees, such as the Palatines, to seek settlement in the American colonies rather than in England itself.

We now begin to see Crusoe's movements in the novel—his migration across colonies and empires—as an expression of Defoe's interest in the extranational settlement of foreigners. Once we begin to observe these movements, it becomes increasingly difficult to view Crusoe as a prototypical Englishman. If anything, he is a free settler and merchant opportunist, affixing himself to global trade networks and settling in foreign lands through legal naturalization. The very figure, then, whom many generations of readers have taken to be the literary epitome of the English nation turns out to also be an expression of all that Defoe saw the nation standing to lose if it did not issue legislation for the naturalization of foreigners. Despite Marx's view of Crusoe as an English *homo economicus*, Crusoe's wealth, which was generated in Brazil while he resided on the island, has very little to do with his own labor and economy (beyond the effort it took him to legally occupy and then reoccupy the Brazilian plantation through naturalization). Instead, Crusoe is the passive and foreign beneficiary of Portuguese empire building. On the island, he is therefore in a position similar to that of a "stockjobber" whose investments in overseas trade are at a personal remove, precisely the kind of adventure capitalist whom Defoe disdained in his writings on trade, but even worse because Crusoe's investments are lodged in a foreign empire.[33]

Nationality as a Necklace

By viewing Crusoe from a limited, ideologically influenced perspective, many literary scholars and writers have neglected to notice how readily his naturalization affiliates him with the complexities of global trade. By seeing him as gloriously individual, on the other hand, they miss Crusoe's paranational identity, the way the novel is attuned to the financial and identity complexities of naturalization. While Watt, in the passage cited at the beginning of this chapter, notes the disparity between thinking of Crusoe as an isolated individual and as a general Englishman, he is the first, and most aggressive, to recommend *Robinson Crusoe* as the foundational novel for what he terms the "modern field of vision," a view that weakens "the traditional group relationship, the family, the guild, the village, [and] the sense of nationality."[34]

Watt is correct that Crusoe's relationship to this family and nationality are "weakened" by his migration from England. But Watt's confident assertion of Crusoe's individuality misses the novel's concern with Crusoe's unclear, unsettled, and unbounded relationship to England. Crusoe begins the novel with an individualizing "I," yet the "I" quickly transforms into a first-person plural "we": "I was call'd *Robinson Kreutznaer*; but by the usual corruption of words in *England*, we are now call'd, nay we call our selves, and write our name *Crusoe*, and so my companions always call'd me" (5). The strange temporality of the "we" here—in a narrative composed from the vantage point of old age, after Crusoe's family are long dead—annuls the view of Crusoe as an autonomous individual divorced from nationality. The "I" that "now" calls itself "we" is a timeless, ghostly "we," a collective, familial, and German "we"—in other words, precisely the "we" that Watt thought was substantially weakened by the individual field of vision that a novel such as *Robinson Crusoe* should foreground. Crusoe's German national identity has been "corrupted," but in England—in the cultural and, perhaps, legal sense—it still signifies. In a single paragraph, Crusoe individuates and affiliates himself with a national group. He is Robinson Crusoe, a unique individual, but also a member of the German Crusoe family.

This maneuver could appear to be an early version of what Étienne Balibar calls "fictive ethnicity," the idea that the individual emerges in the nineteenth century "*in the name* of the collectivity whose name one bears."[35] Yet crucially, Crusoe's naturalization does not embody the "internal collective personality" that Balibar attributes to nationality in the late eighteenth and nineteenth centuries.[36] For Defoe, nationality is not an outward projection of interiority: a personality that one carries no matter where one goes and that fosters collective membership through "ideal signifiers" of patriotism and nationalism, such as "love, respect, sacrifice, and fear."[37] Instead, Defoe, through Robinson Crusoe, argues that national identity can travel and be changed as easily as a goatskin jacket. Nationality is an outward manifestation rather than an inward property that emerges out of a dialectic between the individual and the state. It is for this reason that when Crusoe discovers the body of a drowned boy washed up from a shipwreck, he first examines the body for an outer sign of his nationality, regretting that there is "nothing to direct [him] so much as to guess what nation he was of" (149).[38]

The moment that best illustrates Defoe's voluntarist conception of national identity is when Crusoe discovers that he is about to be rescued after twenty-eight years on the island. This moment works quite differently from Aristotle's concept of anagnorisis, the classic point in an epic when the hero makes a critical discovery about the true nature of an event or discovers the real identity of an individual. Uniquely, the moment of Crusoe's rescue unfolds as a national rather than personal discovery. When Crusoe sees a ship on the horizon, he is not entirely surprised. Days earlier, he bid goodbye to one of the Spaniards he rescued from the cannibals and to Friday's father as they sailed back to the mainland to rescue a group of shipwrecked Spaniards. In order that Crusoe would be able to identify Friday's father and the Spaniard upon their return, Crusoe "agree[s] with them about a signal they should hang out at their return, by which [he] should know them again when they came back, at a distance, before they came on shore" (196). While waiting for his friends to reappear, Crusoe catches sight of a ship, but after scanning it for the familiar signal, he instead sees that the vessel is an English one, rather than the one carrying his friends.

Significantly, the epic turn that brings Crusoe "home" hinges on what Aristotle considered the lowest, most servile, and least epic form of recognition. In the *Poetics*, Aristotle cautions against the use of tokens as a means by which a protagonist could come to recognize his, her, or some other character's true identity and nature. Knowing a character by scar, as in *The Odyssey*, or using an heirloom necklace to reunite a daughter with her family all represent, in Aristotle's opinion, "the least artistic form."[39] One reason for Aristotle's view is the fact that such identifiers are acquired "after birth." That is to say, tokens, unlike honor and rank, are not intrinsic to an individual's born character. Scars, tokens, and necklaces are adornments that lend to an external recognition of various attributes rather than internal discovery. What Aristotle identifies as the least artistic mode of mimesis is therefore another way of characterizing, in an aesthetic sense, what I have been referring to as naturalization. Naturalization involves a change from one signifier of national identity to another—yet the prior signifier is not covered up: it still signals. The linguistic naturalization of Robinson's last name, like his status as a nonnatural born subject in Brazil, is out in the open for all to see. This is ultimately how naturalization works: by means of an open avowal of its artificial quality, by licensing an acceptance of the naturalness of foreigners that is premised on a lie. Crusoe's last name is a naturalized name; it is *made* natural, *made* common for a particular English tongue through repetition and over time.

Generations of scholars have turned to Defoe's novel to culturally substantiate their ideas about economic and philosophical individualism. Yet when we shift our focus away from the island and pay closer attention to the migration of Crusoe's nationality from one place to another, our understanding of national identity revolutionizes: it now takes the form of personal and public property, assessed and atomized by the methods of outward scrutiny. Nationality signals as a flag on a ship or an oath flippantly spoken in court for the sake of a real estate sale. Crusoe's economic settlement and naturalization in foreign territories drive the novel's plot. At each turn, but especially in the final moments before he is rescued, Crusoe understands nationality as a topical identity that can be marshaled for strategic economic advancement. His role as exemplary transnational capitalist in turn has deep consequences for a parallel facet of many nativist *Robinson Crusoe* readings: accounts of the novel that place it within the conscripted and conservative form of Protestant spiritual autobiography.

"Sort of Protestants"

In *Britons*, Linda Colley identifies two factors that cemented Britain's national identity: England's war against France and the emergence of a shared Protestant religious identity. In particular, she notes two influential books: John Foxe's *Book of Martyrs, containing an account of the sufferings and death of the Protestants in the reign of Queen Mary* (1563), reissued in an affordable edition in 1732; and John Bunyan's *Pilgrim's Progress* (1678). According to Colley, both books were instrumental in promoting Protestantism as a shared experience in the eighteenth century: "Through reading or hearing others read Protestant publicists like Bunyan and Foxe, through studying the Bible, or listening to sermons, or leafing through the dog-eared pages of almanacs and homily books, Protestant Britons learnt that particular kinds of trials, at the hands of particular kinds of enemies, were the necessary fate and the eventual salvation of a chosen people."[40]

In a like vein, literary theorists have readily, if sometimes searchingly, cast Protestantism, and Bunyan in particular, as central to the development of the English novel. Many have suggested that Defoe adapted Bunyan's Protestant moralization for *Robinson Crusoe*, turning the novel into a cultural mouthpiece for Protestantism.[41] Current Defoe criticism still does largely read Crusoe's reason for leaving England through the prism of what Crusoe himself refers to as his "ORIGINAL SIN," regarding his departure as an allegory of Christian cosmology and theology (154). By "obeying unruly inclination rather than reason and duty," as G. A. Starr argues, Crusoe reenacts the fall of humanity's first parents.[42] Yet the notion that the novel enacts the linear structure of a Protestant spiritual autobiography, casting Crusoe far away from home to signify his spiritual distance from God, does not account for Crusoe's Brazilian settlement or his interimperial migration. The wealth that Crusoe receives at the end of the novel is not a reward for his religious conversion on the island, or for the Weberian Protestant work ethic that he models while there. The profits that he accrues, as mentioned earlier, derive from his landholdings in Brazil, and the investments that the Portuguese empire makes on those landholdings during his twenty-eight-year absence. Ironically, Crusoe's wealth furthers the interests of the *Catholic* Portuguese empire.

This inconvenient truth undermines earlier scholarly arguments that connect Crusoe's capitalist enterprise with Protestant soteriology. Michael McKeon, for instance, has used the term *naturalization* to describe the process through which Crusoe's outward desire for wealth becomes internalized as religious devotion. McKeon writes, "With the spiritualization of 'deliverance' Robinson's early urge to 'ramble' does not disappear, but it is permanently transvalued for him. . . . Physical mobility is reconceived [in the novel] in spiritual terms, as movement both 'upward' and 'inward.'"[43] In this reading, Crusoe travels outward, far from England, to illustrate an inward movement away from God and his upward financial ascension. The exterior geographical trope becomes symbolic of spiritual devotion. On the island, Crusoe learns to understand his situation as a penance for his aimless past. He dialectically evolves from being an impetuous son bent on defying the advice of his father into a repentant man whose penitence is rewarded with material gain.

However, McKeon's use of *naturalization* to illustrate the dialectic between wealth and spirituality is at odds with the forms of legal and aesthetic naturalization I have discussed. The following passage, which depicts Crusoe's effort to decide where to settle after his rescue from the island, offers grist for both interpretations:

> I had once a mind to have gone to the *Brasils* and have settled my self there; for I was, as it were, naturaliz'd to the place; but I had some little scruple in my mind about religion, which insensibly drew me back, of which I shall say more presently. However, it was not religion that kept me from going there for the present; and as I had made no scruple of being openly of the religion of the country, all the while I was among there, so neither did I yet; only that now and then having of late thought more of it, (than formerly) when I began to think of living and dying among them, *I began to regret my having profess'd myself a Papist* [emphasis added], and thought it might not be the best Religion to die with.
>
> But, as I have said, this was *not the main thing that kept me from going to the* [emphasis added] *Brasils*, but that really I did not know with whom to leave my Effects behind me; so I resolv'd at last to go to *England* with it, where, if I arrived, I concluded I should make some acquaintance, or find some relations that would be faithful to me; and according I prepar'd to go for *England* with all my wealth. (225–26; emphasis in the original unless otherwise noted)

The first paragraph of this passage could handily be cited as evidence of Crusoe's religious conversion in the manner outlined by McKeon. Crusoe admits that before he became a castaway on the island, he "made no scruple" of openly professing himself as a Catholic to leverage property and wealth in Brazil (225). Yet after leaving the island—and after "painfully and imperfectly learning to spiritualize," to borrow from McKeon—Crusoe thinks more critically about his naturalization in Brazil. "I began to regret my having profess'd myself a Papist," he confesses, "and thought it might not be the best religion to die with" (226). McKeon oddly does not discuss this admission, but it certainly qualifies as a rare moment of retrospection wherein, in McKeon's words, "Robinson's mobility gains its religious overtones."[44]

The next paragraph ultimately undercuts this view. Crusoe admits that his fear of dying as a Catholic was "not the main thing" that kept him from permanently settling in Brazil (226). Once more the core reason for his mobility concerns the transfer of wealth through inheritance. He realizes he needs someone "with whom to leave [his] Effects behind" (226). The naturalization occurring here does not conform to McKeon's sense of the term but aligns with the legal trajectory discussed earlier. Here, naturalization is no more than a cheap and convenient way of receiving the rights long associated with birth. After living on the island for twenty-eight years, Crusoe has not progressively interiorized his capitalist desire or sanctified greed through devotion. Instead, he naturalizes that desire in the legal sense rather than in our current cultural sense of the term, using a formal and superficial religious conversion to gain access to lucrative plantation property.

The controversy that once surrounded naturalization and religion in Defoe's time is no longer self-evident, even for many legal historians. Yet it would have been foremost in Defoe's mind when he made the decision to have Crusoe pursue naturalization in Brazil, with the added and doubly emphasized detail of an attendant religious conversion. In fact, Crusoe's hasty conversion playfully imagines the core dynamics of the period's animated debate about naturalization and religion. One of the sharpest criticisms of naturalization in the early eighteenth century was that the legal settlement of foreigners in England would allow Catholics, non-Trinitarians, and atheists to infiltrate England without fear of detection.[45] To many prominent opponents of naturalization, such as Sir John Knight and Roger North, foreignness equaled religious dissent, and religious dissent was a threat to the English nation. This matter had both domestic and international dimensions. In the 1660s the Clarendon Code excluded non-Anglicans from public office and affairs.[46] Though the 1709 Naturalization Act required naturalizing foreigners to take sacrament in the Church of England, many people believed that taking sacrament within the process of naturalization would only produce "pretended Protestants," who could easily be hired by Louis XIV to act as spies and illegal agents.[47]

More than the threat of subterfuge, the perceived cheapening of Protestantism was at stake with naturalization. Defoe was involved in the debate over "occasional conformity," the right of Dissenters to take sacrament while continuing to worship in dissenting conventicles, so they could hold government jobs while maintaining dissenting religious beliefs. Occasional conformity was devised in response to the Corporation Act (1661) and Test Acts (1673), which were passed to prevent Roman Catholics and Protestant Dissenters from occupying government posts. The issues surrounding occasional conformity were also intimately tied to naturalization. A general criticism of naturalization was that it made Protestantism, one of the foundations of English and

British national identity, an acquirable good.[48] Naturalization sold the rights of Englishmen at a cheap price—and while the practice technically required a profession of faith, naturalization compelled outward performance rather than inward devotion. This is precisely why Swift surmised in the *Examiner* that general naturalization would reduce the "birthright of an Englishman... [to] the value of twelve-pence."[49]

For McKeon, the geography of Crusoe's travel is only a metaphor, underlining a point about his distance from God and, by contrast with the island, the interiority of his faith. Yet the existence of Brazil as the place Crusoe travels to both before and after being stranded on the island undeniably complicates what we might call the teleological and "deep" readings of Crusoe's faith. Crusoe has economic reasons for leaving England, and at the end of the novel, his faith remains a matter of financial and external practicality. Crusoe's religious conversion in Brazil is shallow and convenient, a way to amass property through legal naturalization. His voyage to Brazil registers not his distance from God but his closeness to capital. This fact is rendered most succinctly in the retrospective structure of the oath Crusoe recites to resecure the trust of his plantation after his rescue. He swears that he is "the same Person who took up the Land for the Planting the said Plantation at first" (222–23). The progressive or dialectical spiritualization that occurred on the island is swiftly undone by the retrospective structure of legal naturalization, which, like a picaresque narrative, returns Crusoe to an earlier version of himself before he washed up on the island's shores. Crusoe has indeed naturalized his capitalist desire, but not in the progressive or interior manner commonly theorized. Rather, he is retroactively naturalized by the novel to a form of continuous subjecthood that undergirds his discontinuous travels, including his time on the island.

Both the depth and commitment of Crusoe's Protestantism and his attachment to England are pilloried in *The Life and Strange Surprizing Adventures of Mr. D—— De F——*, a parody written by Charles Gildon in 1719, the same year as the publication of *Robinson Crusoe*. Gildon's review, which takes the form of an invented dialogue between Defoe and Crusoe, lambasts Defoe for "making" Crusoe a Protestant in precisely the terms that naturalization was deplored by its critics. In part of the exchange, Crusoe asks Defoe why, as the father who wrote him into being, he cast him as "Sort of a Protestant" and "very fond of Popish Priests and the Popish Religion." Defoe responds that "he always hated the English," and it is for this reason that he Frenchified his English last name from Foe.[50] In a companion piece to this parody, entitled

"An Epistle to D—— D'f——, the Reputed Author of Robinson Crusoe," Gildon, in the name of High Church Anglicans who would have objected to Crusoe's tactical alliance with papacy, takes the real Defoe to task for Crusoe's mixed status, opining that the conversion on the island never succeeds in fully eradicating Crusoe's Catholic tendencies. Even before he is marooned, there is the problem of Crusoe's father, whom Gildon criticizes for not setting Crusoe up with a "settled" religion or finances. Crusoe's religion is so weakly planted that he loses it after only three weeks at sea. Crusoe's father, writes Gildon, issues an "Encomium" about the values of the middle station yet offers nothing of a good settlement that would induce Crusoe to remain at home: "I cannot find that he himself thought that what he was to leave his Son would be sufficient to support him in that Middle State, on which he had made so tedious an Encomium."[51] Gildon does not mention the foreignness of Crusoe's father, or the demerits of naturalization more generally, but it is clear from his presentation of Crusoe as opportunistically Catholic and as a detached Protestant character—"a sort of Protestant"—that Gildon thinks Crusoe's unsettledness is a family rather than an individual affair.

In fact, Gildon's parody turns Defoe into something of a foreign father who "makes" his children in the image of his own unsettled status as a French-styled Englishman. Addressing Crusoe as his son, Gildon's fictional Defoe frames his child precisely as the worrisome subject of occasional conformity: "Then know, my dear Child, that you are a greater Favorite to me than you imagine; you are the true Allegorick Image of thy tender Father D——l; I drew thee from the Consideration of my own Mind."[52] Invoking Defoe's status as a dissenter, and calling him a "Rambling, Inconsistent Creature," Gildon does much to persuade readers that Defoe and his fictional brood are the opposite of natural-born subjects. Thus, one of the earliest reviews of *Robinson Crusoe* saw the novel not as the spiritualized quest or naturalization of Christian ethics into commerce, as critics have claimed, but as a worrying affront to Protestantism. Swift would precisely parody religious shifting of this kind in book 3 of *Gulliver's Travels* in his portrait of the Japanese practice of *e-fumi* ("trampling on the crucifex"), which was introduced as a test for Christians seeking to travel and trade in the country.[53] It is only in the nineteenth century, largely through visual representations of the novel and historical distance from the debates about naturalization, that the reputation of the novel as an instantiation of Englishness—aggressive, imperialistic Englishness—would take hold. Before this period, Defoe reveals Englishness to be more precisely exampled by Crusoe's religious shifting and tactical alliances.

In Whose Name?

I have focused on a renaturalized understanding of England's so-called first novel on the relationship between the individual and the nation and religion and the nation. It is now time to consider how Crusoe's detachable relationship to England reorients the placement of *Robinson Crusoe* within contemporary postcolonial literary genealogies. In 1994 Edward Said officially institutionalized as an imperialized trope James Joyce's characterization of Crusoe as an English colonist into postcolonial literary criticism. While admiring Defoe as the first English writer to release English literature from the yoke of Italian influence, Joyce spoke disapprovingly of Crusoe in a lecture delivered in Trieste, Italy, in 1912 as "the true prototype of the British colonist." "The whole Anglo-Saxon spirit is in Crusoe," said Joyce, "the manly independence; the unconscious cruelty; the persistence; the slow yet efficient intelligence[;] . . . the practical, well-balanced religiousness; the calculating taciturnity."[54] Said leans on this interpretation to retrospectively cast colonialism as central to the inauguration of the English novel. "*Robinson Crusoe*," he claims, "[is t]he prototypical modern realistic novel," adding that this literary landmark "is and certainly not accidentally about a European who creates a fiefdom for himself on a distant, non-European island."[55]

For Said, *Robinson Crusoe* not only inaugurates the genre of the novel but also confirms the central place of imperialism in that genre. In *Culture and Imperialism*, he argues that earlier scholars of the novel overlooked the centrality of colonialism. "Most cultural historians, and certainly all literary scholars," he claims, "have failed to remark the geographical notation, the theoretical mapping and charting of territory that underlies Western fiction, historical writing, and philosophical discourse of the time."[56] To rectify the quietism regarding empire and its dislocation in early British literature, Said calls for a "contrapuntal" approach to reading canonical English novels. Borrowed from musical notation of counterpoint (contrasting melodies played at the same time), contrapuntal reading draws out the hidden colonial labor sustaining bourgeois life in England. It unites "awareness both of the metropolitan history that is narrated and of those other histories against which (and together with which) the dominating discourse acts."[57] For Said, the English novel, as it evolves, works to domesticate colonialism and downplay or erase the metropole's dependence on it. *Robinson Crusoe* is crucial to this formulation for Said, even though it openly, even flippantly, discusses slave labor. Said treats this openness about slavery as proof that, at its core, *Robinson*

Crusoe, and by extension the English novel, participates in imperialism. By beginning his account with Defoe—whose novel is "not accidentally about colonialism"—Said puts forth a clear, unequivocal account of the novel's link to colonialism to bolster his own vision of the novel as the development of ever-more quiet and sublimated relations between colonialism and English domesticity.[58] In this genealogy, *Robinson Crusoe* functions as the nativist point of origin for the English novel, which then progressively—or regressively—becomes involved with a tradition of hiding the imperial engine sustaining its bourgeois and domestic individualism.

The centralization of Crusoe within nationalizing genealogies of the novel is not limited to early postcolonial studies. Recent scholarship on the novel, such as Ning Ma's *Age of Silver: The Rise of the Novel East and West*, which tracks the emergence of multiple modernities across China, Spain, Japan, and England, still upholds—in fact, must uphold for the purpose of transcultural comparison—*Robinson Crusoe* as a canonical instantiation of the English novel and its titular character as representative of an English colonizer. Letting *Robinson Crusoe* stand in for the English novel, Ma emphasizes the belatedness of English modernity in comparison with Chinese modernity, arguing that the English novel was not a "privileged pioneer" of the fictional form.[59] She thus denationalizes the study of the early novel by comparing the English example with Chinese trading economy and narrative. Yet in this new study, *Robinson Crusoe* retains its stature as *the* English novel—in fact, it becomes all the more English in its relation to globalized modernity. Ma calls *Robinson Crusoe* "a self-solidifying narrative" and speaks of Crusoe's kingship on the island as "bound to Britain."[60] As much as Ma demonstrates the so-called belatedness of the English novel in comparison with Chinese literature and trade, thereby offering a welcome expansion of the global trajectories of the early novel, like Said, she still relies on *Robinson Crusoe* to affirm the novel's nativist origin. Even situated within the story of Chinese modernity, *Robinson Crusoe* serves, as she says, "a nationally-symbolic function."[61]

Recognizing Crusoe's ambiguous and multiply exchanged nationality in the early eighteenth century, however, obliges us to reassess twenty-first-century interpretations of his economic boundedness to England. The word *colony* derives from the Roman *colonia*, which means "farm" or "settlement" and referred to Romans who settled in foreign lands but retained their citizenship. The *Oxford English Dictionary* lists this as a definition: "A body of people who settle in a new locality, forming a community subject to or connected with their parent state; the community so formed, consisting of the original settlers and their descendants and successors, as long as the connection with the parent state is kept up."[62] By definition, then, colonialism is a form of domination and settlement that is nationally specific. As I have suggested, however, Crusoe does not keep up a connection with England, and his settlement is far from fixed in any of the national territories he inhabits. Initially, before being shipwrecked, Crusoe joins an expedition for enslaved persons "for the service of the *Brasils*" (32). Then, he profitably invests his money in Brazil, a Portuguese colony. At the end of the novel, while he returns to England to settle his estate with an heir, he finds that he is still "inur'd to a wandering Life" (239) and that his settlement back in England is only "in Part" (240). Crusoe's money circulates outside England far more than it does within it. In addition to the fact that Crusoe's plantation wealth finances the missionary project of the Portuguese vassal state, Crusoe subjugates people not for the sake of the greatness of any particular European sovereign state but for capital itself.

Undoubtedly, Crusoe carries with him, in the words of Christopher Hill, the "mental furniture" of a European white man.[63] He traffics enslaved persons in Brazil and on the island parades himself as a liberator to Friday and his family. Yet, as Peter Hulme notes, on the island Crusoe "throws the whole ideological basis of European colonialism into doubt,"[64] adopting a policy of nonintervention toward the cannibals he meets on the island's beach while chastising "the Spaniards" for "all their barbarities practis'd in America" (136). Defoe more or less confirms Crusoe's disinterest in imperialism in the sequel to *Robinson Crusoe*, the *Farther Adventures*. In this work, Crusoe maintains, "I never so much as pretended to plant in the Name of any Government or Nation ... or to call my People Subjects to any one Nation more than another; nay, I never so much as gave the Place a Name; but left it as I found it belonging to no Body."[65] Based on this evidence, Srinivas Aravamudan speculates that "some colonies, it appears, are exempt from national partisanship when they are founded, and can also involve, as Crusoe's colony does, multinational thought experiments."[66] Historically, however, there is no example of a multinational colony, while there is ample evidence of Defoe's preference for trade, rather than imperialism, as the basis of England's colonial policy. I would suggest, then, that in this moment, Defoe was signaling Crusoe's preference for global trade rather than proffering an experimental engagement in multinationalist colonialism.

In *A Plan of the English Commerce* (1728), written eight years after *Robinson Crusoe*, Defoe contrasts the prosperity of the Portuguese colonies in Brazil and Africa with that of the Spanish to portray commerce as more beneficial to both parties than subjugation and exploitation.[67] This comparison is amply displayed in the novel: Crusoe yields substantial wealth from his plantation in Brazil, benefiting both himself, a naturalized foreigner, and the Portuguese nation; whereas his island colony in the Caribbean, as we know from the novel's sequel, ends in destitution and chaos with the Spaniards begging to be rescued. Similar evidence of Defoe's preference for colonialism based on trade can be found in *A New Voyage Round the World* (1724), where the protagonist claims, "I take the Liberty to recommend that Part of *America*, as the best, and most advantageous Part of the whole Globe for an *English* Colony," because of "the Climate, the Soil, and, above all, the easy Communication with the Mountains of *Chili*."[68] Notably, Defoe has his sea captain in this story recommend the Pacific coast of America for an English settlement because of its climate and location rather than its gold and silver mines. In making this recommendation, Defoe voices suspicion of the uneasy riches of Sir Walter Raleigh's "Guiana" scheme, a colonial project close in territory to the location of Crusoe's island, which looked for quick returns in the form of gold.[69] Defoe was in favor of colonialism, but preferred to make trade its foundation. In "An Essay on the South Sea Trade" (1711), he supported the idea of a venture for an English South Sea colony to deal with the problem of national debt, but he highlighted trade rather than politics as his reason. Defoe unequivocally supports the right of England to "Seiz[e] a place in America, possess'd or unpossess'd as our own," and does so out of a sense that England is losing trading ground to Portugal and Spain.[70] An English colony in America would be the "Foundation upon which may be built an immense trade" both for the inhabitants of the colony and for manufacturing in England.[71] Without much reflection, Defoe advocated for peaceful possession of a colony in America, unlike Christopher Columbus, who "destroy'd the Nations who inhabited the several countries."[72] Defoe's emphasis on commercial advantage, rather than exploitation, is perhaps one reason for his delayed reputation as a colonialist, which did not emerge until Joyce's lecture in 1912. Defoe was interested in cross-national profits and trade, not crass colonial exploitation for the benefit of the "parent state."[73]

Crusoe naturalizes to any state and to any form that promises a good financial return. While he employs English practices on the island, notably the capitalist form of enclosures unique to British history, he utilizes foreign technology, such as an umbrella made of goatskin, which he observed being made while a planter in Brazil. Crusoe also exhibits no national preference for the people he encounters near the end of his time on the island. After his rescue, he leaves the island in the trust of the Spaniards rather than with the band of English mutineers whom he calls his "country-men" (197). Upon returning to the island, Crusoe is satisfied to hear the Spaniards used "violence" against the mutineers to subject them to their authority (240). Throughout *Robinson Crusoe*, and especially in the sequel, *The Farther Adventures of Robinson Crusoe*, Defoe repeatedly depicts the Spaniards as more dependable, judicious, and industrious than the English mutineers. Gildon was especially upset that Defoe cast a golden light on the very people who should be treated as enemies of the English nation and religion.[74]

If Defoe sought to write the novel as a justification for English colonialism, we have to wonder why he set Crusoe's plantation in Brazil rather than in England's colony in South America along the River Surinam. In the novel, against the grain of historical reality, Defoe depicts Brazil as a tolerant and welcoming colony, one that prospers from the incorporation of foreign merchants through naturalization.[75] Crusoe's prosperity in Brazil, and the Portuguese empire's prosperity from his plantation, significantly points to England's economic loss as a result of its refusal to settle the Palatine refugees and other foreigners. Many of the liberal arguments in favor of naturalization, including Defoe's, were that settling foreigners within England would prevent them from taking their wealth elsewhere.

The relationships and exchanges between people and goods in *Robinson Crusoe* exceed the boundaries and interests of a single nation. Of course, we cannot overlook Crusoe's gradual yet forceful command of the island he inhabits, especially his enslavement of Friday, or his own economic investments in and profits from slavery as a European. Yet it is extremely telling that not one of the inhabitants on the island, not even Friday, is indigenous to it. This does not mean Crusoe does not engage in capitalist exploitation and slave trafficking, but it does suggest that Defoe frames Crusoe's dominance on and off the island as something other than the distinctly *English* enterprise Joyce and Said have expounded on to far-reaching effect. The relationship between vassal and metropole, as articulated by Said in *Culture and Imperialism*, emerges as far too linear a model for the global and interimperial relations I have outlined. The geographical notation that Said foregrounds in his reading does not account for the other empires and states into which Crusoe migrates. The narrative of colony to metropole neglects shifts in Crusoe's status as the son of a German immigrant, a convert to Catholicism, and a naturalized subject in Portugal. While Said focuses on what is not in a text—what the text renders invisible in the name of creating a settled bourgeois image of England—

my approach has been to look at what is decidedly denoted in the novel: the legal maneuvers and financial deals that send Crusoe across the world in search of settlement. These maneuvers illustrate Defoe's interest in nationality as a volitional status that can be expatriated.

Global Trade and Volitional Nationality

Defoe's writing on naturalization, and his novelistic depiction of individualism as it travels across nations, reflects the new view of national subjecthood outlined in previous chapters. In particular, Defoe's presentation of nationality as a legal status that can be altered for the transference of personal property bears a striking similarity to Locke's theorization of the autonomous individual who consents to be in a sovereign relationship. In the *Two Treatises*, Locke argues against a natural relationship between sovereign and subject, which he allegorizes through the relationship of father and son:

> A *child is born a subject of no country or government*. He is under his father's tuition and authority, till he comes to age of discretion; and then he is a freeman, at liberty what government he will put himself under, what body politic he will unite himself to: for if an *Englishman*'s son, born in *France*, be at liberty, and may do so, it is evident there is no tie upon him by his father's being a subject of this kingdom; nor is he bound up by any compact of his ancestors. And why then hath not his son, by the same reason, the same liberty, though he be born any where else? Since the power that a father hath naturally over his children, is the same, where-ever they be born, and the ties of natural obligations, are not bounded by the positive limits of kingdoms and common-wealths.[76]

While the *Two Treatises* does not address naturalization directly, it is clear from this passage that Locke views allegiance and nationality as part of a social compact; as a legal contract rather than an imagined, cultural community. Before the "age of discretion," a man can leave the nation of his birth just as easily as he can voluntarily enter a new one.[77] Birth is a condition that can be altered. Applying Locke's allegory of the father-and-son relationship to *Robinson Crusoe*, we readily see Crusoe as precisely the kind of free agent central to Locke's political view on nationality. While Crusoe's German ancestors still signify at the beginning of the novel, Crusoe holds no compact with them. Instead, he has the right to forsake allegiance to his father and his ancestors, striking out in the direction of new economic interests.

In addition to empowering England with more labor, Locke maintains that naturalization would help England expand its commercial society through international trade. Like Defoe, he argues against conquest as a means of advancing national wealth: trade rather than land, he insists, forms the basis for a prosperous nation. And like Defoe, Locke considers naturalization the best means of ensuring a good supply of labor within England. Both writers speak in the republican tradition interested in the use of trade rather than colonialism.[78] In *Robinson Crusoe*, there is no pronounced distinction between Englishmen and foreigners. For certain contemporary critics, the double signification of naturalization was a problem. According to the doctrine of perpetual allegiance, an original allegiance can never be tapped out, and for this reason it persists as a threat to the English nation. Defoe follows Locke in disregarding this as a problem. The following justification for naturalization written by Locke could easily be mistaken for a passage from one of Defoe's pamphlets on the Palatine migration: "Besides when they are once naturalized how can it be said that they eat the bread out of our people's mouths? When they are then in interest as much our own people as any the only odds is their language w[hi]ch will be cured too in their children & they be perfect Englishmen as those that have been here ever since William the Conqueror days & came over with him. For tis hardly to be doubted but that most of even our Ancestors were Forainers."[79] Locke counteracts the fear that foreigners will taint the English nation with their prior natural allegiance by insisting that individuals are guided by an interest that is vested in the self and can be transferred. Once in England, a naturalized subject will make the self-interest of England their own. Becoming English is not tied to affective feelings for the nation, which become the measure of nationality in the nineteenth century. For Locke, Englishness is a legal and economic contract rather than the basis of an organic, cultural-linguistic community.

One signal difference between Locke and Defoe, however, is that Defoe takes volitional national identity from outside England into account. Indeed, while David Armitage identifies Locke as a "specifically *English* international thinker who was committed to the common interest against the Catholic Bourbon threat," Defoe represents something of the reverse.[80] With *Robinson Crusoe*, he gives a portrait of a specifically *international* Englishman who is often weakly committed to Protestant power and order and whose financial dealings traverse empires, not to mention countries. Crusoe is born in England—he fits the definition of a "true born Englishman"—but his national allegiances are everywhere in question: he is quickly a Catholic when lucrative trade demands it and bequeaths his precious island to Spanish friends rather than to English countrymen. It would be naïve to call Crusoe a cosmopolitan "citizen of the world"; he moves between nationalities easily but not fluidly or without need of external aid and legal settlement. Allegiance and religion matter in this novel. Naturalization was a privilege, not a right, but a privilege that Defoe clearly thought should be extended out of national self-interest. Allegiance and religion also matter enough that Defoe included legal nomenclature about naturalization procedures in the stray few paragraphs he granted to Crusoe's Brazilian venture. Defoe understood the consequences of the fiction he bestowed on Crusoe's plantation in Brazil: in allowing Crusoe to settle there, the Portuguese were enriched. Nationality lacks cultural, linguistic depth; it operates as a community of convenience. In this sense, too, we can see Crusoe's migration as a more potent assertion of paranationality—nationality that is not closed to the outside but forged in positive relation to it—than the John Bull Englishman inscribed by nineteenth-century receptions of the novel, or the aggressive nationalism located in many twentieth-century accounts.

Many readers of *Robinson Crusoe* have insisted that nationalism and individualism are the organizing categories of Defoe's fiction, even though Defoe portrays Crusoe as an individual whose defining traits—faith and economic prosperity—are just as easily affixed, or naturalized, to Catholicism as to Protestantism, and to the benefit of the Portuguese empire as to the English. Crusoe naturalizes in plain sight. There is nothing hidden about the act; we are merely unable to see it because we have not paid careful attention to how Crusoe's Brazilian settlement figures in the novel and, beyond that, because we have lacked an essential understanding of early legal history, or have not made ample use of Defoe's journalistic writings. By realigning *Robinson Crusoe* with its global trajectories, I hope to reorient the field of early novel studies by showing that a novel believed to be a national allegory for England is in fact a portrait of an alternative conception of national belonging, one that took root in literature long before it ever gained lasting hold in law.

Far from cementing a national tradition, *Robinson Crusoe* registers and offers an aesthetic form for the early modern conditions that were rendering nationality as part of an emerging capitalist system of exchange. When we attend to the novel's legal forms of eighteenth-century naturalization, *Robinson Crusoe* emerges as a work of paranational fiction, a formal experiment that leaves national membership open. Defoe's novel merits this description not because it literally crossed geographical and linguistic borders in its translated or adapted forms (as with the Robinsonades of the nineteenth century) but because it depicts an opportunistic willingness to exchange national identities, a willingness that will begin to disappear in the nineteenth century as nationality becomes something deep, bordered, and indelible. To return to the age of naturalization, to the messy beginnings of the novel and modern nationality, is to see that it was not so much interiority that formed the basis of participation in the nation or the novel but rather the ability to appear as a plausible subject—the ability to be naturalized by artifice.

I have argued that we should pay more attention to the porousness of national identity in Defoe's adventure fiction and to the expandable form of nationality he forged alongside Locke's thought. In the next chapter, I turn to a more unlikely fictional substantiation of naturalization: the so-called interior-facing "domestic" genres of sentimental, epistolary, and gothic fiction.

CHAPTER 4

Open-Door Domestic Fiction

The previous chapter recontextualized the nativist mythologies that became attached to *Robinson Crusoe* in the nineteenth and twentieth centuries. I now want to turn to a wider range of authors and subgenres to provide broader evidence of both a continued and complicated concern with paranational issues in prose fiction across the second half of the eighteenth century and into the Romantic period. The novel continued to explore the idea and possibilities of fictionalized nationality and subjecthood, though by midcentury it had taken up a variety of subjects and plot lines concerning religion, gender, and race, at precisely the moment that the law itself was closing off the possibilities of naturalization. What we see is that the fiction of the second half of the century, into the Romantic period, both indexed this closure and worked against it.

Tobias Smollett's third novel, for example, *The Adventures of Ferdinand Count Fathom* (1753), comedically amplifies for midcentury readers the concerns about naturalized nationality that gripped writers and philosophers in the first half of the eighteenth century. Assuming the role of historian, the novel's narrator imagines how the obscure origins of its novel's hero might have been explained in an ancient and chivalric age. Perhaps, the narrator speculates, the protagonist's unclear ancestry would have been taken as a sign of divine parentage. Quickly, however, the narrator is forced to acknowledge that the history of Ferdinand Fathom, or lack thereof, can only be comprehended within the social and political specificities of his own era: not only is Fathom an illegitimate child whose mother "could never pitch upon the person from whose loins [he] sprung,"[1] his nationality has been rendered legally unclear by the ridiculous event of his birth: "He was brought forth in a waggon and might be said to be literally a native of two different countries; for though he saw the first light in Holland, he was not born till the carriage arrived in Flanders; so that all these extraordinary circumstances considered, the task of determining to whose government he owed allegiance, would be at least as difficult, as that of ascertaining the contested birth-place of Homer" (46–47). The idiosyncratic study of allegiance that opens *Ferdinand Count Fathom* obliquely recalls the unsettling debates about nationality that emerged in *Calvin's Case*, which concerned the status of the Scots in England after the Union of the Crowns. If territory of birth entails allegiance, then Fathom can plausibly, if preposterously, lay claim to dual allegiance, a legal impossibility in the period, by means of natural law. His head arrives in Holland and his feet emerge in Flanders. Complicating matters, though, is the fact that Fathom's mother is an Englishwoman. She bestows on her bastard son the name of a hastily married German trooper and then makes no effort to teach him English. Fathom, like Victor Frankenstein's nameless monster, only learns "the language of his forefathers" by hearing it spoken among Scottish and Irish guests at a cabaret in Prague (51). He grows up claiming England as his "native land" without ever having set foot in it (124). He is as English as Robinson Crusoe is German.

Smollett's rogue protagonist, who was vilified by readers as the starkest literary villain since William Shakespeare's Iago, comes to index fears of naturalized identity run amok and of Englishness as liberated capital rather than natural right. Fathom moves autonomously between European nations and governments disguised, at turns, as "a man of family," a musician, a French gentleman, a German nobleman, and a Polish count (127). As he travels, leaving ruin and destitution in his wake, speculation arises about his nativity. To this gossip, Fathom responds with his own view of allegiance as predicated on time rather than space: "At present," he says, "I have the honour to be of England" (207). When his interlocutor responds that "good citizens" can never forget or change their country of origin, Fathom vocalizes the liberalized view of naturalization held by John Locke and others that bad citizens are those who are incapable of escaping the conditions of their birth (208). For Smollett's hero, an individual's ability to change their early life history and override the foreign conditions of their birth, as the legal fiction of naturalization was thought to do, provides a more practical way to live as an individual in the world. Fathom's way allows for maximal personal gain and the ability to escape censure by moving to another country when one's cover is blown or credit ruined. Thus, *Ferdinand Count Fathom* vivified many readers' worst nightmares about naturalization: that the ability to assume a national allegiance would lead to large-scale swindle and deceit, and a "swarm of the most useless and contemptible people under the sun" would descend on the country.[2]

Yet Smollett's novel is not purely a vituperation of naturalization. Although it appears to enliven popular assumptions about the liberties of naturalized people, it is also contains sentimental portraits of foreigners residing within England: an old French Huguenot refugee at a coffee house; a destitute foreigner orphan named Monimia (who is later revealed, in proper romance fashion, to be Serafina, the long-lost daughter of a Spanish aristocrat); Renaldo, an Austrian count whose father raised Fathom and whose inheritance Fathom has tried to steal; Joshua Manasseh, a "benevolent Israelite," who lends money to foreigners despite their lack of credit (and is one of the first sympathetic portrayals of a Jewish person in English fiction); and a Castilian named Don Diego, who at the end of the novel heretically resolves to marry an English woman and convert to Protestantism (294). These foreigners are both legally and morally settled in England at the end of the novel. After Fathom is captured and shipped off to the North of England to do penance for his misconduct (a punishment he stunningly accepts after hundreds of pages of pure, unreflective villainy), the novel concludes with an image of a "box of foreigners" at the opera who are held up by the English audience as paragons of beauty, virtue, and humanity (443). Smollett sought to resist an easy for-or-against ideological position on naturalization. Anti-naturalization, while a popular opinion in newspapers and caricatures of the Jew Bill, was not a nuanced enough response to the traffic of migration and wealth that was also venerated by the public in the forms of fashion and art.

Smollett's engagement with the particularities of national allegiance and naturalization brings to mind Chapter 3's argument about the developmental tension between the supposed foundation of the "English" novel (Robinson Crusoe as the English colonizer of land and fiction) and the displayed paranational proclivities of characters independent of national allegiance (Robinson Crusoe as a naturalized Catholic and Portuguese plantation owner). *Ferdinand Count Fathom* shows readers more precisely how far the novel was from abandoning a paranational viewpoint by midcentury. Paranationality, we will recall, is a distinct perspective from internationalism and transnationalism; it signals uncertainties about national allegiance from perspectives both within and outside the nation. For many scholars, however, the openness displayed by Smollett's novel will be seen as merely a remnant of romance, and as hardly representative of the dominant trend of fiction in the second half of the eighteenth century. Indeed, one of the more intractable "rise of the novel" theses, asserted by a variety of scholars and writers, from the historicists of the 1950s and postcolonial scholars of the 1980s to the distant readers of today, is that older genres, such as romance and picaresque, were gradually suppressed in the second half of the eighteenth century by the advance of domestic realism.[3] As the development of narrative modes for representing particular and private life followed the rise of individualism more generally in European culture across the eighteenth century, the public aims and common causes of chivalric heroes were gradually overshadowed.[4]

This turn toward particularized descriptions of private life has been regarded by many scholars as representative of a wider turn away from public, communal, and national perspectives. When the genre of the novel turned inward to examine the subjective thoughts of individuals, its spatial and social ranges were also thought to constrict. Srinivas Aravamudan, for instance, following Edward Said, argues that, after Daniel Defoe, novels tended to "favor the closed-door domestic fiction that in fact is an evasion or even an occlusion of the historical realities that were creating much wealth and leisure that support the social world in the novel."[5] Collecting features of the novel from the likes of Catherine Gallagher, Michael McKeon, and Ian Watt, Aravamudan assigns domestic fiction the following traits:

NOVELS MAKE READERS
into addicts of reality
love home
keep company with fellow citizens
moral/immoral
responsible
experience an "open" genre
treat characters as fetishes
into national narcissists
autoaffective[6]

This narrative, which argues that the cosmopolitanism of early travel narratives and romance was gradually repressed by the inward turn of realistic prose fiction, echoes how otherwise methodologically diverse scholars have comprehended the eighteenth-century novel as primarily domestic in scope and, in that more limited and private orientation, as conservatively related to the ascension of the bourgeois middle class.[7] To recall an example from the introduction, Franco Moretti argues that the novel only rose to national importance in the nineteenth century by resolving the tension between cosmopolitan travel narratives and interior-focused private fiction. "It is only at the very end of the century," writes Moretti, "that the contraction of narrative space" into the nation-state "becomes finally visible."[8]

Smollett's *Ferdinand Count Fathom*, however, is not merely an outlandish holdover of paranational concerns from earlier in the century. The novel renders comically obvious a thread of interest in and concern with voluntary nationality that continued to characterize much canonical literature in the second half of the century. The paranational perspectives of prose fiction were by no means foreclosed or jettisoned by a turn to private and domestic life in the middle of the century; in fact, the novel, in contiguity with the broader legal and political culture of the mid-eighteenth century, became more concerned with the surface dimensions of nationality. For this reason, the category of "domestic fiction" misrepresents much canonical English fiction as *willfully* uninterested in paranational issues in order to usefully set the novel up as a purveyor of nationality in the nineteenth century—it has also been used as something of a straw man for the current interest in globalizing the study of English literary history. The story about the rise of domestic fiction, useful as it has been for political and literary theorists alike, appears as entirely too simple once we consider how the individualist agendas of so-called domestic fiction were part of the continued interrogation of the relationship between national allegiance and unbounded mobility.[9] Indeed, the "domestic" ideas attached to the novel were primarily assigned by some of the dominant scholarly projects of the 1980s and 1990s: new historicism and feminist criticism, whose important recovery efforts had the effect of overlooking the ways in which these genres also offered engagements with questions of religious and national allegiance both *in* and *outside* the nation. Even scholars with global and transnational investments who are interested in expanding the geographical radius of eighteenth-century fiction, such as Aravamudan, have not been attentive to the specific national frameworks, legal references, and geographical coverage in prose fiction that continued to enliven debates about nationality long after Defoe had written his novels and pamphlets.[10]

To establish a deepened interest in paranationality in the second half of the eighteenth century, I adopt a somewhat unique approach in this chapter. I turn to the *last*-written novels of several canonical authors who have been roundly understood as English domestic writers: Samuel Richardson's *Sir Charles Grandison* (1753), Laurence Sterne's *Sentimental Journey through France and Italy* (1759), and Frances Burney's *The Wanderer; or Female Difficulties* (1817). What we see when we examine the late novels of allegedly domestic fiction writers is an individualist framework of domestic fiction *opening* onto paranational concerns about national and religious allegiances. Canonical eighteenth-century writers, that is, have tended to become more interested in migrating selves, not less, as their writing careers have worn on. This dilation has gone unnoticed, however, either because these novels have been viewed as their respective authors' less famous or available work or because they have been compressed into interpretations that avoid issues such as migration, allegiance, and nationality law. By deliberately taking up these canonical authors, rather than less represented or non-English authors, I want to emphasize how novelists affiliated with domestic fiction display continuities with, rather than departures from, the concerns about national allegiance foregrounded by Defoe and Smollett.[11] In other words, I want to disrupt the thesis that canonical eighteenth-century writers turned inward and away from paranational perspectives. Once this thesis is disturbed, the idea of globalizing the canon of English literature in opposition to domestic fiction, or of calling out the novel's inattention to transnational identities and movements, stands out as in need of methodological repair. Fictional interest in paranationality was not hidden, repressed, or expressed solely in genres separate from the English novel in the second half of the eighteenth century.

Undoubtedly, the novel was important to the development of individualism in the eighteenth century, especially through its creation of new narrative forms for the depiction of interiority and subjectivity. Yet domestic concerns with interiorization and privacy were not at the expense of views of national self-presentation. Indeed, as Michael McKeon notes in another context, the figurative meaning of the verb *domesticate* is "'to naturalize' or 'to familiarize' the great, the distant, the worldly, the strange, or the foreign by 'bringing it home'—through the medium of the little, the proximate, the local, the familiar, or the native."[12] For epistolary and sentimental novels trained on women's conduct and function within the bourgeois family, a focus on private life often enabled a more precise, rather than limited, epistemological engagement with questions about the extent and depth of national allegiance. The novels studied in this chapter explore questions about how individuals can exist and persist as individual selves in other national territories, from a man seeking to marry a woman of another faith, to a traveler who wants to preserve the portrait of his beloved, to a female refugee's quest for asylum among well-connected, middle-class English families. As these novels navigate national identity from within the walls of domesticity, they locate the bonds of fellow feeling not just in the depths of the individual human heart but, more importantly, in the public procedures and processes of national law. As Sir Charles Grandison, Yorick, and Juliet Granville, and other paranational characters discussed in this chapter, all demonstrate—along with many a lovelorn couple filing immigration papers with the US Department of Homeland Security today—before a private individual can be thought to marry or travel for love, their religious and national allegiances must be publicly clarified by law. They remind us, that is, there is no subjective and interior life of an individual without also a legible outward form of allegiance.

The last-written novels of Richardson, Sterne, and Burney not only tell a less parochial story about the relationship between domestic fiction and the rise of the nation-state, they also collectively outline how the idea of naturalization was complicated in the second half of the eighteenth century as it encountered subjects and scenarios that had not figured in earlier legal debates. Each of these novels, in addition to tracing a continued paranational experiment in the second half of the eighteenth century, offers a different touchstone or landmark for the story of naturalization as it changed in the second half of the eighteenth century: from the naïve and romantic nostalgia expressed by Richardson's Grandison for a natural-law understanding of human connection, to the growing codification of nationality under conditions of war experienced by Sterne's protagonist in midcentury France, to Burney's exploration of naturalization's limits in the plight of Black servants and enslaved persons who immigrated to England toward the end of the century. These novels track, across a range of responses, both the possibilities and limits of naturalization, and they do so by exploring the subject as it roams beyond its familiar, domestic spaces.

Love and the Law of Nations

Richardson's reputation as a domestic novelist has long rested on his first two epistolary novels, *Pamela* (1740) and *Clarissa* (1748), both of which concern the dangerously private and individual lives of women as written from their own perspective. In 1747 Richardson advertised *Clarissa* as featuring "the most Important Concerns of Private Life; and particularly showing, "the stresses that may attend the Misconduct both to parents and children in relation to marriage."[13] Yet Richardson's status as a domestic novelist is something of a rearward projection, having much to do with the lack of availability—and sheer length—of his final epistolary novel, *The History of Sir Charles Grandison*, which was written in 1753, the same year as Tobias Smollett's *The Adventures of Ferdinand Count Fathom* and the same year in which the bid for Jewish naturalization was brought before the English Parliament.[14] While the letters in *Pamela* are almost entirely written from the perspective of its titular character—a one-sidedness that did much to create a new sense of interiority in fiction—in *Grandison*, letters are written by many people and enclosed, shared, and translated across a wider geographical distance. Significantly, these letters function less as a means to externalize private thoughts and feelings—to bring felt interiority to the surface—than to translate and traffic information across national territories. As is evident in a letter from Dr. Bartlett to Harriet, the sharing of letters among a greater variety of people across national territories is an assumed practice in the social world of the novel: "The next morning, early, Mr. Grandison received the following Letter from his friend Signor Jeronymo. I translated it, my good Miss Byron, at the time I received it. I will send you the translation."[15] Here Dr. Bartlett explains and translates a letter from Grandison's Italian friend for Harriet in England, who is not the letter's primary recipient.

Over the course of Richardson's epistolary fiction, in fact, social and geographical spheres grow rather than contract in relation to the legal and literary concepts of naturalization that developed during the period. Richardson expressed approval for the legal naturalization of Jewish people in his private correspondence, and his final novel, *Grandison*, was written concurrently with the Jewish Naturalization Bill, which was brought before Parliament in the same months Richardson was revising *Grandison* for press.[16] The bill allowed Jews to become naturalized by an application to Parliament. Richardson initially welcomed the act. As the months wore on, however, he fell quickly in line with senior Whigs' opinions in opposing the legislation on the grounds that it had raised too much public outcry.[17] His fiction, however, appears to tell another story. During the months that Richardson made these remarks about naturalization, he also actively revised his draft of *Grandison* so that its Jewish character, a libertine named Solomon Merceda, could represent the threats posed by Jewish naturalization.

Yet Richardson's engagement with naturalization extends beyond the topical debate about Jewish naturalization. His epistolary novel also picks up the thread of a discourse about naturalization that first appeared and was substantiated in *Calvin's Case* and the cases related to the estate of the earl John Ramsey. As we saw in Chapter 1, the Ramsey cases provided two competing explanations for how Scots might be considered subjects of the king of England after the Union of the Crowns. The first followed Francis Bacon's argument in *Calvin's Case* that "by the law of nature all men in the world are naturalized one towards another.... It was civil and national laws that brought in these words, and differences, of civis and exterus, alien and native."[18] Bacon understands naturalization as the ultimate natural process—men exist in the state of nature before the development of civil and natural law and differences. Naturalization is but a return to a natural state they once occupied. The second understanding of naturalization, which was explored in Defoe's *Robinson Crusoe* in the previous chapter, challenged the idea of allegiance as entirely derived from natural law, holding a contrary view that nationality could also be created or engineered, ex nihilo, by parliamentary statute. This was the republican view of naturalization as the individual's right to traffic across national boundaries without the burden of perpetual allegiance. While Smollett's *Fathom* and Defoe's *Crusoe* entertain the liberal view of naturalization, Richardson's novel appears to side with Bacon's earlier view.

Grandison principally concerns the life of an Englishman, Sir Charles, who finds himself gripped by a "divided or double Love" with marriage prospects in both England and Italy (3:76). Before meeting Harriet Byron, a young English orphan whose family estate has been entailed to a foreigner, Sir Charles had been living in Italy, where he had promised his hand to an Italian woman named Signorina Clementina della Porretta. The marriage offer, however, is fraught with religious and national differences. Clementina's family, and Clementina herself, do not favor a marriage between a Roman Catholic Italian and a Protestant Englishman, and Sir Charles is reluctant to convert. In examining issues of transnational marriage, Richardson takes a wider social and political view than in his earlier novels, examining the national situation of his protagonists and the political events determining their lives as individuals.[19] Much has been written about the tolerance Richardson extends toward Italian Catholics in *Grandison*, but in making a marriage between individuals of two different religions and allegiances the novel's centerpiece, he also shows himself to be interested in the complications of tolerance for legal institutions such as marriage.[20] These interests are particularly underlined in the passage where Grandison ruminates on how he might make compromises with Clementina and still conform to his Protestant faith. He says he is "Entirely satisfied" in his faith and loves his "native country" (2:130). He cannot sacrifice either of them. Grandison attempts to satisfy his Protestant faith and the faith of his future sons by compromising with Clementina on the country of his residence and on the faith of their future daughters. To marry Clementina, he proposes alternating between living in England and Italy if he and his future sons can remain Protestant.

Clementina, however, objects to these proposed articles, and to the marriage in general, as too heretical. Thus, in the end, Grandison's Protestant faith and English allegiance are not sullied, and in this sense, the novel might be thought to avoid the problems of naturalization entirely. Grandison abandons the paranational plot and marries an Englishwoman. Yet the fact that Richardson broaches these compromising ideas in his novel, and makes them the focal point of its action, drew, at the time, significant attention. Even though the novel resolves with a felicitous marriage between two English subjects, Grandison's proposed marriage amendments to Clementina were the subject of major outcry. Richardson received several letters from readers who worried about the damage these articles might do to Grandison's Englishness and moral character. In a response to one reader, Richardson highlighted that it was important that Grandison not appear too punctilious with his faith. By acquiescing to the concerns of Clementina's Italian family, Grandison shows himself to be a moral person rather than a bigoted one. Clementina's family, he maintained, faces a greater concession in agreeing to let their grandsons—the inheritors of property in England and Italy—be raised as Protestants. He also argued that the effort at compromise conformed more readily to his reader's generic expectations of romance: had Grandison not compromised on the purity of his religious and national allegiance, he maintained, readers would not believe the extent of his love for a lady of merit and fortune. In other words, it was more natural, in Richardson's opinion, for Grandison to negotiate his nationality and faith than ruin his moral character.[21] In an editorial "Concluding Note," which Richardson added to subsequent editions of the novel, he made clear that Grandison's actions, especially as they relate to his refusal to engage in a duel, were "imperfection[s]" that made him all the more natural.[22]

Not only does Richardson suggest that Grandison's studied consideration for his faith and native home is natural, but he also links Grandison's natural behavior to "the Laws of all nations" (465). Before the nineteenth century, the "law of all nations" referred to the law of nature, as international, national, and domestic spheres were not yet analytically distinct.[23] Richardson thus responds to objections about Grandison's transnational marriage concessions by framing the protagonist as a subject of less tainted, more universal natural law, rather than of "silly modern custom."[24] This is a move we already witnessed in Chapter 1's investigation of the Ramsey cases, in which jurists considered how it might be possible for a foreign Scot to be made into a natural subject without overturning the feudal basis of the laws of allegiance. Several of the jurists answered, in a reflection of Sir Edward Coke's complicated and contradictory reading of *Calvin's Case*, that men are subjects of natural law before they are subjects of allegiance to a crown. Because of this view, an individual can be thought to change their allegiance without being considered heretical. Men exist in nature before they exist in a state of law, and as a result individuals can be naturalized as political and religious subjects without compromising the natural order. What appears as unnatural excess is, in fact, a truer expression of the natural order.

As Defoe does in *Robinson Crusoe*, Richardson demonstrates in *Grandison* an awareness of the legal and political barriers to transnational settlement, especially as they concern the transfer of property and religious practice across national territory. But in distinction to Defoe, who follows Locke in emphasizing the contractual and liberal nature of allegiance, Richardson genuflects to the prior view of Coke and Bacon: all men are naturalized to one another before they are natural members of a nation. Harriet encapsulates this position about Grandison at length in a letter to Lucy:

> Sir Charles has seen more of the world, it may be said, than his sister has. He has travelled. But is not human nature the same in every country, allowing only for different customs? Do not love, hatred, anger, malice, all the passions, in short, good or bad, shew themselves by like effects in the faces, hearts, and actions of the people of every country? And let men make ever such strong pretensions to knowledge, for their far-fetch'd and dear-bought experience, cannot a penetrating spirit learn as much from the passions of a Sir Hargrave Pollexfen in England, as it could from a man of the same or like ill qualities, in Spain, in France, or in Italy? And why is the Grecian Homer, to this day, so much admired, as he is in all these nations, and in every other nation where he has been read, and will be, to the world's end, but because he writes to nature? And is not the language of nature one language throughout the world, tho' there are different modes of speech to express it by? (1:184)

As Lisa O'Connell argues, Lucy's position here "is a vernacular statement of the fundamental presupposition of natural law theorists."[25] Before men are carved up into members of different national cultures, they are steeped in the same nature. Homer, whose birthplace was the subject of much speculation and contestation, is not a writer who proclaims the interests of a single nation; he writes from the state of nature itself. It is this original nature that makes it possible for individuals like Grandison to change or compromise the particulars of their allegiance or religion without sullying their character. Recall that the process of understanding Grandison's "unnatural" excesses as "more natural" expressions of the social order was an aesthetic maneuver already discussed in Chapter 2 in relation to Richardson's first novel, *Pamela*, where the concept of naturalization as a technique of empowering individual liberty over aristocratic hierarchy is shown to be substantially borne out in the creative and inherently fictional power of Pamela's account of her capture: the way the letters she writes progressively naturalize her as an authority against social and sexual conflict, and how, through that process, she acquires the authenticity of a subject speaking in her own right. *Grandison* is a decidedly more paranational novel, yet, in many ways, its naturalization of religion succeeds to a far lesser extent than the naturalization of class in *Pamela*. At its conclusion, the characters remain discriminated along national lines.

Indeed, the marriage between two upper-class English subjects in *Grandison*, unlike the class-crossing marriage of Pamela and Mr. B, requires no naturalizing effort. As if to prepare for the impossibility of transnational marriage, in the novel's opening material, Richardson divides *Grandison*'s characters into three types—Men, Women, and Italians—a typology that, by turning nationality into a gender or, vice versa, gender into nationality, signals the divided geographical sphere of the novel just as it indicates the formative importance of national origin for the recognition of marriage between men and women. The novel introduces a foreign third term into the domestic institution of marriage that can never entirely be shaken off: indeed, the marriage—the event that completes so much English fiction—is only the penultimate event of this novel. The final pages unwind with letters discussing the unsettled marital state of Clementina as she visits England and resides with Grandison and his new wife. The novel then wraps up with Grandison escorting his former Italian love to France, extolling the future harmonization of their two countries: "Friendship, dearest creatures, will make at pleasure a safe bridge over the narrow seas; it will cut an easy passage thro' rocks and mountains, and make England and Italy one country" (8:454). While Grandison still fervently believes in the inherent ability of the individual to transcend religious and other divides, the plot of the novel moves otherwise, leaving its Italian heroine in paranational ambiguity.

Although Richardson was—and continues to be—understood as a primarily domestic fiction writer, when his complete oeuvre is considered, we see how a conception of naturalization emerged alongside an epistolary structure overriding national and religious difference through the paper conduits of letters. It is striking how plaintively the novel harks back to the possibility of naturalized allegiance in conformity with Bacon's view that "by the law of nature all men in the world are naturalized one towards another."[26] Naturalization in this view does not fictionalize a new national subject through a civil process. Rather, it recalls the original naturalness of individuals under natural law, enabling the overlooking of national and religious difference for a deeper claim to resemblance and recognition through human nature. In contrast to Lockean writers and thinkers who see allegiance as radically contractual, in his final novel, Richardson suggests naturalization cannot exist as a means of connection without the "more natural" agreement of human nature. While we may want to sanction this view of the world as an airy aristocratic cosmopolitanism, or as outright contradictory, as indeed it appeared when Coke first assembled the argument, the combination of proposed national and religious compromise in Richardson's final work invites us to delineate the historical conditions under which it was possible for love and marriage between individuals to transcend the legal and social constraints of their time. Thus, in the immediate aftermath of one of the century's biggest challenges to a legal naturalization act—the bill for Jewish naturalization—we find Richardson retreating not inward but more broadly backward to an ahistorical idea of natural relations.

The Sentimental Passport

In *Grandison*, Richardson reasoned the case that individuals were naturally acquainted before they were defined as national subjects. Six years later, Sterne would test the opposite proposition in *A Sentimental Journey through France and Italy* (1759). The national identification of individuals, Sterne contends in this wry, sentimental novel—a favorite of Thomas Jefferson's—is more important than the anterior fellowship they are thought to share as humans. *A Sentimental Journey* was published only a few years after *Grandison*, but already it shows a strikingly more nuanced and realistic appreciation of nationality law in England and France. Principally, the novel concerns Yorick, an obtuse English traveler who is contrasted to Smellfungus, the sobriquet Sterne invented to make fun of Tobias Smollett's own acerbic travel narratives. In the first volume, Yorick arrives in Dover on his way to Calais, only to immediately discover he cannot pass into France on his own ("It never enter'd my mind that we were at war with France").[27] He then begs a count to let him travel in his suite. Once in Paris, Yorick quickly forgets how he smuggled himself into the country and becomes engaged in a variety of sentimental encounters: with a monk begging alms for his friar, with a dead ass on the road, and with a mysterious woman in Calais. In the second volume of the novel, however, Yorick's servant informs him he must produce a passport for the French chief of police. Fearful he might be thrown into the Bastille, Yorick appeals to a local count, identifying himself by pointing to the appearance of his namesake in Shakespeare's *Hamlet*. This fictional identification is sufficient to warrant the issuance of the legal document that allows Yorick to settle in France as a naturalized foreigner (121).

The plot of Sterne's sentimental novel is thus concerned with an effort at naturalization. This fact has barely been recognized by generations of scholars, partly because the novel appears as almost plotless. Like Richardson, Sterne has been designated primarily as a domestic writer. The sentimental genre he helped develop and popularize, which reached its peak in the 1770s and 1780s, was primarily associated with female writers, and, as contemporary scholars have long insisted, it is historically and ideologically entwined with the making of the English middle class.[28] Yorick's acutely tender regard for an abandoned désobligeant in a coach yard and his burst of tears for a dead ass on the road have seemed too glaringly bathetic to scholars to be taken seriously as evidence of larger social and political concerns. Many characterize Yorick's sentimentality as disingenuous, hypocritical, narcissistic, and apolitical, concluding that Sterne wrote the novel to consciously critique the ideological motivations of sentimentalism or otherwise carelessly cavort with them. Terry Eagleton, for example, argues that the ambiguity attached to Sterne's critical vision is the problem of sentimentalism as a domestic genre in general. Distracting readers from grim economic and political realities, "sentimentalism, and the literature produced by it, tends to be whimsical, digressive and idiosyncratic, preferring the pale sheen of a snowdrop to prison reform. It is in every sense a luxurious ethics."[29]

In its attempt to navigate the issue of Yorick's national status in a cross-border context, however, *A Sentimental Journey* very clearly outlines the legal problems of sentimental travel and posits a dramatic text—Shakespeare's *Hamlet*—as a resolving rather than mystifying end point. To understand how fiction comes to facilitate Yorick's naturalization, we must understand the reference to French nationality law in the novel's first sentence: "Strange!" exclaims Yorick, "that one and twenty miles sailing, for 'tis absolutely no further from Dover to Calais, should give a man these rights—I'll look into them" (3). Like *Robinson Crusoe*, *A Sentimental Journey* is framed by a law about strangers. In the very first lines of the novel, we learn that in traveling to France, Yorick has become the subject of a law that commands that the king is entitled to all his property should Yorick die in France. The "rights" Yorick refers to here are the *droits d'aubaine*, a French law stipulating that "all the effects of strangers (Swiss and Scotch excepted) dying in France, are seized . . . tho' the heir be upon the spot—the profit of these contingencies being farm'd, there is no redress" (3). In the eighteenth century, the droits d'aubaine was the opposite of naturalization. While naturalization restored or granted property rights to foreigners, the droits d'aubaine executed the right to take property away; it was a negative rather than a positive right; a right of pillage rather than passage; a right that turned the stranger into a passive subject rather than an energetic agent. As Yorick goes on to say, "The whole world could not have suspended the effects of the *Droits d'aubaine*—my shirts, and black pair of silk breeches—portmanteau and all must have gone to the King of France—even the little picture which I have so long worn, and so often have told thee, Eliza, I would carry with me into my grave, would have been torn from my neck" (3–4). It is tempting to see Yorick's regard for his property in this passage as evidence of petit bourgeois self-interest. But as his engagement with nationality law here reveals, the travel from Dover to Calais is in fact a disenfranchisement of his class and nationality. The droits d'aubaine represents the passage from the rights and privileges of a gentleman to the empty status of the stranger. In the course of events as they occur in the novel, Yorick's regard for sentimental objects—such as his cherished portrait of Eliza—is occasioned by the loss of his status as an English gentleman, rather than an indulgence in its privileges. The droits d'aubaine is a French nationality law that cancels the possibility of sentimentality as luxurious personal indulgence.[30]

From this discussion of an exploitative French property law, we may begin to theorize how Sterne's sentimental novel, which has generic roots in the travel narrative, strengthens rather than diminishes the general novel's investment in paranational perspectives, in particular the politics of nationality as surface and depth first explored by Defoe in *Robinson Crusoe*. In Sterne's novel, sentimentality emerges as a universalist discourse that can override the brutal nationalist laws of absolutist France. Yorick is frustrated less by the potential loss of property presented by the droits d'aubaine than by a feeling that this law is contrary to a universal principle of sentimentality he has always associated with the French people: "Ungenerous!" says Yorick, addressing himself to the absent king, "to seize upon the wreck of an unwary passenger, whom your subjects had beckon'd to their coast—by heaven! SIRE, it is not well done; and much does it grieve me, 'tis the monarch of a people so civilized and courteous, and so renown'd for sentiment and fine feelings, that I have to reason with" (4). Yorick's use of "beckon'd" here sets up a dramatic comparison between the French king, who "seize[s]" Yorick's possessions based on the letter of the law, and his gentler and more "civilized" subjects who mutely welcome Yorick to their shore. Beckoning is both an active and passive mode of signaling between two parties. It is physical—a waving of the hand, for example—and intuitive, such as the involuntary feeling of being drawn in by no force at all. If we now regard Yorick's sentimental idealization of the French people as a defense against a law that would shift his identity to the empty category of a foreigner, John Mullan's theorization of sentimentalism as an exceptional and privatizing connoisseurship appears inadequate.[31] Not only does Yorick become unpropertied in France, but he is also, as the very beginning of the novel announces, rightless. And in this preposterous way, Yorick's statusless status is on par with many of the pathetic victims whose suffering he seeks to represent and identify throughout the novel.[32] In casting Yorick as an overambitious and impractical sentimental statesman, these views, and others like it, have overlooked Sterne's exposure of sentimental travel as beset by the problem of legal nationality.

Sterne's framing of an opposition between an authorized law that restricts movement, on the one hand, and a nebulous and anonymous force with no boundaries, on the other, corroborates Peter Sahlins's historical research into the disjunction between official legal discourse and vernacular notions of nationality in eighteenth-century absolutist France. Specifically, Sahlins argues that in the eighteenth century the political significance of the droits d'aubaine extended beyond its function as a feudal tax on foreigners. Before 1789, there were no citizenship laws in France. As in England, the common link between French people was not their status as political subjects but their shared subjection to the same king. Lacking an official way to differentiate his subjects from foreigners, the droits d'aubaine furnished the king with the ideological material necessary for a definition of the "royal model of the citizen": "The droit d'aubaine, in an expansive and political definition of the practice, became the centerpiece of French nationality law. This was the case in practice, in the bureaucracy of naturalization. But it was also the case in politics, where the crown appropriated the droit d'aubaine to tax the alien population of the kingdom, and thus to mark the divisions of citizens and foreigners."[33] Effectively, Sahlins argues that the droits d'aubaine emerged as the primary means of establishing the native French person in binary opposition to the foreigner. This is quite a different trajectory from the history of nationality law explored in the English context in Chapter 1. Because the state bureaucracy of France defined citizenship in political or legal terms, the only appeal for foreigners seeking naturalization was an appeal to more essential and primordial feelings of social and cultural belonging. These more essential feelings, which we can see in Yorick's suggestion that he has been "beckon'd" into France by its people, are posited as anterior to, and more primary than, the identifying structures of the law. What I want to emphasize here is that Yorick's sentimentalism surfaces in the first half of the novel as an attempt to redress—rather than to ideologically simplify, mystify, or confirm—an authoritarian strategy of repression. By rhetorically placing his sentiments before and above the language of the legal system, Yorick suggests an active engagement with the so-called political reality of France at the very beginning of the novel. But as we shall see, unlike *Grandison*, Sterne's novel ultimately finds sentimentalism lacking as a place from which to bridge national divides.

Yorick's early encounters in France betray a pronounced tension between a form of identification that recognizes others through concrete and objective particulars, such as those pertaining to national allegiance, and a more anonymous and body-based recognition that precisely suspends the particulars on which pity often depends. In the second half of *A Sentimental Journey*, this tension becomes more acutely complicated—but more imaginatively effective—when sentimentality moves from a basis in the body to an aesthetic logic. In the first half of the novel, Yorick's sentimentalism is figured primarily in the body—in the ability, for example, to feel for a poor monk based on the whims of his humors, or in the dilation of his nerves and arteries upon seeing a young woman in a remise. By the second volume, however, with the increasing burden of his status as a foreigner in France, Yorick finds himself needing to give an exterior account of himself. Returning to his hotel after an unsuccessful attempt to buy a set of Shakespeare's plays, Yorick is informed by his servant, La Fleur, and the master of the hotel that the "Lieutenant de Police" has been looking for him. Only at this point does Yorick admit that he has been traveling without a passport. At first, he shrugs the matter off, stubbornly maintaining his sentimental outlook that he "shall do very well" without a passport in Paris: "Poo! said I, the king of France is a good natured soul—he'll hurt no body" (98). La Fleur, however, kindly reminds Yorick that the king's authority cannot be cavalierly refused, whispering in his ear that "no body could oppose the King of France" (98).

In many ways, Yorick's dilemma regarding his passport represents the prototypical Sternean impasse between the threat of being captured within a bureaucratic language and the threat of giving oneself over to a digressive chaos wherein every conclusion is suspended. Just as the threat of death in *Tristram Shandy* functions to lengthen rather than expedite Tristram's writing, the social and political "reality" in *A Sentimental Journey* occasions the episodic nature of Yorick's sentimentalism. Tristram, however, can endlessly defer telling the story of his life, while Yorick, as becomes increasingly certain in the second volume of the novel, must give an account of himself before the law. Indeed, Yorick comes to understand that his passport, in being "directed to all lieutenant governors, governors, and commandants of cities, generals of armies, justiciaries, and all officers of justice," is paradoxically the one document that will secure his private existence, allowing him to "travel quietly along" (116). Sterne presents the dilemma of nationality in *A Sentimental Journey*, then, as twofold: If Yorick endorses himself as a friendly foreigner who is safe, he concedes that the king has a right over him—a preexistent right that is contrary to his sentimental ethos. If, however, Yorick refuses to answer to the question of his name, he risks deportation, or worse, imprisonment in the Bastille. At a moment such as this, Sterne goes out of his way to demonstrate that the sentimentalism in his novel is useful for exploring, rather than ideologically sealing, the fissures presented by national allegiance in the eighteenth century. It is precisely in the reactive space between Yorick's refusal to give up his privileged singularity and his need to surrender himself to an external representation that Sterne locates an imaginative possibility for the transnational allegiance.

To understand this possibility, it is necessary to recall that passports in the eighteenth century did not contain a description of a person's physical appearance. The passport that Yorick seeks in Paris would be limited to a single sheet of paper, headed by a coat of arms, containing a script written in the name of the monarch requesting in florid language that the traveler be able to pass in France unimpeded. Physical identifiers such as eye color, hair color, and height were not standard features of passports in France until 1915. For obvious logistical reasons, the practice of basing passports on familiarity was given up in the more globally mobile and increasingly populous nineteenth century.[34] I invoke this historical background to stress that the determinants of national allegiance in the eighteenth century were vested in language rather than biometrical imaging. It is the authority of an external person that guarantees recognition under the law rather than a person's fidelity to an image or set of personal markers. It is this fact, I contend, that helps to explain why Yorick chooses to give an account of himself by strategically connecting his name to the most famous Yorick in English culture:

> There is not a more perplexing affair in life to me, than to set about telling any one who I am—for there is scarce any body I cannot give a better account of than of myself; and I have often wish'd I could do it in a single word—and have an end of it. It was the only time and occasion in my life, I could accomplish this to any purpose—for Shakespear lying upon the table, and recollecting I was in his books, I took up Hamlet, and turning immediately to the grave-diggers scene in the fifth act, I lay'd my finger upon YORICK, and advancing the book to the Count, with my finger all the way over the name—*Me, Voici!* said I. (118)

In one and the same motion, Yorick approaches the Count de Bissy as himself—he is named Yorick—and presents this self in the name of Yorick from *Hamlet*. Because the Yorick of the play appears only as a skull, the Count elides the reference to Shakespeare in Yorick's self-identification and decides (quite incoherently) that the Yorick in front of him is another Yorick still, the famous Danish court jester: "Had it been for any one but the king's jester," the Count tells Yorick after he returns with his passport, "I could not have got it these two hours" (121). Equivocating on the link between a name and an identity, Yorick's pointing to a name in *Hamlet* simultaneously suggests that he is the king of Denmark's jester, the gravedigger's skull in *Hamlet*, and also himself, joking that he is both—and, of course, neither. By using the play *Hamlet* to identify himself, Yorick reveals and conceals his identity at the same time. He locates his identity in a fictional reference while also obscuring that reference. Yorick doesn't convince the Count that he is a legitimate subject by authentically appearing as himself; instead, he connects himself, a comic figure, to one of the greatest tragedies in English literature. This is ultimately how naturalization worked in this moment: by avowing its artificial quality, by licensing an acceptance of the naturalness of foreigners that is premised on a lie. Naturalization involved a change from one signifier of national identity to another—yet the prior signifier is not covered up: like Robinson Crusoe's German name, it still signals. The capacity to be misread or mistaken by the Count as a jester allows Yorick, a comic figure, to naturalize into the tragic plot of *Hamlet* and receive all its rights and privileges.

It is the certain genius of Sterne to equivocate the truth and falsity of Yorick's passport, allowing Yorick to distance himself from his truth claim—indeed he *is* jesting, he tells the Count—and to hold on to that claim as authentic: the Count really does believe, or will not hear claims to the contrary, that the man before him is actually the Danish court jester. But the joke is not only at the Count's expense, nor is it an ironic underscoring of the difference between jester and jest. The multiplication of meaning in the word *jest* has the effect of opening for the reader fundamental questions about the identification of national allegiance. Yorick's jest reveals the scripts that summon and siphon personal identity into national identity and suggests the ways in which all of these identities are intentional and passive, artificial and natural, manufactured and discovered, necessary and superfluous. Most importantly, the jest allows Yorick to retain the ambiguity, the central mystery, of his core person even as he satisfies the exterior question of his person to the law.

A Sentimental Journey is a novel concerned with political and aesthetic borders: the territorial border between France and England, the linguistic border between proper and common names, the narrative border between reality and fiction, and the generic border between tragedy and comedy. It is also a work about illegal occupations: a foreigner who is not supposed to be in France and a comedic figure who should not be in Shakespeare's great tragedy. With Sterne, we are given a demonstration of sentimentality that overruns domestic borders toward the comically improbable. Yorick expresses emotions toward people and objects that appear "out of order." At times, he depicts "pity without an object"; "sadness without any apparent occasion," in Robert Burton's phrase; or "misery to no purpose," to use Samuel Johnson's term.[35] But far from ridiculing Yorick's mode of engagement with people and objects in France, Sterne exploits the gap between his expressions of sensibility and the reader's "sense" of reality to show how Yorick emerges as a subject within the social and political order of the text, precisely because he refuses to compromise his feelings of a self who is identified by sympathy rather than name.

Sterne's sentimental novel locates the possibility of recognition for subjects who cannot (or should not) be "seen" by official discourses and genres. Playing two meanings of *plot* against each other—as a narrative sequence governed by a knowable logic and as a secret, subversive act—Yorick's passport demonstrates the gap that allows an imposter to pass into the "real" based on a jest. Yorick enters France legally from the illegal place of fiction, but we, the readers, like the count to whom Yorick tells his story, are left to sort the difference: "*Pardonnez moi*, Mons. Le Compte, said I—I am not the king's jester,—But you are Yorick?—Yes.—*Et vous plaisantez?*—I answered. Indeed I did jest—but was not paid for it—'twas entirely at my own expense" (121–22). Ultimately, what we see in *A Sentimental Journey* is that self-contradiction does not stall Yorick's progress; rather, it ensures his survival. Yorick is indeed, as he says, a singular traveler, but one with a plan to overthrow national singularity itself. It is true that his "ethic" of sentimental sociability is not a practical way of getting along in—much less improving—society, but it may now be considered an imaginative response to a practical and delimiting political and national necessity. Yorick relies on sentiment to extend relations beyond personal, epistemological, and territorial limitations, specifically in a situation in which individual rights cannot be depended on to secure his safe passage or legitimacy.

In turning now to an early nineteenth-century novel, Frances Burney's *The Wanderer; or Female Difficulties*, we can see how naturalized allegiance and its attendant fictional forms of communication continued to evolve in three ways: as a fictional experiment concerned with the insularity of English middle-class society, with racialized migration as it attached to the French and English empires, and in relation to the deprivations of female private life.

"Black, Patched and Pennyless"

In 1802 Burney, then an established writer known for the novels *Cecilia* and *Evelina*, moved with her husband, General Alexandre D'Arblay, to France. Unlike Yorick in Sterne's *Sentimental Journey*, who steals himself into Paris at the height of the Seven Years' War, Burney migrated during a period of relative peace between the two countries. As hostilities resumed, however, she would find herself exiled in Paris for the next ten years. Eventually, in 1812, while Napoleon was off campaigning in Russia, authorities granted Burney permission to leave France for America (though her husband had engineered passage for her on a ship that would make an illegal stop at an English port). As Burney waited for the ship to set sail, she wrote her husband asking him to forward a manuscript she had been working on. General D'Arblay obtained permission from the Police Office, assuring the authorities, "upon his Honour, that the Work had nothing in it political, or even National . . . and possibly offensive to the government."[36] Nevertheless, in her journal, Burney recorded the rage of a Dunkirk customhouse officer who, after discovering the manuscript in her portmanteau, accused Burney of "traiterous [sic] designs."[37] The manuscript was only allowed to pass customs because of the timely intervention of an English merchant living in France, whom Burney called on to vouch for her person to the French authorities—just as Yorick more ridiculously calls on Shakespeare's *Hamlet* to recommend him to the French count.

Obviously, much had changed for migrants traveling to and from England in the early decades of the nineteenth century. In previous centuries, rich merchants possessed the freedom to travel largely unimpeded across Europe—borders were unclear and unpoliced, reflecting the limits of a sovereign's physical control rather than the territorial reach of their jurisdictional authority.[38] The French Revolution and Napoleon's rule strongly altered this openness, putting into play immigration protocols that would fundamentally reorient the relationship between states and their citizens. In 1793 English Parliament passed the Aliens Act, a law requiring that all foreigners who arrived in England register at the customs office before disembarking and then wait for a passport to be granted by the home secretary or a local magistrate.[39] The 1793 Aliens Act was a legislative reaction to the arrival of thousands of French émigrés into England seeking to escape French tyranny. It was also in this period that the Home Office was consolidated.[40] Unlike the 1709 Foreign Protestants Naturalization Act, which had been devised to grant rights and privileges as part of an effort to lure foreign craftspeople into England, the 1793 Aliens Act was entirely restrictive. Many members of the British government feared that spies would come into England disguised as supplicating migrants. As Burney remarked in her diary, the event of the customs officer almost seizing her manuscript occurred "during a period of such unexampled strictness of Police Discipline with respect to Letters or Papers, between the Two Nations."[41]

One could not ask for a better description of the nineteenth-century nationalizing shift identified by the likes of Benedict Anderson and Franco Moretti than Burney's diary entry. In it, the author evidences how the nation-state emerged from the policing of borders and the essentialization of national cultures. Yet the novel Burney was working on while waiting for her ship to disembark from France would ultimately sidestep this nationalizing shift, experimenting instead with the fear and freedom of paranational allegiance. In the dedication to the manuscript that would eventually be published in 1814 as *The Wanderer; or Female Difficulties*, Burney insisted, as if speaking to the customs officer who had confronted her in Dunkirk, that *The Wanderer* had nothing political or national in it: "I should leave all discussions of national rights, and modes, or acts of government, to those whose wishes have no opposing calls; whose duties are undivided; and whose opinions are unbiassed [sic] by individual bosom feelings."[42] For Burney, there was nothing national or nationalistic—nothing particularly dismissive or congratulatory of the French or English nations—in her novel, not because it avoided political or national themes (it is chock full of them), but because it does not prioritize a certain national perspective.[43] At precisely the moment that many scholars argue novels were beginning to consolidate nationalism in cultural form, Burney attested that her novel eschews a national perspective. *The Wanderer* is simply a "composition upon general life, manners, and characters; without any species of personality, either in the form of foreign influence or of national partiality," because it shows no unique national attachments.⁴⁴ The novel is not designed to *engender* national community; rather, it examines the problem of divided allegiance at a precise moment of intense nation-state building.⁴⁵

When considered alongside Richardson's pious gentleman hero and Sterne's equivocating jester, the wandering heroine of Burney's novel emerges as the most serious limit case for naturalization we have thus far encountered. In the opposite migration pattern of Sterne's *Sentimental Journey*, the novel chronicles the travel of a female French refugee—a "female Robinson Crusoe," as the narrator styles her—who seeks safe passage among a group of English passengers fleeing Robespierre's terror.⁴⁶ This is how the novel opens: "During the dire reign of the terrific Robespierre, and in the dead of night, braving the cold, the darkness and the damps of December, some English passengers, in a small vessel, were preparing to slide silently from the coast of France, when a voice of keen distress resounded from the shore, imploring, in the French language pity and admission" (11). The English passengers are vexed by the self-presentation of the woman who emerges from the dark: she appears French based on the language she speaks but quickly tells them she is from England. She is dressed in rags but has the airs and accomplishments of a person of high breeding. Her face looks dark, covered in black patches and bruises—leaving the passengers to wonder if she hails from "the settlements in the West Indies? or somewhere off the coast of Africa" (19)—yet in England, "the woman's face appears to change from a tint nearly black, to the brightest, whitest, most dazzling fairness" (43). The refugee refuses to reveal any information about her name, national origin, racial identity, class, or social connections. The lack of clarity surrounding the woman's identity, especially her race, troubles the English passengers for two reasons. The first is that, without familial connections, the nameless woman has no "receipt" to credibly introduce her into English society as a respectable person (14). The second is that, far worse than her lack of history, the woman seems to repeatedly alter her self-presentation. She is a "frenchified swindler" who can "swell into a duchess, or . . . swindle into a beggar" (52, 111). She can swivel between races, traveling with "black and white outsides" (45). "Pray," asks the imperious Mrs. Ireton, "have you kept the same face ever since I saw you in Grovenor Square? Or have you put it on again only now . . . ?" (485). To make the woman's name and race more concrete, the English passengers adopt a blend of assignations from romance and travel literature. She is dubbed "Incognita" (12), "tawny Hottentot," "tattered dulcinea" (13), "adventurer," "walnut-skinned gypsey" (52), "vagabond," "black insect," "native enemy," and "double face" (251). Like Smollett's antihero Fathom, the multiple appearances of Burney's nameless heroine, specifically her French-accented claim to possess an English birthright, unsettle established protocols of determining national belonging.[47]

If, for the passengers, the problem posed by the refugee is that she cannot be slotted into firm racial, class, and national categories, then the predicament faced by the anonymous heroine is that of naturalization. After rejecting the nameless wanderer—who is dubbed Ellis on account of a letter she receives bearing the initials L. S.—Mrs. Maple spitefully observes that "Ellis seemed to be naturalized at Brighthelmstone, where she was highly considered, and both visited and invited, by all who had elegance, sense, or taste to appreciate her merits" (241). The sense of *naturalization* spoken of here recalls the meaning used by Defoe in reference to Crusoe's acclimatization to island life, though Ellis's naturalization to middle-class English society is far less cumulative and stable. Housing, employment, and neighborliness do not become progressively more secure for Ellis the longer she resides in England, whether because her foreign identity triggers gossip among neighbors, because she lacks the means to pay for her accommodation, or because her unprotected status makes her the continual prey of a libertine baronet and other men. Ellis's naturalization in England is thus not one that can be determined by length of residence or adaptation to a country's mores and customs—it is not a matter of acclimating to a new environment. By the end of the novel, Ellis is (re)installed as a person of eminent distinction when it is revealed that she is Juliet Granville, the exiled daughter of the English Lord Granville. But Ellis's restoration to upper-class English society is rather beside the point. What the novel does is update the romance genre to explore at length why nativity and family title should matter for the public recognition of its heroine's worth. Beyond Ellis's singular person, the novel brings into view other anonymous subjects of domestic life—most prominently, Black enslaved persons and servants brought to England from the British colonies and poor women laboring in shops or sewing circles—who cannot be transformed or naturalized by a romantic ending.

Burney's novel draws out the interplay between the depth and surface of nationality in a different manner from what we have previously witnessed. If other subjects of naturalization emphasize the fictionality of national allegiance by overtly highlighting how easily and openly nationality can be donned and taken off through law, Ellis's refusal to yield answers to anyone about her origins and personal history, even to those sympathetically predisposed to her situation, and the deferral of her history until the sixth volume of the novel, turns nationality into a buried secret. Ellis is adamant that her refusal to talk is not because she wishes to disguise a deeper truth: "I have no false coloring," she says, "I am only not open" (340). Here, she offers a very different idea of openness: one that is structured based not on personal confession or the excavation of interior thinking but rather on the value of general anonymity. As Ellis describes her decision not to narrate her life history, even to those she might trust not to reveal it elsewhere, she centralizes the idea that a foreigner's hospitable reception should be premised on surface facts alone—on the traits, behaviors, and dignities of her self-presentation, rather than on the revelation of historical, social, and national connections. The belief that familial and national histories are not necessary precursors for social and national acceptance thus positions Burney's anonymous wanderer between Richardson's Grandison and Sterne's Yorick: between, that is, a naïve and cosmopolitical belief that people are all connected in an anterior state of nature and the ironic elision of national identification altogether.

Complicating all of this, however, is the matter of race. When Burney's heroine first appears on the shores at Calais, she is described as having "hands and arms of so dark a color, that they might rather be styled black than brown" (19). Several scholars have remarked how, in blackening Ellis's initial appearance, Burney refers to the violent migrations produced by the American, French, and Haitian revolutions at the end of the eighteenth century, which brought approximately ten thousand former enslaved persons to England and Ireland. Burney does indeed draw several parallels between the plight of unprotected women such as Ellis and the treatment of Black domestic servants in England. When Ellis serves as companion for the irascible Mrs. Ireton, for example, she witnesses the mistreatment of Mungo, a young Black domestic servant whom Mrs. Ireton orders "stripped" and threatens to have "shipped back to the West Indies" after he stifles a laugh at her bathetic attempt to drum up sympathy for her muddied lapdog (285). But the idea that Ellis herself might metamorphize or naturalize from a Black migrant into a white native in the same manner Yorick transforms from an English traveler to Danish court jester, or Crusoe casts himself as a Catholic papist in Brazil, is ultimately exposed as far too gimmicky for an early nineteenth-century novel to bear. The fluctuations of Ellis's racial appearance do not elasticize race in the same way that Crusoe, adapting the view of Locke and other liberal proponents of general naturalization, affirms the individual right to change one's religion and national allegiance. Race ultimately cannot be liberalized in the same manner as nationality. As Roxann Wheeler, Felicity Nussbaum, Nicholas Hudson, and others have shown, the eighteenth century was still very much influenced by theories of "racial plasticity" rooted in the idea that skin pigmentation could be changed with a generational change in climate.[48] But scientific racism, or the idea that racial appearance confirmed biological and cultural inferiority, would gain more traction in the late eighteenth and early nineteenth centuries. Burney's novel might, as Tara Czechowski suggests, reflect the tension of these shifting understandings of race in the period, but ultimately race will emerge as patently unnaturalizable.[49]

In the seventeenth and eighteenth centuries, race had not factored into legal and literary debates about naturalization. In 1695 proponents of a "universal naturalization" advocated naturalization for "all Persons of all Nations, of all Religions, Protestants, Papists, Jews, Mohametans, Turks, Moors, [and] Pagans."[50] When the English Parliament devised the idea of a general naturalization act to attract skilled foreigners, it had not thought to add racial criteria; it was more concerned with admitting religious differences than racial ones. At this time, as we have seen in previous chapters, economic and political writers were worried about population shortages in England and a surplus of waste lands in England itself. By the middle of the eighteenth century, however, after the outrage surrounding the Jewish Naturalization Act, legal naturalization began to wind down as an idea designed to make settlement in England and the colonies more attractive. By the end of the century, with the abolition of slavery, and the migration of thousands of Black royalists and enslaved persons to England from America, Britain began to overtly racialize naturalization. In 1771 the abolitionist Granville Sharpe argued that skin color should not impede the naturalization of Black enslaved persons and servants as British subjects because "every person who, in any respect, is in subjection to the laws, must undoubtedly be a subject."[51] But ultimately, the Committee for the Relief of the Black Poor settled on the Sierra Leone Resettlement Scheme, which proposed shipping the "Black Poor" to Britain's new colony in Sierra Leone in exchange for citizenship rights in the colony.[52] Like the Palatine refugees before them, whose refugee camp in London led to the overturning of the 1709 Naturalization Act, but with greater and more far-reaching consequences, the "Black Poor" in England could not be permitted recognition as subjects.

Burney's novel is not naïve (as Richardson's) or crafty enough (as Sterne's) to bypass the fissures of these rising challenges to general naturalization; instead, it examines the complications and hypocrisies of naturalization within the context of racialized migration in England. Perhaps the most profound way the novel registers the racial inequalities of naturalization is with its artificial and unsatisfying ending. Harleigh, the man Juliet marries, is one of the most stale and uninteresting love interests a novel of manners has ever coughed up. He is hardly compensatory for all that Juliet experienced as a poor, racialized refugee. And the revelation of Juliet's identity as an English heiress hardly arrives as a meaningful transformation for people such as Lord Melbury and Lady Aurora, who loved Juliet before she was known to share their blood. Indeed, the marriage plot that is meant to restore harmony to the social order, and to establish Juliet's place as a rightful protagonist, feels inadequate in the face of the larger social world the novel chronicles, especially regarding the Black and Brown bodies that Ellis/Juliet essentially doubles or proxies, without really embodying, and whose suffering is not transformed by her status change at the end of the novel.

Burney's final novel thus rests thematically and formally closer to earlier narratives concerned with naturalization as a voluntarist model of association than with the conceptualized national communities of the nineteenth century foregrounded by Anderson and others. Burney's fiction yields a different focus on individual and domestic life from what scholarly critics of the novel have typically discussed, conflating the situation of a foreigner in a new country with the plights of unprotected women and Black enslaved persons and servants. *Domesticity* is a word that is often used to refer to family life in scholarly accounts of eighteenth-century fiction and politics, but Burney's *The Wanderer* invites us to consider the word in three distinct yet collocated meanings. If we consider *domesticity* in senses not invoked by most critics, as "relating to one's own country or nation" and "as a laboring servant or attendant," rather than strictly "belonging to the home, house, or household," we can observe how Burney's novel extends beyond preoccupations with private female life, shallow middle-class society, and individual character development. To understand how Burney mobilizes multiple meanings of *domesticity*, however, we must comprehend her use of a plot about an unknown migrant in England as a vehicle to explore other forms of gendered and racial exploitation in the period. The novel's paranational perspective—its examination of the domestic contexts of the English nation from the perspective of an outsider who newly enters both middle- and lower-class English life— declines the nationalism of revolutionary romanticism and instead revisits the older, eighteenth-century interests in and anxieties about wandering nationality. Burney is able to more precisely explore the hardships faced by middle- and lower-class women through the figure of a racialized and foreignized newcomer encountering these hardships, and who cannot be saved from them (as her class status should allow), because her birth and race cannot be verified. This postulation of an abstract union between foreignness, gender, and race reveals that Burney was, after all, committed to fictionalizing national and political scenarios, albeit in a very different way from the jingoism she was accused of by the customs officer in Dunkirk.

Mobile Selves

One of the benefits of seeing naturalization as a heuristic for prose fiction is that it can help scholars make sense of the novel's disparate parts. There is still a good deal of debate about what a novel is, when and where it began, and how the novel's investment in individualism and interiority can be reconciled with the persistence of older, nonrealistic modes, such as romance, the picaresque, and the gothic. Modern critics, writing from the retrospective viewpoint of the age of the rights of citizens and nation-states, tend to understand the rise of the novel according to the rise of characters' interiority—people such as Sir Charles Grandison making personal decisions (even if they are bad ones) as the potential participants in a newly conceptualized civil and national society. But the creation of felt belonging through interiority is not a significant component of a national society before the nineteenth century. Rather, in the eighteenth century, allegiance is centralized as the tragic and comedic problem to the point that interiority can often seem remarkably beside the point. The interiorized spaces, subjective thoughts, and particular feelings of the self are perforated by the need to give politically and economically opportunistic accounts of the self.

Sir Charles Grandison's feelings do not override his understanding of the importance of his outward expression of allegiance in the same way that Pamela's might be said to do (though as we saw in Chapter 2's discussion of *Pamela*, her challenge is to demonstrate her inner worth as of equal importance to outward, social rank). And like Crusoe before him, who thinks nothing of swearing on paper to be a Catholic Portuguese subject when it suits his economic interests, Sterne's Yorick exploits the rules of naturalization in a mobile, emergent global age. He uses a great English tragedy to present himself in France. *A Sentimental Journey* is more astutely read as a commentary about the fictionality of national allegiance: about the slapstick narratives used to present and identify oneself beyond the domestic range of the self, and the inability, or refusal, to present oneself as a singular rather than communal being. With Burney, the fictionality of the subject gives way to the fictionality of the novel itself, to the insufficiency of romance to support the logic of a natural subject, but also to the insufficiency of realism to convey the fictional dimensions of these problems.

The study of these paranational novels allows us to comprehend how the dominant reception of the novel in theories and history is inadequate to the task of understanding how so much fiction was interested in the self as it migrates. As I have shown, the rise of the individualism narrative and its accompanying claims about interiority and subjectivity tells only one side of the story about the novel's formal development. Indeed, the other side—the side concerned with crossing into new lands and identifying oneself to new institutions and people as "safe"—requires more outward and ready-to-hand demonstrations of allegiance. From Smollett's picaresque tomfoolery, Richardson's archaic naturalism, Sterne's comedic jesting, and Burney's buried interiority, we can see how prose fiction in the eighteenth and early nineteenth centuries intersected, rather than shrank from, the age's legal shift toward forms of paranational allegiance. In the next chapter, we will see how novelists went beyond representing the law's insufficiencies, to trying to repair them.

PART III

RELATIONS OF NATURALIZATION

CHAPTER 5

Unnatural-Born Subjects

In the first book of the *Annals*, the Roman historian and senator Tacitus recounts the speech of a rebellious soldier named Percennius, who, in the reign of Tiberius, instigated a mutiny among the legions in Pannonia. Percennius, Tacitus narrates, was once "a busy leader in the embroilments of the theatre" but is "now a common soldier."[1] According to the German literary scholar Erich Auerbach, Tacitus's narration of Percennius's story in the *Annals* allows a common Roman legionary to enter the Latin discourse of historiography. And yet, as Auerbach argues, Tacitus's interest in Percennius's speech is "purely aesthetic."[2] Tacitus does not care about Percennius's political position or the demands he makes on behalf of his fellow soldiers. Before representing the soldier's energizing speech, Tacitus has already labeled him an "incendiary" with a "petulant, declaiming tongue," as well as an imposter who has unjustly assumed the "character of a lawful Commander."[3] The overall effect of this framing, according to Auerbach, is to strip "[Percennius] of his reasons and his voice, of his belonging to a common history and his own speech."[4]

While Auerbach argues that Tacitus's narration erases Percennius from history, the philosopher Jacques Rancière offers an alternative reading of this moment, one that prompts us to consider how narrative functions as an important form of naturalization in the absence of legal and political recognitions. Rancière argues that Tacitus's narration of Percennius's speech amounts to a radical form of narrative equality, which naturalizes the rebel soldier into the community, even though it is evident Tacitus himself thinks he is a deviant rabble-rouser. "What will interest us in Tacitus' discourse," says Rancière, "is not its effect of exclusion, underscored by Auerbach, but, on the contrary, its power of inclusion: the place it gives, through its own agency, to what it declares to have no place."[5] He continues, "Percennius is not, for Tacitus, among those whose speech counts, to whom his fellows speak. And nevertheless, he makes Percennius speak in the same mode as the others." While Tacitus does not recognize Percennius as a legitimate political subject,

Rancière identifies the Roman author's summary of the soldier's speech as an instance of a writer unintentionally introducing an excluded person into the discursive field of politics. Tacitus gives Percennius speech "in this 'indirect style,' which is the specific modality according to which he effects the equilibrium of narrative and discourse, and holds together the powers of neutrality and those of suspicion." According to Rancière, Percennius is granted political representation, indirectly, by means of his speech's inclusion in Tacitus's narrative, rather than through the historian's engagement with his revolutionary demands. In the summary of Percennius's revolt, the slave himself "doesn't speak; rather Tacitus lends him his tongue."[6] In a narrative effort to state and recount the speech of another, Rancière locates a discourse that brings both speakers, legitimate and illegitimate, into equal relation, even if they are not considered of the same kind—a relation that doesn't claim the speakers have the same origin but allows them equal standing.

Another way of describing this modality is what I have been calling *naturalization*, though this theorization strongly differs from the narratological understanding of naturalization considered in Chapter 2, where it was theorized by Jonathan Culler and others as a process of assimilation and domestication that stifles the singularity of texts. In Tacitus's *Annals*, it is precisely the homogenizing, flattening effect of historical writing—precisely its inability to render the singularity of individual existence into writing—that enables the introduction of new subjects into a shared community. "The appropriation of the other's speech," concludes Rancière, "can be reversed. . . . Tacitus does more than give [Percennius] a historical identity. He also creates a model of subversive eloquence for the orators and simple soldiers of the future."[7]

Turning now to what I will call *narrative naturalization*, this chapter examines two novels from the early nineteenth century that also historicize subjects who have been cast out of a political community. These novels go further than those we have encountered so far, not only registering the cultural impact of new legal understandings about national allegiance, or imagining new scenarios for the legal fiction of naturalization, but also attempting to use the genre of prose fiction itself to redress failures of legal naturalization to represent and incorporate religious and racial outsiders. The first novel, Maria Edgeworth's *Harrington* (1817), does this in a straightforward way: the novel adopts the genre of autobiography to tell the story of a man who disowns the anti-Semitic and anti-naturalization prejudices of his childhood, particularly the bigoted dictum that Jewish people cannot be naturalized because "you can't naturalize what's naturally unnatural."[8] Edgeworth's protagonist overturns this "logic" only after he understands the role of literary representation—specifically William Shakespeare's *Merchant of Venice*—in creating hostile views of Jewish naturalization. Through a dramatic text, Edgeworth provokes a revelation about the binary of unnatural and natural within her novel, which readers realize through the understanding of the protagonist, that she then follows with a gimmicky ending that leads to what I call narrative naturalization—one form thus embedded within and creatively working on another to expose and facilitate subject formation.

The second novel, Mary Shelley's *Frankenstein; or, The Modern Prometheus* (1818/31), which I treat at greater length, presents a more innovative combination of autobiography and biography in an epistolary format with a double frame to achieve naturalization for a racialized being who has been othered by all national communities. *Frankenstein*'s complex structure serves to naturalize a subject who is unnaturally born in two senses: Victor Frankenstein's Creature does not issue naturally from a womb; his body parts (like Tobias Smollett's Fathom) belong to different countries, and he cannot be claimed as a member of any nation-state. Critics have suggested that the frame narratives of Shelley's novel, like Tacitus's framing of Percennius, underscore the Creature's dislocation and ejection from human society by making it impossible for him to directly represent himself. Yet upon closer study of Shelley's literary influences, especially Plutarch's *Lives*, we will find that her unique narrative style is in fact a sophisticated vehicle for the aesthetic naturalization of the Creature. The narrative frames of the novel, which have long confounded scholars, not only register the discrepancy and abstraction between speaking for oneself and being spoken of but also articulate the power of narrative to indirectly produce new subjects. It is indirect narration, appearing in the words and language of someone else, rather than sympathy, that ultimately enables the Creature to become a subject, rather than object, in literature.

My readings of these novels will demonstrate that the novel functioned as more than a commentary on the failures of legal naturalization in the period. These narratives shaped history by creating new possible subjects of literature. Both Edgeworth and Shelley draw parallels between received modes of literary representation and the legal and historical dynamics that contiguously determined who could and could not be recognized as a national subject. Their novels each seek to redress a historical failure to incorporate religious and racial outsiders—in Edgeworth's case, the Jewish Question produced by the repeal of the 1753 Jewish Naturalization Act, and in Shelley's, the exclusionary immigration politics of Geneva, where the novel is partly set. Edgeworth and Shelley employ narrative's power of naturalization (of re-representing, re-shaping, redistributing, and reframing who appears as a subject) as an extra-legal means of confronting and ameliorating legal injustice and political prejudice. They do so unequally, however. Even though Edgeworth's novel is directly and more thematically concerned with the politics of naturalization, her effort for the most part weakly assumes the power of naturalization to lie with the personal intentions of the author and character rather than, as I argue, the bizarre and impersonal deus ex machina she concocts for the novel's ending. By contrast, Shelley's layered, innovative literary experiment enables a truly radical act of subject creation and change.

Inverted Sympathy and *Harrington*'s Cheap Trick

In 1815 a Jewish American educator named Rachel Mordecai wrote a letter to the famed Anglo-Irish author Maria Edgeworth. In it, the teacher questioned how Edgeworth could publicly write about the significance of early childhood education with justice and broadmindedness while at the same time delivering in her fiction hostile and bigoted depictions of Jewish people. In her response, Edgeworth acknowledged the justness of the educator's assessment. Her earlier fiction was indeed riddled with anti-Semitic stereotypes, from the protagonist of her most famous novel, *Castle Rackrent* (1800), who refers to his wife as "my pretty Jessica," after the seduced daughter from Shakespeare's *Merchant of Venice*, to the short stories she had written for children, such as "The Prussian Vase" and "The Good Aunt," which feature tightfisted and malicious Jewish characters, including Mr. Carat, a miserly Jewish jeweler who helps plot the robbery of a rich Christian woman. Struck by the accuracy of Mordecai's judgment, Edgeworth assured her American reader she would "make all the atonement and reparation in [her] power for the past."[9]

Two years later, in 1817, Edgeworth made good on her promise, publishing *Harrington*, an autobiographical novel about a young man who learns to overcome his childhood prejudice against Jews after falling in love with the daughter of a benevolent Spanish Jew. As she prepared the draft of *Harrington*, Edgeworth read an array of materials related to the historical status of Jews in Britain and Europe, familiarizing herself especially with the legislative battles Jews faced regarding naturalization. In 1753 a bill was presented before Parliament with the object of allowing Jews to be naturalized after three years of residence in England. Though the bill itself would have only affected a select group of Jewish financiers who had demonstrated loyalty to the administration, naturalization bids, as we have seen, were catalysts for expressions of wider anxiety about the unwritten natural laws of nationality. In this case, a flurry of pamphlets arguing for and against the naturalization of Jewish people generated intense public debate within England about allegiance and religious tolerance more generally. Many of these pamphlets' authors cited the tract *Reasons for Naturalizing the Jews in Great Britain and Ireland* (1714), written after the 1709 Naturalization Act, in which the Irish philosopher John Toland made the case for Jews as natural subjects, "hav[ing] no common or peculiar inclination distinguishing 'em from others; but visibly partake of the Nature of those nations among whom they live."[10] Edgeworth seems not only to take up Toland's argument in her novel but to crucially expand on it to include a discussion of religious tolerance more generally: the novel is bookended by the furor surrounding the 1753 Jewish Naturalization Act and the 1780 Protestant Gordon Riots protesting the passage of the 1778 Papists Act (which, like the Jewish Naturalization Act did for Jews, sought to reduce official discrimination against British Catholics by granting them select liberties, such as the right to serve in the British Navy and Army).

No other novel in the anglophone tradition appears as closely aligned with the politics of early legal naturalization as *Harrington*. At the end of the novel, in a scene that is meant to be reminiscent of the Gordon Riots, an angry mob attacks the house of Mr. Montenero, a benevolent and wealthy Jewish American man who has recently moved to England, with the chant, "No Jews, no wooden shoes!" (wooden shoes were associated with Catholic domination in France). The mob seeks to oust not only him and his Jewish family but also two wealthy women he has sheltered who the mob believes are Catholics. In this reinterpretation of the riot, Edgeworth records the affinity in the public imagination between the legal and political disabilities suffered by Catholics and Jews in England and recommends a wider discussion of the prejudices linked to the dominant Protestant religion and Englishness that gripped naturalization politics in the eighteenth century. The scene of the Gordon Riots in the novel also registers a correspondence between Edgeworth's own biography and that of her Jewish characters. In 1798, during the United Irishmen uprising against British rule, Edgeworth's father sought escape for his family from the Catholic rebels in the Protestant-protected town of Longford, where he was quickly suspected by Protestant leaders of being a French spy and nearly lynched.[11] Edgeworth reverses this outcome in her novel, having the Jewish and Catholic characters save the lives of the petulant and prejudiced Protestants. Through this reversal, and others, the novel probes not only the political and emotional dimensions of some of the most important controversies about naturalization in England but also how fiction works to rewrite these histories.

Crucial for the purposes of this book, Edgeworth's fictional narration of the Gordon Riots raises a question about her effort to "make all the atonement and reparation in [her] power for the past": What is the unique value of the novel for reckoning with the recorded events and discriminations of legal and political history? Edgeworth turns decisively to the novel as the genre that can best atone for the violent outcomes and prejudices attached to the Jewish Naturalization Act and the Papists Act—it is the genre, in the words of her father, that best functions as "an *amende honorable*"—because the novel is capable of allowing Jews to appear, sympathetically, as fully realized human subjects.[12] This is to say, Edgeworth's father proposes the novel as a genre that can help make new subjects in the real political world on the basis of sympathy: seeing characters represented in fiction as suffering individuals. By contrast, I have deliberately resisted throughout this book any relational or instrumental claims about novels and the social and political world, as these claims tend to portray the novel less as a prose narrative genre, with specific conventions and relations to literary history, than as, in the words of Lynn Hunt, an "experience" that "spread[s] the practices of autonomy and empathy."[13] Authors such as Daniel Defoe and Samuel Richardson, I have argued, while proponents of legal naturalization in their nonfiction and fictional writings, did not possess the force of law to change who could be recognized as a national subject in their novels, nor was the express purpose of their prose fiction to generate new emotional reactions toward foreigners (indeed, Sterne, as we saw in the previous chapter, comedically thwarts this very proposal). Yet as Edgeworth recognized, professions of sympathy for new subjects involve the positing of new literary representations against older literary protocols about who can be a subject. In practice, Edgeworth's attraction to the novel as "an *amende honorable*," which she submits to Rachel Mordecai as reparative and justice-oriented, is intently mindful of how narrative fictions are often responsible for generating one-dimensional representations of Jewish people and other foreigners.

For Edgeworth, the prejudicial treatment of Jews in English political life can only be redressed by considering how they have been represented in literature. From one angle, the history of literary representation is analogous to, and informative of, political discrimination against Jews: it is fictional writing that inculcates political prejudices in the first place. Indeed, Harrington's early phobia of Jews arises after his childhood nurse dresses some Christian beggars to look "like the traditionary representations and vulgar notions of a malicious, revengeful, ominous looking Shylock" (79). Later, when Harrington begins reading, this dramatized association of Jews with maliciousness is reinforced by the representation of Jews he discovers in traditional and modern fiction (83). Harrington's alignment of the dramas and books of his youth with the psychological phobia he experiences of Jews articulates the linked ideas that characterized the public outcry against the Jewish Naturalization Act. As James Shapiro has shown, Shakespeare's portrayal of Shylock as a vengeful usurer in *The Merchant of Venice* was used as an authoritative portrait to successfully argue for the repeal of the Jewish Naturalization Act in 1753.[14] Edgeworth mirrors the association between literary representation and politics in the novel when she has the fictional ideas that grip Harrington's early life, in turn, find an outlet in his father's obnoxious anti-naturalization politics: "A subject apparently less likely to interest a child of my age than this Act of Parliament about the Naturalization of the Jews could hardly be imagined; but from my peculiar associations it did attract my attention" (83). Here, Harrington's subterranean fear of Jews, an antipathy he declares to be psychologically compulsive, reappears as politically logical. When asked by his father's confederates why the Jews should not be naturalized, Harrington attempts to string an irrational correlation into a political argument: "Because the Jews are naturally an unnatural pack of people," he says, "and you can't naturalize what's naturally unnatural" (87).

This is a "logic" we have seen at work throughout the chapters in this book, especially in the reports from the seventeenth-century court cases about the naturalization and estate of the Scot John Ramsey. Naturalization, several justices argued, cannot permit the political toleration of the natural enemies of the English Crown because nature cannot be naturally altered. *Harrington*, however, exposes this logic as tautological. During a performance of *The Merchant of Venice*, Harrington comes to understand that the distinctions he has long held to be compulsively and inescapably natural are the products of fiction. This realization first occurs in a moment of mediated sympathy when Harrington watches Mr. Montenero's daughter, Berenice, as she painfully observes the stereotypical portrayal of Jews on stage: "My imagination formed such a strong conception of the pain the Jewess was feeling, and my inverted sympathy . . . so overpowered my direct and natural feelings that at every fresh development of the Jew's villainy I shrunk, as though I had myself been a Jew" (136–37). "Inverted sympathy" arises in this moment as another way of describing the work and effect of naturalization. As Harrington observes Berenice's pained expressions as if they were his own, he reads and interprets her as a new text, one with a different set of associations and manifestations. Harrington once spoke of his terror at the sight of a Jew as "involuntary" (75) and "invincible" (91), yet watching Berenice watch *The Merchant of Venice*, he comes to see how fictional representation mediates his desires and antipathies. It is through this recognition of the fictional basis of antipathy that Edgeworth seeks to rewrite the history of the Jews in literature.

If Harrington's mediated experience of Jewish suffering gives him and us a fictionalized understanding of the interconnection between representation, politics, and sympathy, Mr. Montenero's explanation for prejudice against Jews offers a more productive opposition for understanding the biased intersection of literary texts and the symbolism and bureaucracy of politics. After the play's performance, Harrington discusses with Mr. Montenero the relationship of Shakespeare's work to depictions of Jews more widely, blaming the prejudices of Shakespeare's age for influencing his representation of Jews. Mr. Montenero counters with a surprising fact: Shakespeare reversed the source story for the play and transferred what had originally been a Christian's vengeful demand for a "pound of flesh" to a Jewish character. "We Jews find it peculiarly hard," Mr. Montenero laments, "that the truth of the story on which the poet founded his plot should have been completely sacrificed to fiction, so that the characters were not only misrepresented but reversed" (144). In effect, by revealing this fictional reversal to Harrington, Mr. Montenero retroactively reinscribes the naturalness of a representation of Jews as, in fact, "unnatural."

Yet this reversal of the reversal is ultimately undone by Edgeworth's final plot twist, which echoes the return of social order in the conclusion of Frances Burney's *The Wanderer*. It is a twist that Edgeworth's critical correspondent Rachel Mordecai (in a follow-up letter to the author) described as especially shocking and egregious, considering the author's pledge to atone for past representational misdeeds.[15] After Harrington asks for Berenice's hand in marriage, and Harrington's family moves to accept a Jewess as their daughter-in-law, she is revealed by Mr. Montenero to be a Christian after all. As with Juliet in *The Wanderer*, Berenice's reward for acceptance into middle-class English society appears to be the discovery that she was always already a member of the society that rejected her as foreign. But unlike Burney, whose fictional ending was meant to feel insufficient in the context of wider racial and class tensions, Edgeworth believed her novel's conversion narrative would ultimately satisfy readers—indeed, she implied as much in a response to Mordecai's second letter asking for a justification of the novel's romantic ending. "I really should be gratified," Edgeworth told Mordecai, "if I could have any testimony even if it were ever so slight from those of your persuasion that they were pleased with my attempt to do them justice."[16]

While Edgeworth defended what she saw as her reversal of expectations through a conventional ending, Mordecai's follow-up letter proffered an alternative view of the novel's conclusion: by having Mr. Montenero keep Berenice's Christian birth a secret (and bring up his daughter in the faith of two religions), Edgeworth demonstrates his "united liberality": his concern for "justice, benevolence, and morality" and religious tolerance.[17] We have seen this line of thinking before, in the letter Samuel Richardson wrote to readers concerned about Grandison's religious purity after the character briefly considers raising his unborn daughters in another faith. (Edgeworth actually makes reference to this reading of *Grandison* in her novel, when Harrington's friend Lord Mowbray protests that, unlike Grandison, he would "have no religious scruples" in marrying a Jewish woman if he were in love [220]). In Mordecai's reading of the novel's end, Edgeworth turns Berenice into a Jewess not to satisfy Christian or Jewish readers but to cast the heroine as *both* Jewish and Christian, neither naturally one nor the other. She adapts a conventional story ending, that is, to make a comment about religious tolerance and to naturalize, in narrative if not in law, a Jewish heroine as a Christian one.

Edgeworth's undoing of the distinctions between Jewishness and unnaturalness is admittedly clunky. Early reviewers were less accommodating and creative in their interpretations of the novel, accusing Edgeworth of unrelenting didacticism at the expense of belief. More pointedly, Harrington's extreme phobia of Jews has struck more than a few historical and modern readers as overly psychological and neglectful of the political issues surrounding the Jewish Question in England.[18] For Catherine Gallagher, the novel "all too often makes the Jewish Question seem like a private obsession."[19] But as I have argued throughout this book, naturalization makes new subjects possible by revealing the impossibility of refusing them. The overt fictionality of naturalization, its calling attention to the way new subjects are created, challenges sacrosanct rules and traditions by showing how easily they can be mimicked. In the end, Edgeworth makes Berenice a subject, not with the eloquence of persuasion or logical insistence (as she herself would have believed), nor through sympathy from the reader (as Hunt and others would want), but through the cheap trick of a reversal. She retrospectively naturalizes her Jewish heroine not by making her realize, conform to, or covert to Christian principles or demonstrate her "humanity" but by simply and indecorously announcing her to be so. In this way, Edgeworth's ending reflects the work of naturalization itself, which, as we have learned, was considered scandalous by many for appearing to naturalize new subjects in England by the gimmick of a parliamentary act alone. Shelley's *Frankenstein*, to which I now turn, is an even more remarkable example of how the novel can function as a creative means of national and narrative incorporation in the absence of law, especially because its narrative trick is harder to disentangle from history itself.

Changing the Subject: *Frankenstein*'s Frames

Mary Shelley's *Frankenstein* appears at first to be a strikingly unusual example of naturalization. The novel's anonymous Creature has appeared to many readers to be the very essence of an unnatural aberration, a warning not to sport with the natural circumstances of life or travel beyond the confines of one's native home. Compared with the novel's other two foreigners—Elizabeth, Victor Frankenstein's fiancée, and Safie, the Arab Christian refugee whose education the Creature observes from his hovel in the countryside of Switzerland—the Creature lacks nativity: he has neither a native land nor a native language. Though Victor himself is, famously, after the first line of Jean-Jacques Rousseau's *Confessions*, a "citizen of Geneva," his Creature comes to life anonymously in Ingolstadt, Germany, and, after pursuing Victor to Switzerland, learns to speak the French language from a family taking refuge in the countryside of Switzerland, without ever stepping foot in France.

Two changes Shelley made to her novel in 1831, though, underline the possibility, if not crucial importance, of viewing the Creature's position in the novel from the perspective of legal and literary naturalization. In the 1818 version, Shelley describes Victor as simply "by birth a Genevese" (18). In the 1831 edition, Shelley shifts his birthplace to Naples, where he is born while his parents are traveling (precisely the inverse of Robinson Crusoe's position at the beginning of Defoe's novel). Second, in the 1831 edition, Shelley recasts Victor's fiancée, Elizabeth, as an Italian German orphan discovered by Victor's parents while abroad. Thus, in the second edition, Elizabeth and Victor are placed in a similar foreign position to Safie, the Arab Christian refugee adopted by the De Lacey family from Turkey, whose education the Creature observes in secret.

Frankenstein, like many of the novels I have considered, teems with people who travel beyond the confines of their native homes and who subsequently naturalize into new ones. In this respect, it is no accident that Shelley chose Geneva as the country where the Frankenstein household resides. In the sixteenth century, Geneva was one of the most cosmopolitan cities in Europe, serving, under the influence of John Calvin, as a model of the ideal city-republic and as a benevolent host for thousands of French and Italian refugees. The city held a current of unrest, however. The number of Geneva residents who qualified as citizens had become smaller as the population grew in the seventeenth century: by 1700, only about 1,500 of Geneva's 5,000 adult males could become citizens. Catholic inhabitants, who made up the country's majority, were excluded from civil rights and privileges and denied access to all the most lucrative trades and professions. In the nineteenth century it was felt by many that Geneva could no longer claim to offer the international, Calvinist leadership that had led it to once extend religious solidarity to the Huguenot refugees.[20] Geneva, therefore, was a city on which the highest ideals of naturalization had been posed—indeed it is idealized as such in the novel when the Swiss Frankenstein family decides to let the French Justine live with them: "Justine, thus received in our family, learned the duties of a servant; a condition which, in our fortunate country, does not include the idea of ignorance, and a sacrifice of the dignity of a human being."[21] But Geneva also operated as a site of massive exclusion from the rights of citizenship. Shelley herself spoke of the passports required to enter Geneva in several of her journal entries.[22]

Too often, Shelley's Creature has been misunderstood by critics and readers as a symbol of the limits of humanity and language, his monstrosity the embodiment of the failure of kinship and sympathy (and therefore an emblem of a failed political vision) to overcome difference. Yet by juxtaposing the Creature's exclusion from both Geneva and Switzerland to the integration of the novel's other foreigners, notably Safie, we can begin to understand *Frankenstein* as a project in which Shelley seeks to expose the hypocrisy of national exclusions and also how the Creature might be "naturalized" into a nonnational community by means of narrative rather than law. This narrative naturalization does not occur through the powers of human sympathy ("No sympathy may I find," says the Creature at the end of the novel), though it does for Safie (as well as for *Harrington*'s Berenice) (159). Neither does it unfold via legal process, as it does for Victor and Elizabeth, who naturalize in Geneva shortly after their birth. Instead, Shelley makes naturalization operative for the Creature in *Frankenstein* at the level of the novel's narrative.

Just as the Creature is concatenated from various body parts across Europe, Shelley assembled *Frankenstein* from a variety of literary techniques and genres: the confessional structure of the Godwinian novel, the historical novels of Walter Scott, and the physiological and fantastic mechanisms associated with gothic fiction. Shelley's journals reference several literary works read either before or during the composition of *Frankenstein*, many of which have been thought of as possible influences for the framed narrative of the novel. Between 1815 and 1816, Shelley read all three of Richardson's epistolary novels: first *Clarissa*, then *Pamela* and *Sir Charles Grandison*. In 1817 she read a French translation of *Arabian Nights*, famous for its framed form. Shelley's husband, Percy, read aloud to her from the *Female Revolutionary Plutarch*, an adaptation by Stewarton Lewis Goldsmith of the Plutarchan style of biography for the purposes of telling and comparing the lives of certain female revolutionary figures. Shelley also read Charles Brockden Brown's epistolary novel *Wieland, or the Transformation* (itself heavily influenced by her father's *Caleb Williams*) and may have found in it an important source for her frame structure, as well as a thematic concern for the monstrosity of imitated speech.

But what is without precedent, certainly in terms of genre classification, is Shelley's combination of a biographical and epistolary frame narrative.[23] *Frankenstein* is composed of letters written by Captain Robert Walton to his sister Margaret Saville in England. These letters tell three different stories: Walton's firsthand account in English of his experience as the captain of an arctic exploration; Victor's confession to Walton, also in English, of his hideous laboratory creation; and the Creature's tale of his abandonment and autodidactic education, told to his maker in what we must presume to be French, the only language that he ever mentions being able to speak. Victor relays both the tale of his scientific labor and his interview with the Creature to Walton, his amanuensis, after the Englishman has rescued him from an ice floe at the North Pole. Walton, in turn, compiles both stories in one long letter to his sister dated between August 19 and August 26, 17—. All three histories are delivered with the first-person pronoun, but only Walton's account is written rather than spoken, though Victor makes unknown edits to the narration before it is delivered to an unknown addressee and compositor of the text.[24] The three narrators of *Frankenstein* are ostensibly autobiographers, yet in execution, Shelley sets two modes of writing—confessional autobiography and historiographical biography—in opposition to each other. In one, Victor confesses his story to Walton, using his own credibility as a citizen of Geneva to vouch for his authority and the monstrosity of his creation. This self-exculpating autobiographical effort, however, has the unwanted effect of producing a biography of the anonymous Creature, which is then renarrated by Walton, who writes the parallel stories of Victor and the Creature to his sister as a "record" for mass consumption by a posthumous public (176).

For generations, scholars have looked to Rousseau's *Confessions* as the key intertext for explaining Shelley's vexing narrative formation, but it is no accident that Plutarch's *Parallel Lives* is among the books that the Creature first discovers and reads in his woodland hovel.[25] The significance of this shelf mark in the Creature's woodland library is quite the opposite of that of Rousseau's *Confessions*.[26] Plutarch models a vision of the self that "surpassed" singular "understanding and experience," teaching the Creature to transcend the sphere of self-reflection and situate himself among a larger historical community (90). Unlike Rousseau's declaration of sui generis existence at the beginning of his autobiography ("I am not made like any one I have seen"), *Parallel Lives* features twenty-two (surviving) biographies of famous Greek and Roman rulers and statesmen—men belonging to different nationalities—paired together through a device of comparison known as *synkrisis*.[27] As Tim Duff writes, "Equality is one of the most striking features of the Plutarchan *synkrisis*.... The emphasis is not so much on the differences between the two protagonists as on the qualities which the two men had in common and which they manifested within their own particular milieu."[28] With this emphasis on parallelism, synkrisis shares a similar structure to what I am calling naturalization. Like synkrisis, naturalization is a structure of correspondence rather than sameness, a form of finding commonality amid difference—it is a parallel structure that, like Tacitus's narration of Percennius's story, holds subjects in common relation, even if they are not entirely of kind. Using narrative frames, *Frankenstein* explores narrative naturalization as the remedy for the Creature's exclusive, singularizing foreignness.

Most film adaptions of the novel have tended to strip the Creature of his capacity for language, even though in the novel, Shelley repeatedly points to the fact that it is language that overcomes the singular horror of the Creature's appearance, and it is her experiment with language that ultimately allows her innovation in form to succeed. One early example emerges in the dream Victor has shortly after his first encounter with his experiment. Victor fixates on the potential communication initiated by the Creature, first through the eyes, and then through the mouth: "I beheld the wretch—the miserable monster whom I had created. He held up the curtain of the bed; and his eyes, if eyes they may be called, were fixed on me. His jaws opened, and he muttered some inarticulate sounds, while a grin wrinkled his cheeks" (36). Concentrating on the more immediately fearsome structure of the jaw rather than the mouth (the jaw is an inherently violent mechanism, whereas the mouth can be invitational and erogenous), Victor replaces the possibility of the Creature's speech with sheer noise. This fear of language is displaced in the next sentence onto an image of bodily excess: "He might have spoken, but I did not hear; one hand was stretched out, seeming to detain me, but I escaped, and rushed down the stairs" (36). It is not clear from the sentence whether Victor flees the threat of the Creature's body—the arms that "seem" to want to detain him—or the potential auditory threat of the Creature's voice. These sounds, if he stayed to listen, might be heard as language, and if they were heard as language, Victor might be put into a communicative relationship with the Creature, a relationship of exchange that would demand certain responsibilities and, at the bare minimum, recognition of shared human traits. Fleeing the room instead, Victor dismisses the possibility of a linguistic relationship between himself and his creation.

"He might have spoken, but I did not hear." This sentence comes to define the political and formal problem in Shelley's novel. Victor deliberately *unrecognizes*, deliberately *unhears* the Creature's voice as noise rather than comprehensive language. To put the predicament in figurative terms, the Creature's situation in the novel models the rhetorical structure of what I will call a *reverse apostrophe*. An apostrophe is an address directed toward an object that cannot respond to or even hear the human speech addressing it. In the case of Shelley's Creature, we have the example of a nonhuman "being" addressing a human actor (Victor, primarily) who cannot hear what the speaker says as anything other than "inarticulate sounds" issued from a "filthy mass that moved and talked" (103). Through reverse apostrophe, the object speaks, but the subject will only hear what it says as noise. The first task of the Creature, then, is to render his bodily difference invisible so that he can be recognized as a member of a national community. Thus, to overcome the stultifying effects of reverse apostrophe, the Creature must seek a form of narrative naturalization.

Indeed, the first thing that the Creature learns from his earliest contact with other humans is that he needs to disguise, rather than singularize, the uniqueness of his body: "for I easily perceived that, although I eagerly longed to discover myself to the cottagers, I ought not to make the attempt until I had first become master of their language; which knowledge might enable me to make them overlook the deformity of my figure; for with this also the contrast perpetually presented itself to my eyes had made me acquainted" (78). The Creature wants to become the "master" of a language that is not his own by right of birth so that he can persuade others to overlook his physical deformity. He goes on to admit that his "voice was very unlike the soft music of their tones" (79), then likens himself to the ass in Aesop's fable "The Ass and the Lapdog," who understands his physical difference from the small dog, yet thinks this difference can be mitigated through an effort at mimicry: "Surely the gentle ass," says the Creature, "whose intentions were affectionate, although his manners were rude, deserved better treatment than blows and execration" (80). The Creature realizes that his speech might be only a "rude" approximation of the speech he hears, but it is in the staging of his capacity for speech, rather than the mimesis of its sound, that the Creature seeks to warrant the recognition of his place in a shared community. He wants to learn language so he can enact a kind of a parallel structure that would hold him in common with others, if not entirely in kind.

This parallelism is most overtly on display in the Creature's first encounter with the blind old man De Lacey:

> "By your language, stranger, I suppose you are my countryman;—are you French?"
>
> "No; but I was educated by a French family, and understand that language only. I am now going to claim the protection of some friends whom I sincerely love, and of whose favour I have some hope."
>
> "Are they Germans?"
>
> "No, they are French. But let us change the subject. I am an unfortunate and deserted Creature; I look around, and I have no relation or friend upon earth. These amiable people to whom I go have never seen me, and know little of me. I am full of fears; for if I fail there, I am an outcast in the world for ever." (93)

The Creature's claim for protection is not a bold or declaratory utterance. It is an appeal for a joint project ("let us"), a collaborative venture, rather than an individual demand or claim for recognition. Though obvious to the reader, it is not clear to De Lacey that he is one of the "friends" to whom the Creature has directed his claim for protection. Affecting the kindness of a stranger, the Creature appeals to the old man in the language of one of his "countrym[e]n." To request the protection and sympathy owed to a being "with no relation or friend upon earth," the Creature categorically addresses his would-be protectors as already "friends whom [he] sincerely love[s]." (Sterne's Yorick would manage a similar strategy in *A Sentimental Journey*, using a text he does not belong in, that of Shakespeare's *Hamlet*, to present himself to the French count as foreigner who is already a friend. Indeed, the Count mistakes Yorick for a court jester he already knows.)

To be sure, this strategy is something of a rhetorical ploy. It is dependent on the inversion of associations (friend and stranger, friend and enemy) that determine the identity of individuals as much as on the old man's physical blindness: "By your language, stranger, I suppose you are my countryman;—are you French?" The Creature cannot claim to be French by way of birth, but by speaking in the French language, and *only* in the French language ("I was educated by a French family, and understand that language only"), the Creature disorganizes the deductive logic that leads the old man to make smooth equations between language, national identity, and friendship. Thus, it is by speaking in a language not his own that the Creature displays the arbitrariness of the disjunction that denies a speaker of a language membership in its corresponding national community. As the Creature's conversation strategy here emphasizes, national communities (the French, the English, etc.) are predicated on—indeed named after—the ability of their members to speak a certain language. In making this primary connection between community and language evident, the Creature forges a link between the subject of national and social belonging (he speaks in a language he is not supposed to be a "subject" of) and the subject of himself as a "stranger" without a home or community in the world. He reveals that there is no authorial reasoning that could comfortably exclude his being from a community with rules of membership determined by language. That is to say, the Creature stages his membership in a national community by revealing the impossible logic that would try to reject him from it.

The change of subject requested by the Creature is therefore not so much a change of perspective or a turn in the direction of the conversation, or indeed the kind of fantastic reversal we saw at the end of *Harrington*. The Creature does not want to hasten De Lacey away from a discussion of how friends and countrymen might be identified by their language—"Are they Germans?"—to an entirely new topic, his own desertion and homelessness. Rather, the purpose of the "change of subject," as the Creature initiates it, is to forge a connection, or transference, between two terms, *friend* and *stranger*, which are supposed to be antithetical. In figurative terminology, we could say that he displaces the metaphorical logic of autobiography—the idea that the perception of likeness between two terms determines their membership together—to the logic of metonymy, where meaning is transferred and resemblance devised "on the basis of associations that develop out of specific contexts rather than from participation in a structure of meaning."[29] If, within the context of his conversation with the old man, the Creature can demonstrate himself as already a "friend" by way of language, in what sense, his logic pleads, could the old man, or anybody, retroactively reject him as a "stranger"?

The conversation between De Lacey and the Creature provides insight into the ways that the naturalization of language—its inability to represent singularity—actually works to stage a common world shared with others. On the one hand, the Creature's interview with the old man suggests the autobiographical impossibility of his coming to speak directly for himself as a person worthy of reception. And yet on the other hand, it suggests that the use of a shared (albeit "stolen") language will overpower the estranging effect of his physical appearance: "My voice, although harsh, had nothing terrible in it; I thought, therefore, that if, in the absence of his children, I could gain the good-will and *mediation* of the old De Lacey, I might, *by his means* be tolerated by my younger protectors" (92; emphasis mine). Recognizing that he cannot make his own appeal directly, the Creature looks to the old man to "mediate" his case to the wider community ("I might, by his means, be tolerated"), just as he hinges the success of an introduction to the De Lacey family on the reduplication of language lessons that were intended only for Safie:

> "If you unreservedly confide to me the particulars of your tale, I perhaps may be of use in undeceiving them. I am blind, and cannot judge of your countenance, but there is *something in your words* which persuades me that you are sincere." . . . .
>
> "Excellent man! I thank you. . . . You raise me from the dust by this kindness; and I trust that, by your aid, I shall not be driven from society and sympathy of your fellow-Creatures." (94; emphasis mine)

In De Lacey, the Creature seeks a quasi-Adamic "raising from the dust." In the hope of being born again in someone else's language, the Creature will "unreservedly" confide or confess the details of his story to the old man. Yet this story can only be authorized and authenticated to a wider community by the old man himself, who ostensibly lends its words his personal credibility and thereby "undeceives" it for his family, just as Walton does for the English public.

It might be argued that this linguistic laundering cannot ultimately save the Creature from judgment and rejection. As all readers of *Frankenstein* know, the plot ushers in the Creature's doom faster than it pauses to hear his story.

At precisely the moment that the old man seems poised to accept the Creature's account, agreeing to make a plea on his behalf, his children enter the cottage and chase the Creature away, battering him with sticks. This ending might then give us recourse to agree with poststructuralist scholars such as Gayatri Spivak and Barbara Johnson, who claim that, because the Creature is dependent on others' words and categorizations to broadcast his story about being a French-speaking foreigner and motherless being, he cannot satisfyingly register the contradiction of his identity in language. Johnson argues that the novel's iconic frame narrative is symbolic of the inability of female authors to satisfy the contradictions of themselves in language.[30] Spivak meanwhile insists that *Frankenstein* does not help readers imagine the Creature's history as anything other than his master's history. The very resources that mark out the Creature as a colonial subject in the novel—Victor's "unhallowed science," the great books about empire and civilization that the Creature reads in his hovel, and the French language that he eventually learns to speak—are for Spivak the same resources that taxonomically deny him a home in a shared social and national community.[31]

I am suggesting, however, that there is a way in which the Creature's narrative requests for inclusion in the human community can be considered successful. Narrative naturalization is not simply the effect of speaking on behalf of someone else, nor of using one's personal authority to secure rite of passage for a less secure other. Narrative naturalization is also a form that verifies the sincerity of words and the equality of their meaning: "There is *something* in your words which persuades me that you are sincere," says old man De Lacey to the Creature. When words become ambiguous, when they resonate to the old man from a familiar yet unknown authority, when they become "something" rather than precisely one "thing," they can be seen as open and available to anybody for occupation. By way of the "thing," truth and sincerity become extended and attached to the anonymous prefix *some*-, a prefix that changes the particular identity of a thing into a generality, just as the particularity of the "thing" lends to the "some" a frame of reference by which it might be recognized. The word *something* thus transforms what one particular person says into "something" anybody might say. The Creature's conversation with De Lacey, and De Lacey's response to its request, reveals the meanings that can be transferred when people who are not supposed to be in possession of them occupy the very terms that determine the use of language.

This logic of metonymy becomes overtly politicized in the Creature's first interview with Victor. The logic of identity and speech that the Creature uses to speak of his existence in his private exchange with De Lacey is at this point linked to political rights: "Listen to my tale: when you have heard that, abandon or commiserate me, as you shall judge that I deserve. But hear me. The guilty are allowed, by human laws, bloody as they may be, to speak in their own defense before they are condemned. Listen to me, Frankenstein. You accuse me of murder; and yet you would with a satisfied conscience destroy your own creature. Oh praise the eternal justice of man" (69). The metonymy performed by the Creature in this passage can be usefully described by what Hannah Arendt calls, in her analysis of the situation of stateless people after the Second World War, a claim for "a right to have rights."[32] Like the Creature's appeal for friendship from old man De Lacey, the claim here is structured as a paradox: How can a "monster" who cannot be recognized as a human being demand a legal right that is itself premised on his recognition as a human being? The Creature cannot be seen as a man by the persons he encounters, making it impossible to regard him as a holder of legal rights. This is precisely the point made by the constable whom Victor approaches to arrest and arraign the Creature: "Who can follow an animal which can traverse the sea of ice, and inhabit caves and dens, where no man would venture to intrude?" (144). When the Creature speaks to Victor on the basis of a right to human justice he does not have, he forges for himself a link to humanity: "The guilty," he says, "are allowed by the rights of human justice to speak in defense of themselves" (69). The Creature challenges Victor with a logic similar to that which he employed with De Lacey: if you and the constable can call me a murderer, then you have already admitted that I am a human since only human laws can make murderers; therefore, by calling me a murderer, you have already admitted that I am human, and since I am human, you are obligated to assist me, to defend me, to protect me. Like his address to De Lacey in French, a language he cannot own by right, the Creature's use of a legal argument not intended for him stages his membership in linguistic and political communities at precisely the same moment that it reveals his vulnerability to these groups.

Nonetheless, it might be argued that the Creature's rhetorical attempt to convert what one person says into something that anybody might say is ultimately a failure. Susan Lanser, for example, argues that, in terms of gender politics, "*Frankenstein* enacts the rejection of a politics, a refusal to make a part among speaking bodies for the Creature who has no part."[33] Fairly soon after promising to make the Creature a companion, Victor destroys the half-made-up body. At the end of the novel, the Creature is seen receding into the distance, alone. Among his final words are these: "I shall collect my funeral pile, and consume to ashes this miserable frame, that its remains may afford no light to any curious and unhallowed wretch, who would create such another as I have been" (161). The Creature says his remains shall have no light. He will leave no record of himself behind. Though he represents himself as a friend and as a subject of rights, his claims to both ultimately fail because neither Victor nor De Lacey can act as an external guarantor. They cannot "recompense" him, as he says at one point, by representing his speech and his story to the larger community and then, in a separate but connected act, by making both equivalent to those of other human beings (69).

Yet if we foreground the Creature's linguistic encounters—first with the books he discovers in the forest and then with De Lacey and Victor—we can see more clearly the parallel structure of the novel's narrative and the level at which the Creature's entrance into a social community actually succeeds. A question that has long puzzled *Frankenstein* scholars is why Shelley uses Walton as the novel's "initial and ultimate narrator" (to borrow Peter Brooks's phrase).[34] The plainest answer is that Walton's relationship to Victor creates a valuable parallel perspective allowing readers to see the hypocrisy of Victor's refusal to extend sympathy and community to his creation. The novel begins with Walton celebrating the values of friendship with Victor. Crucially, the sympathy that Walton seeks with Victor is not based on a correspondence of their persons. He recognizes that they are not entirely like each other. Yet, as with Plutarch's paired biographies, the connection between them transcends differences of nationality, education, and class. Walton refers to Victor as a "stranger," and he mentions that he feels very much inferior to him: "I am self-educated, and perhaps I hardly rely sufficiently upon my own powers. I wish therefore that my companion should be wiser and more experienced than myself, to confirm and support me" (16–17).

The relationship between Victor and Walton is not predicated on precise or mimetic resemblance; it is not the kind of sympathy that Harrington experiences with Berenice when he comes to see himself as if he were her. Walton admits that he is an autodidact and that Victor's friendship might correct his faults. He desires a sympathetic relationship of codependency and collaboration, which parallels the connections the Creature wishes to make with Victor and old man De Lacey. It is evident, however, that Victor's "strangeness" does not impede Walton's love in the way that the Creature's physical ugliness blocks every path to friendship. Although the Creature insists that he is "fashioned to be susceptible of love and sympathy" (158), and while he easily finds himself in sympathetic agreement with the De Lacey family, whom he watches in secret from his hovel ("When they were unhappy, I felt depressed; when they rejoiced, I sympathized in their joys"), he is refused the sympathy Walton offers to Victor (77).

Walton thus emerges as a figure from whom we can detect the hypocrisy of Victor's ethics. But he also represents something else. In addition to ironizing Victor's relationship to the Creature, Walton's position as master narrator goes further, providing a parallel demonstration of the connection between Victor and the Creature within writing itself. Walton records Victor and the Creature's story in letters for posterity. While his sister may read his "manuscript" for "pleasure," Walton writes so that, in the future, he can read the full account with "interest and sympathy" (18). For Walton, who has positioned himself as the biographer of both monster and man, the challenge in writing this story becomes how to avoid narrating the raw life of a monster so as to make him equal to the paradigm of man, whom the author wishes to set apart. That is to say, the challenge for Walton, the biographer of two autobiographies—that of Victor and that of the Creature—is how to keep his subjects distinct from each other and from himself. It is important to recognize that Walton approaches the Creature's story in the same way that Tacitus had that of the soldier Percennius, without any regard for fairness or political equality. But where the Roman historian merely saw his subject as an illegitimate political actor, Walton (like Victor) thinks of the Creature as less than human. While writing his final letter to his sister, for instance, Walton describes being interrupted by the sudden appearance of the Creature in his cabin. Switching to the present tense, he writes, "I am interrupted. What do these sounds portend? It is midnight; the breeze blows fairly, and the watch on the deck scarcely stir. Again; there is a sound as of a human voice, but hoarser" (157). Shortly after Walton writes about the mysterious humanlike "sounds" (the "sounds" as of a human "voice"), he goes on to record the Creature's parting words to his creator: "Oh, Frankenstein! generous and self-devoted being! What does it avail that I now ask thee to pardon me?" (158). Walton's narration here rushes onward, breathless and seemingly unadulterated, giving readers the impression that his narrative is artless (it reminds me of a moment in Burney's *The Wanderer* when the young Lord Melbury writes an urgent letter while riding on a horse). But the reader cannot avoid detecting a gap between Walton's perception of the Creature's mysterious humanlike sounds and the eloquent presentation he then gives of the monster's final words to his creator. Regretfully, readers cannot hear these inhuman sounds. Unlike the Wedding Guest in Samuel Taylor Coleridge's "Rime of the Ancient Mariner," who "cannot choose but hear" the story he is told, readers of Walton's narrative cannot hear, but can only know of, the inhuman sounds the captain describes. In writing, Walton simply has no way of representing or demonstrating his perception of the Creature's vocal difference from other humans. He cannot articulate sonic difference; he can only weakly suggest it through the analogy of the "as if." And so, by narrating the Creature in the same language and mode as Victor, Walton cancels their differences at the level of narrative: he *blinds* the reader to their difference.

Whether he wants to or not, Walton cannot avoid equalizing the Creature's voice with Victor's, even at the very moment that he wants to express its inhumanity. He frames the story of the Creature and Victor in a way that allows readers to naturalize and accept the "monster" as a sympathetic human being, according to the discourses of nationality and friendship that are natural for the characters in the novel to express. And further, Walton's narration makes it possible to identify what Victor designifies as noise as relatable human language, enabling readers to recognize narrative in what they are told not to hear and see as nonnarrative. Many critics view the ending of *Frankenstein* as the ultimate confirmation of the Creature's failure to become a realized subject; in Spivak's terminology, for example, the Creature is condemned to be "without history" rather than in "national history."[35] But when we begin to see how Shelley frames community as a possibility made available by narrative form, our measure of the success and failure of the Creature's rhetorical claims for recognition takes a radical turn. What we see is a presentation not so much of how self-representation forfeits itself to the framing devices and referents of language but rather of the equality that is staged precisely by way of these failures and indirections. In the process of telling a cautionary story about a scientist's unnatural creation, Shelley demonstrates how an art form might make intelligible the very creation it would deem too horrible for representation in its own story. The result of Walton's writing about the nameless Creature is narrative equality. By allowing the Creature to appear in the guise of his writing, and later in the "manuscript" (18) that his letters will complete, Walton creates a model of Rancière's idea of "subversive eloquence" for a being who is not supposed to speak. By providing a frame that makes the Creature legible in language, he gives the Creature a historical identity, even though the Creature does not have the right to one based on birth or nationality. Walton wants to write the life of a monster, but the result is that he stages the remarkable formal accident of realizing a human subject while trying to create a monster.

I have reread the nineteenth century's most famous narrative of exclusion and denial as one that fosters inclusion within history. In doing so, I have sought to emphasize the power of narrative naturalization: though the law cannot naturalize the Creature, as it can Victor and his cousin, it is ultimately a self-conscious narrative, rather than a spectacle of sympathy, that enters the Creature into history, making it impossible, through its framework of seeing and unseeing, to view him as separate from those who would challenge his belonging. While *Frankenstein* addresses legal and political naturalization less directly than Edgeworth's *Harrington* does, Shelley's novel provides a more sophisticated narrative framework for the comprehension and fulfillment of naturalization outside law. Edgeworth wished to rewrite literary history to change who could count as a subject—she sought to use the novel to directly change history itself. However, she did so through a hackneyed plot twist that, while emphasizing the anxieties about naturalization's secular procedure that had been permeating for over a century, resorts to a miraculous intervention to advance her greater ambition of atoning for her own anti-Semitic past. Shelley, on the other hand, understood that the only political intervention that the novel can plausibly lay claim to is its power of inclusion: its ability to bring the familiar and the foreign into common relation through the unique parallelism afforded by narrative.

By the early nineteenth century, legal routes to naturalization were being closed off. Jewish naturalization had failed, and other naturalization acts were beginning to outline further racial and religious exclusions. In this context, Shelley's complex portrayal of narrative naturalization highlights the widening divide between the discourses of law and of literature. As English law began to codify more exclusionary forms of immigration, the novel evolved in an opposite direction, toward a modernist reverence for total freedom and openness to all subjects. The contiguity between law and the novel, which was founded on the structure of naturalization in the eighteenth century, begins to grow distant.

CODA

The World of Yesterday

This book began by asking readers to consider the analogy Hannah Arendt used to describe how immigration changed with the advent of the First World War. Before the war and after, she said, a separation occurred "not like the end of an old and the beginning of a new period, but like the day before and the day after an explosion."[1] Arendt was largely concerned with the modern fallout from this "explosion"—when, in her unforgettable phrasing, naturalization became an "appendage to the nation-state," a mere stooge to fascist and frightened national agendas.[2] I have instead turned to what came before. Examining the forgotten early modern history of naturalization, this book has shown how the concept emerged as a legal fiction designed to liberalize settlement and subjecthood in England.

Yet even though the chapters in this book reconstruct what Arendt thought was a "happier" history of immigration, one that in many ways functions as a quaint foil for modern border control practices, I do not want to don the rose-colored glasses worn by the likes of early twentieth-century writer Stefan Zweig and economist John Maynard Keynes. The world before 1914 was not a lost time when "the earth belonged to the entire human race . . . [and] [e]veryone could go where he wanted and stay there as long as he liked."[3] To conclude with an emphasis on such an overly forlorn and nostalgic trajectory would be to deny the many ways that early cultural and legal ideas about naturalization do survive, and can be recuperated, for the modern era. It is thus with an eye to our current moment that I conclude here with two brief speculations about what the early idea of naturalization might mean for modern legal and literary studies.

The first is directed firmly at historians of immigration, though not without interest for literary critics insofar as they often passively borrow ideas of the nation-state from historians and political theorists. The regimes of naturalization and denaturalization that Arendt saw as bluntly cleaved in 1914 are not as disconnected as one might think. Early naturalization was part of a powerful tilt toward a contractual understanding of political community. It is no exaggeration to say that it is because of the fiction inherent in naturalization—the idea that a person could be treated *as if* they were a natural-born subject—that the American revolutionaries were able to conceptualize a right to break with what was supposed to be their perpetual allegiance to the British Crown and form a new kind of country and citizenship.[4] It is also because of this fiction that people without any biological or territorial attachment to a nation today potentially have a path to becoming full members within it. Early naturalization made it possible to break old bonds of belonging and invent new ones.

The relaxation of allegiance in the early modern period and its reconfiguration as a manufactured commodity, however, also paved the way for an era of extreme forms of nationality loosening. We have seen how, beginning in the seventeenth century, nationality was reconceived as something that could be given freely to resolve the political and economic tensions inherent in a rapidly modernizing world. Today, this same need persists under the conditions of global capitalism. In 2011 the German American entrepreneur and investor Peter Thiel, like Robinson Crusoe's naturalizing in Brazil to participate in the Portuguese slave economy, bought citizenship in New Zealand to purchase a sheep ranch for the purpose of building a global apocalypse bunker. Long after John Locke and other Enlightenment figures philosophized about a fundamental liberty to leave the country of one's birth and contract with a new one elsewhere, a thriving market has grown up for the buying and selling of passports and citizenship between poor countries in need of revenue and ultra-rich individuals wishing to offshore their assets.[5]

There is a more singular legacy for early naturalization in our contemporary era than its use as a means of nationality acquisition. More disturbingly, early naturalization reconfigured nationality into a kind of personal property that, as Arendt frighteningly laid bare, could be lost. Naturalization adapted to the conditions of national sovereignty that were introduced with the nineteenth-century nation-state paradigm, but the die for the severance of nationality was cast earlier when naturalization followed the larger transformation of political contract. Once nationality was no longer naturally and inherently tied to a person's birth and parentage, it could just as easily be conceived as a privilege that could be taken away. The 2006 Immigration, Asylum and Nationality Act, for example, grants the home secretary the power to revoke nationality on the dangerously ambiguous grounds that it is "conducive to the public good."[6] Since its passage, Britain has embraced citizenship stripping with gusto, denationalizing some 464 people.[7] At stake here is not national security but the propensity of a state to sever connection to its own people.

Just as national identity was becoming a contract that might be acquired or broken, the expansion of empire, industrialization, and war accelerated racialized fiction-making in law and literature. As we saw in the chapters on Frances Burney's *The Wanderer* and the Jewish Naturalization Act, if naturalization was once a liberal and universal idea in theory, it evolved into an effective tool for nations to defend their decisions *not* to integrate certain populations, including Jews, Black Americans, and Indigenous peoples, converting what was supposed to be a universal policy into a racially selective one. Race was both the limit case of liberalized naturalization and the basis on which it was transformed. But given the fact that common law's first immigration legislation was the naturalization and denization of aliens deemed foreign to the English Crown, and given further that a major grievance driving the American Revolution was a lack of freedom to control membership in the colonies by way of naturalization, it is hard to explain the xenophobia and racism of contemporary immigration laws—which have made it increasingly harder for migrants from African nations, the Middle East, Afghanistan, and Central America to settle in the United States and the United Kingdom—through recourse to nineteenth-century law alone. In the interest of a better understanding of the often-disturbing uses to which the fiction of naturalization has been put, we must look further back in time. The development of forced migration under conditions of capitalism and nationalism evolves both in contrast and in relation to the fictional imaginary of naturalization under study here.

Yet a return to the early history of naturalization reveals more than the origins of the restrictive immigration practices and adventure capitalism with which we live today. This book makes its way into the world at a time of ever-larger migrations of refugees. The almost certain threat of climate catastrophe on the horizon, as well as the outbreak of war in Europe as I write, make understanding the long history of naturalization ever more important. One of the reasons I have focused on the positive creative force of naturalization as a legal fiction is that our current circumstances, especially at a time when popular nationalisms are on the rise worldwide, compel us to rethink the fictions so many countries use to deny settlement for millions of people. The case here does not take the form of policy proposals or legal amendments, and might therefore be considered weaker, inconsequential, or merely historical. Yet remembering how nationality was powerfully reconceived in the

Enlightenment period as a flexible bond is no small feat. Many across the world regularly view national citizenship through a patriotic lens, as a God-given natural right that is born with them on their native soil and that excludes those who were not, without realizing that such an understanding of nationality would have been foreign to their nation's founders. By writing this book, I want to remind readers of certain resources in naturalization's past that can be marshaled to fight against new forms of cultural nationalism. The flexibilities afforded by naturalization need not be limited to the interests of elites and powerful governments; naturalization is a tool of inclusion that could be used in the interest of many more people.

The second intervention that this book hopes to make concerns critical reading practices. For a long time, the idea of what is natural has been construed as a problem for aesthetics. Naturalization has long been the name to describe—and deride—a process whereby the aesthetic is used to pass off a social or political agenda as timeless and natural. What would it mean, however, to think of nationality *not* as a cultural construction but as something else? More pointedly, must naturalization be an ideological process at all? Must it refer to actors disguising political ideas of national belonging and presenting them as timelessly natural? Or is it possible for naturalization to avoid challenging the idea of a natural community? What might *that* kind of naturalization—not as an epithet but as creative thought—look like? I ended this book with a dramatic rereading of Mary Shelley's *Frankenstein* as a novel that naturalizes a nameless and homeless being into national literary history against those very agendas of so many who are determined to see him as inhuman. In other chapters, I pursued equally revisionist rereadings of famous "English" novels, showing how these novels expose—rather than reify—various political logics that seek to exclude certain beings from subjecthood. In other words, naturalization, this book shows, is also a process whereby texts bring new subjects into being through overtly creative fictions.

Seeing how new subjects are brought into being in literature sounds conspicuously like recent accounts of affirmative reading. Over the past decade, affirmative reading has emerged in literary debates as an alternative to symptomatic reading and other critical modes of reading texts. Like affirmative reading, this book is interested in naturalization as a thing that texts do to introduce new subjects against older logics and empathizes with the call to critical disarmament. Yet this book has also asked advocates of positive ways of reading whether such affirmative readings are possible in relation to larger and more forceful political and legal discourses. Can affirmative readings of texts, without historical or empirical bedrock, seriously challenge political and legal arguments, whose power substantively relies on normative claims? I suspect not.

The overall goal of this book has been to ask readers, especially those who are literary scholars, to question why the artificial creation of nature is something to be feared and exposed rather than something that is itself creative and generative. By returning to early modernity and showing how naturalization, in law and literature, was regarded as a stubbornly artificial process and one that made new subjects in complete opposition to natural hierarchies of the social order, I propose an alternative to highly idealized and ahistorical calls for more positive ways of reading. I recommend what we might think of as *strong* forms of reading in every sense: empirical, historical, and fully bidisciplinary (as recognizing and embracing the strengths of one field, while working to fully absorb and understand the strengths of another). I have argued that rethinking what we mean by naturalization requires extending the archives, texts, and histories that we read while also overcoming the nationalist reading protocols we have inherited.

The various texts and documents brought together in this book have been corralled for the purpose of drawing law and literature closer together. Thinking with and against each other, law and literature together help us imagine new possibilities for hermeneutics and history. Just as we need to make sure our affirmative readings are more deeply historicized, practitioners in law and literature owe it to one another to read each other more carefully, with respect for disciplinary rigor and knowledge. Literary historians today are everywhere trying to dismantle what are perceived as provincial, Anglocentric, and nationalist disciplinary agendas in the name of "global" or transnational literature. Yet often they seek to introduce new methodological focus points without an empirical, historical, and legal understanding of how nationality works. Law itself fictionalized nationality long ago, well before borders were actively enforced by sovereign nation-states and growing imperial regimes began collapsing distinctions that had earlier grounded national belonging. At the same time, legal theorists often too quickly reach for the ruling to support modern immigration practices, ignoring at their own peril the literary creativity their forebears deployed to devise legal arguments and which—even if these eventually proved to be short-lived or unsuccessful—had lasting cultural influence.

Whatever their causal relation, novelists and judges of early modernity were simultaneously engaged in an enormous challenge to rules of national belonging. Whether in the plots and formal freedoms of prose fiction or in legal and political scenarios concerning naturalization, legal and literary practitioners looked to naturalization to license new bonds—and in some cases they supplemented the failures of legal argument with their own forms of narrative naturalization. Rather than smooth over the questions generated by legal naturalization, literature enlarged the consequences of these expanded national rights. Literature persisted alongside legal thinking, not just in the continuum of historical time, but in the critical imaginations that reflect on legal, political, social, and cultural ideas with significant purchase on everyday lives, from the narratives we use to account for our relationship to one another to the logics we use to exclude certain people from the rewards and privileges of subjecthood. It is thus with an eye to the future, and with a rich historical sense of the critical relationship between the power to invent and the power to understand, that we might think anew the conditions from which subjects are born and made.

Introduction

1. Hannah Arendt, *The Origins of Totalitarianism* (San Diego: Harvest, 1968), 267.
2. "The Postwar 'Stateless,'" *Social Service Review* 20, no. 3 (1946): 403.
3. Arendt, *Origins of Totalitarianism*, 267.
4. See Mervyn C. Jones, *British Nationality Law and Practice* (Oxford: Clarendon, 1947), 39; John Hope Simpson, *The Refugee Problem: Report of a Survey* (London: Oxford University Press, 1939), 265; and W. E. Wilkinson, "Some Changes in the Laws of Naturalisation," *Law Magazine and Review: A Quarterly Review of Jurisprudence* 40, no. 2 (February 1915): 187–95.
5. Daniel Defoe, *Roxana*, ed. Melissa Mowry (Toronto: Broadview, 2009), 45.
6. *Sundry considerations touching naturalization of aliens whereby the alledged advantages thereby are confuted, and the contrary mischiefs thereof are detected and discovered* (London, 1695), 3.
7. Caroline Robbins, "A Note on General Naturalization under the Later Stuarts and a Speech in the House of Commons on the Subject in 1664," *Journal of Modern History* 34, no. 2 (1962): 168.
8. William Arthur Shaw, William Minet, and Susan Minet, *A Supplement to Dr. W. A. Shaw's Letters of Denization and Acts of Naturalization*, Publications of the Huguenot Society of London, vol. 35 (Frome, England: printed for the society by Butler and Tanner, 1932), 11.
9. Walter Allen Knittle and Ryan Fox Dixon, *Early Eighteenth Century Palatine Emigration: A British Government Redemptioner Project to Manufacture Naval Stores* (Philadelphia: Dorrance, 1937), chap. 4.
10. *Sundry considerations*, 3.
11. Granville Sharp, *Extract from a representation of the injustice and dangerous tendency of tolerating slavery, or admitting the least claim of private property in the persons of men in England* (London: [n.p.], 1771), 5.
12. See Peter Fryer, *Staying Power: The History of Black People in Britain* (London: Pluto, 1984).
13. Naturalization Bill, H.R. 40, March 4, 1790.
14. J. Willard and Massachusetts Historical Society, *Naturalization in the American Colonies: With More Particular Reference to Massachusetts: A Paper Read before the Massachusetts Historical Society, at the July Meeting* (Boston: printed by J. Wilson and Son, 1859), 5; Robbins, "Note on General Naturalization," 170.
15. John Locke, "For a General Naturalization," in *Political Essays*, ed. Mark Goldie (Cambridge: Cambridge University Press, 2004), 325.
16. Daniel Defoe, *Lex Talionis* (1698); Daniel Defoe, *The History of the Kentish Petition* (London, 1701); Daniel Defoe, *More Reformation: A Satyr upon himself. By the author of The True born English-man* (London, 1703); Daniel Defoe, *The shortest-Way with the dissenters* (London, 1702); Daniel Defoe, *Giving Alms no Charity* (1704); Daniel Defoe, *Defoe's Review*, 9 vols., ed. John McVeagh (London, 2003–11), vol. 6. (no. 34, June 21, 1709). Although *A Brief History of the Poor Palatines Lately Arrived in England* (1709) is often attributed to Defoe, it has been deattributed by P. N. Furbank and W. R. Owens in *Defoe De-attributions* (London: Black, 1994), 35. For an overview of Defoe's writing about naturalization, see generally Marc Mierowsky's unpublished manuscript "Defoe and Naturalization" and Daniel Statt, "Daniel Defoe and Immigration," *Eighteenth-Century Studies* 24 (1991): 293–313.
17. Thomas Babington Macaulay, *The History of England from the Accession of James the Second: Popular Edition in Two Volumes* (London: Longmans, 1889), 2:477.

18. Jonathan Swift, *The History of the Four Last Years of the Queen: By the Late Jonathan Swift, D. D. D. S. P. D. Published from the Last Manuscript Copy, Corrected and Enlarged by the Author's Own Hand* (London: printed for A. Millar, 1758), 222–23. Swift was one of the most excoriating critics of naturalization, writing in the *Examiner* in 1711 that "Some Persons, whom the Voice of the Nation authorizeth me to call her Enemies, taking Advantage of the general Naturalization Act, had invited over a great Number of Foreigners of all Religions, under the Name of Palatines; who understood no Trade or Handicraft; yet rather chose to beg than labour; who besides infesting our Streets, bred contagious Diseases, by which we lost in Natives, thrice the Number of what we gained in Foreigners." Jonathan Swift, *The Prose Works of Jonathan Swift, D.D.*, ed. Temple Scott (London: George Bell and Sons, 1902), 293.

19. Samuel Johnson, *A Confutation of a Late Pamphlet Intituled, A Letter Ballancing the Necessity of Keeping a Land-force in Time of Peace, with the Dangers That May Follow on It. The Second Edition Corrected* (London: printed for A. Baldwin, 1698), 27, 23.

20. Johnson, 22.

21. Johnson, 31.

22. There were, however, ways to remove people from the kingdom. Cities and towns often used banishment, deportation, and transportation to remove vagrants and beggars from local communities. Matthew Gibney suggests this punishment "presaged contemporary migration controls" but only at the local level and not exclusively for noncitizens (as with modern deportation power). Importantly, with the exception of "perpetual banishment," which resulted in a form of "civic death" for the offender, these forms of punishment did not result in a transfer of allegiance or loss of membership. Gibney, "Banishment and the Pre-history of Legitimate Expulsion Power," *Citizenship Studies* 24 (2020): 287.

23. Johnson, *Confutation*, 28.

24. Two recent books that provide excellent general examinations of these topics are Samantha Seeley, *Race, Removal and the Right to Remain: Migration and the Making of the United States* (Chapel Hill: University of North Carolina Press, 2021); and Charlotte Sussman, *Peopling the World: Representing Human Mobility from Milton to Malthus* (Philadelphia: University of Pennsylvania Press, 2020).

25. Will. 3, c. 3, s. 3.

26. Ian Watt's *Rise of the Novel: Studies in Defoe, Richardson and Fielding* (Berkeley: University of California Press, 2000) has been the most influential in promoting the novel as a genre that produces a psychological portrait of the subject as a private individual. As Sandra Macpherson notes, this thesis, though it originated in the 1950s, still prevails in much criticism. Macpherson, *Harm's Way: Tragic Responsibility and the Novel Form* (Baltimore: Johns Hopkins University Press, 2010), 2. See also Dror Wahrman, *The Making of the Modern Self: Identity and Culture in Eighteenth-Century England* (New Haven, CT: Yale University Press, 2004), 181.

27. Samuel Johnson, *A Dictionary of the English Language*, 4th ed. (London: W. Strahan, 1773).

28. Quoted in James H. Kettner, *The Development of American Citizenship, 1608–1870* (Chapel Hill: University of North Carolina Press, 1978), 41.

29. Daniel Statt, *Foreigners and Englishmen: The Controversy over Immigration and Population, 1660–1760* (Newark: University of Delaware Press, 1995), 32.

30. Lon Fuller, *Legal Fictions* (Stanford, CA: Stanford University Press, 1967), 7.

31. Simon Stern, "Legal and Literary Fictions," in *New Directions in Law and Literature*, ed. Elizabeth Anker and Bernadette Meyler (New York: Oxford University Press, 2017), 323.

32. Roberto Esposito, *The Machine of Political Theology and the Place of Thought* (New York: Fordham University Press, 2015), 114.

33. Lorraine Daston and Fernando Vidal, *The Moral Authority of Nature* (Chicago: University of Chicago Press, 2004), 2.

34. Erich Auerbach, *Mimesis: The Representation of Reality in Western Literature* (Princeton, NJ: Princeton University Press, 2013), 22.

35. The democratization of the novel has generally been theorized in the context of nineteenth-century fiction, most admirably by Isobel Armstrong in *Novel Politics: Democratic Imaginations in Nineteenth-Century Fiction* (Oxford: Oxford University Press, 2017). See also Jacques Rancière, *The Lost Thread: The Democracy of Modern Fiction*, trans. Steve Corcoran (New York: Bloomsbury Academic, 2016).

36. In *Bardic Nationalism*, Katie Trumpener remaps the origins of the historical novel by showing that, during the late eighteenth century, antiquaries in Ireland, Scotland, and Wales made nationalist arguments for cultural preservation that both shored up and resisted imperialism and influenced the history of the novel, especially the writing of Walter Scott. Trumpener, *Bardic Nationalism: The Romantic Novel and the British Empire* (Princeton, NJ: Princeton University Press, 1997).

37. Tim Watson, "The Colonial Novel," in *The Cambridge Companion to the Postcolonial Novel*, ed. Ato Quayson (Cambridge: Cambridge University Press, 2016), 17; Carolyn Vellenga Berman, *Creole Crossings: Domestic Fiction and the Reform of Colonial Slavery* (Ithaca, NY: Cornell University Press, 2006), 5–6.

38. Oliver Goldsmith, *The Traveller, or A Prospect of Society* in *The Poems of Thomas Gray, William Collins, Oliver Goldsmith*, ed. Roger Lonsdale (London: Longmans, Green, 1969), 651; Charles Churchill, *The Farewell* (London, 1764), 5.

39. For an extended reading of critical reactions to Defoe's *The True-born Englishman* in the context of Defoe's support for general naturalization, see Mierowsky, "Defoe and Naturalization." As Mierowsky observes, later in life Defoe turned to "the opportunities afforded by prose fiction" to examine the moral "dimension" of naturalization, a notion he could only have "gestured more fully to" in prose fiction than in *The True-born Englishmen* and in his political writings. Mierowsky, 23.

40. Peter Sahlins's *Unnaturally French: Foreign Citizens in the Old Regime and After* (Ithaca, NY: Cornell University Press, 2007) is a standout exception, but it covers the field of French naturalization in the ancien régime, barely mentioning the practice in English common-law tradition. James Kettner's *Development of American Citizenship*, which has long been a staple for understanding early immigration law in both America and Britain, schematizes the history of naturalization in early America.

41. C. B. Macpherson, *The Political Theory of Possessive Individualism: Hobbes to Locke* (Oxford: Clarendon, 1962).

42. Watt, *Rise of the Novel*, 61.

43. Franco Moretti, *Atlas of the European Novel, 1800–1900* (London: Verso, 1998), 17 (emphasis in the original).

44. Moretti, 51.

45. Robbins, most prominently, in "Note on General Naturalization"; James Kettner, *The Origins of American Citizenship*; Statt, *Foreigners and Englishmen*; Clive Parry, *British Nationality Law and the History of Naturalisation* (Milano: Giuffrè, 1954).

46. Linda Colley, *Britons: Forging the Nation, 1707–1837* (New Haven, CT: Yale University Press, 1992).

47. E. P. Thompson, "The Making of a Ruling Class: *Britons: Forging the Nation, 1707–1837*, by Linda Colley," *Dissent*, Summer 1993, 380.

48. Benedict Anderson, *A Life beyond Boundaries: A Memoir* (New York: Verso, 2016), 19.

49. Anderson, 19. Literary and cultural theorists have remained especially beholden to Anderson's thesis, even if to critique it, for the link it formalizes between the rise of print capitalism and a new national consciousness. See generally Pheng Cheah and Jonathan D. Culler, *Grounds of Comparison: Around the Work of Benedict Anderson* (New York: Routledge,

2003); and Nancy Armstrong and Leonard Tennenhouse, *Novels in the Time of Democratic Writing: The American Example* (Philadelphia: University of Pennsylvania Press, 2017), 3–4, 77. Rebecca Walkowitz has engaged Anderson's understanding of translation, arguing that "philosophers of the nation have to ask how the translation of literary texts into more languages and faster than ever before establishes networks of affiliation that are less exclusive and less bounded than the nation's 'community of fate.'" Walkowitz, *Born Translated: The Contemporary Novel in an Age of World Literature* (New York: Columbia University Press, 2015), 25.

50. See Margaret Cohen and Carolyn Dever, *The Literary Channel: The Inter-national Invention of the Novel* (Princeton, NJ: Princeton University Press, 2002); Mary Helen McMurran, *The Spread of Novels: Translation and Prose Fiction in the Eighteenth Century* (Princeton, NJ: Princeton University Press, 2010); Margaret Anne Doody, *The True Story of the Novel* (New Brunswick, NJ: Rutgers University Press, 1996); and Nicholas Paige, *Before Fiction: The Ancien Régime of the Novel* (Philadelphia: University of Pennsylvania Press, 2011).

51. Guido Mazzoni, *Theory of the Novel*, trans. Zakiya Hanafi (Cambridge, MA: Harvard University Press, 2017), 66.

52. Étienne Balibar and Immanuel Wallerstein, *Race, Nation, Class: Ambiguous Identities* (New York: Verso, 1991), 86.

53. For a review of the modern and traditional understandings of the nation, see Azar Gat, *Nations: The Long History and Deep Roots of Political Ethnicity and Nationalism* (Cambridge: Cambridge University Press, 2013), 1–18.

54. Moretti, *Atlas of the European Novel*, 17.

55. Moretti, 17. In Moretti's construction, the eighteenth century was the period through which the novel rose to national importance in the nineteenth century, beating out conflicting cosmopolitan narratives that were largely domestic and private in their scope. "It is only at the very end of the century," he argues, "that the contraction of narrative space" into the nation-state "becomes finally visible" (55). Moretti's claim adapts Anderson's argument about how the emergent novel, alongside the growth of print media and other technological innovations such as the newspaper, helped individuals understand themselves within the confines of a bordered national community. Yet Anderson's position largely rested on the nineteenth-century novel, especially José Rizal's *Noli Me Tangere* (1886). It is not entirely clear, then, how Moretti conceptualizes the novel before the nineteenth century. He speaks of Jane Austen as the first novelist to have the "intelligence" to devise a symbolic form capable of making sense of the nation-state (17). He also talks of a "clash" in the eighteenth century between the novel and "other geographical matrixes," such as the Robinsonade; local love stories, such as *Pamela*; and national or cosmopolitan texts, such as *Moll Flanders* and *Wilhelm Meister* (53). It seems that, before the nation-state, Moretti locates two impulses reflected in the novel: the domestic, isolated, individual scope—what we could call the *Pamela* scope; and the cosmopolitan scope, represented by novels and oriental tales that consider other worlds beyond England. The two are at odds in the eighteenth century, but according to Moretti, they are collected and reconciled by the nineteenth-century novel.

56. Nancy Armstrong, *How Novels Think: The Limits of Individualism from 1719–1900* (New York: Columbia University Press, 2005), 54.

57. Armstrong, 53–54.

58. As new guises of nationhood took hold between the eighteenth and nineteenth centuries, Britain and England were used sometimes interchangeably, hence Armstrong's conflation of "being British" and "remaining English." But the seventeenth and early eighteenth centuries pinpoint a dynamic that has returned with current debates about devolution and Scottish independence. To be British is (and was) to belong within a composite polity. To be English is

(and was) to make a claim on an altogether distinct ancestral, ethnic, and geographic identity. John Havard, email message to author, January 21, 2022.

59. Ning Ma, *The Age of Silver: The Rise of the Novel East and West* (New York: Oxford University Press, 2017).

60. Srinivas Aravamudan, *Enlightenment Orientalism: Resisting the Rise of the Novel* (Chicago: University of Chicago Press, 2012), 57. See also Margaret Cohen's *The Novel and the Sea* (Princeton, NJ: Princeton University Press, 2010), which proposes to rethink the novel not in terms of nationalities and nation-states but in terms of seas that unite territories.

61. Andreas Wimmer and Nina Glick Schiller, "Methodological Nationalism and Beyond: Nation-State Building, Migration and the Social Sciences," *Global Networks* 2, no. 4 (2002): 301–34.

62. David Armitage, *Foundations of Modern International Thought* (Cambridge: Cambridge University Press, 2013) 42.

63. Luca Scholz, *Borders and Freedom of Movement in the Holy Roman Empire* (Oxford: Oxford University Press, 2020), 5. As Daniel Statt also writes, "Before the nineteenth century, no general, or at least permanent, restrictions on the entry of immigrants to England existed, and almost no records were kept of comings and goings." Statt, *Foreigners and Englishmen*, 27.

64. Jones, *British Nationality Law*, sec. 1.

65. See Hannah Weiss Muller, *Subjects and Sovereign: Bonds of Belonging in the Eighteenth-Century British Empire* (New York: Oxford University Press, 2017). I agree with Muller's suggestion that *subjecthood* is a better word for discussing bonds of belonging in the eighteenth century, especially with regard to empire (6). As the naturalization debates make clear, the interpretation of who could be a subject of the king was the occupying question of England's earliest nationality law.

66. *Oxford English Dictionary Online*, s.v. "para-, prefix," December 2021, https://www.oed.com/view/Entry/137251?rskey=O2NeYW&result=10.

67. Doody, *True Story*, 294.

68. Scholz, *Borders and Freedom*, 5. See also John Torpey, *The Invention of the Passport: Surveillance, Citizenship, and the State* (Cambridge: Cambridge University Press, 2000), 3.

69. Aamir Mufti, *Forget English! Orientalisms and World Literatures* (Cambridge, MA: Harvard University Press, 2016); Ragini Tharoor Srinivasan, "The Nation We Knew: After Homi Bhabha's 'DisseMiNation,'" Post45 Contemporaries, May 19, 2020, https://post45.org/2020/05/the-nation-we-knew-after-homi-bhabhas-dissemination; Matthew Hart, *Extraterritorial: A Political Geography of Contemporary Fiction* (New York: Columbia University Press, 2020); Pheng Cheah, *Inhuman Conditions: On Cosmopolitanism and Human Rights* (Cambridge, MA: Harvard University Press, 2006).

70. Sussman, *Peopling the World*, 8.

71. An early version of the notion of contiguity was presented at the Harvard Radcliffe Institute in December 2018 and at the Western Society for Eighteenth-Century Studies Conference in February 2019 in Tempe, Arizona. In Tempe, Joshua Swidzinski encouraged me to adopt Hume's notion of contiguity to clarify the relation between law and literature with regard to naturalization. I am grateful for his suggestion and for the "Exodus and Exile: Migrants, Refugees and Asylum Seekers 1750–1850" conference at the Clark Memorial Library on February 22, 2019, where I was able to present an early version of this notion.

72. David Hume, *A Treatise of Human Nature* (Oxford: Clarendon, 1888), 12.

73. David Hume, *An Enquiry concerning Human Understanding* (Indianapolis: Hackett, 1993), 14.

74. For a thought-out consideration of this problem, see Elizabeth Anker and Bernadette Meyler, introduction to Anker and Meyler, *New Directions*, 1–25.

75. Guyora Binder and Robert Weisberg, *Literary Criticisms of Law* (Princeton, NJ: Princeton University Press, 2000), 3.

76. Simon Sterne, email correspondence, January 30, 2022.

77. Lisa Lowe, *The Intimacies of Four Continents* (Durham, NC: Duke University Press, 2015), 76.

78. Lowe, 76.

Chapter 1 · Naturalization in History

1. Several scholars have sought to dispel the notion that it is only after the nineteenth century that immigration became allied with matters of racial policy and national security. There have been arguments for a range of continuities between law and history before the nineteenth century and the present immigration order. See Gerald L. Neuman, "The Lost Century of American Immigration Law (1776–1875)," *Columbia Law Review* 93, no. 8 (1993): 1833–901; Anna O. Law, "Lunatics, Idiots, Paupers, and Negro Seamen—Immigration Federalism and the Early American State," *Studies in American Political Development* 28, no. 2 (October 2014): 107–28; Kunal Madhukar Parker, *Making Foreigners: Immigration and Citizenship Law in America, 1600–2000* (New York: Cambridge University Press, 2015); and Aziz Rana, *The Two Faces of American Freedom* (Cambridge, MA: Belknap Press of Harvard University Press, 2010).

2. See Robert Hope Simpson, *The Refugee Problem: Report of a Survey* (London: Oxford University Press, 1939), 265; Ann Dummett and Andrew Nicol, *Subjects, Citizens, Aliens and Others: Nationality and Immigration Law* (London: Weidenfeld and Nicolson, 1990), 40; and W. E. Wilkinson, "Some Changes in the Laws of Naturalisation," *Law Magazine and Review: A Quarterly Review of Jurisprudence* 40, no. 2 (February 1915): 187–95. On deportation, see Adam B. Cox and Cristina M. Rodríguez, *The President and Immigration Law* (New York: Oxford University Press, 2020), 8.

3. Cox and Rodríguez, *President and Immigration Law*, 8.

4. Hannah Arendt, *The Origins of Totalitarianism* (San Diego: Harvest, 1968), 284.

5. Colin Kidd rightly questions whether any model of interiority is idiomatic, let alone helpful, in the early modern period: matters of allegiance and religion were primary forms of recognition, he argues, and therefore "identity" is anachronistic. See Kidd, *British Identities before Nationalism: Ethnicity and Nationhood in the Atlantic World, 1600–1800* (Cambridge: Cambridge University Press, 2003).

6. Alexander James Edmund Cockburn, *Nationality, or, The Law Relating to Subjects and Aliens: Considered with a View to Future Legislation* (London: W. Ridgway, 1869).

7. William Blackstone, *Commentaries*, vol. 1, chap. 10. See also Samuel Kliger, "The 'Goths' in England: An Introduction to the Gothic Vogue in Eighteenth-Century Aesthetic Discussion," *Modern Philology* 43, no. 2 (1945): 107–17.

8. As Polly Price clarifies, in the late sixteenth and early seventeenth centuries, the doctrine of precedent did not yet exist: "Coke's use of the term 'precedent' in *Calvin's Case* was purely to stress continuity with the past—a desire to show consistency with historical legal practices, but with no reciprocal view that historical examples (whether cases, statutes, or custom) were controlling, nor that the reasoning of any case was binding." Polly J. Price, "Natural Law and Birthright Citizenship in *Calvin's Case* (1608)," *Yale Journal of Law and the Humanities* 9, no. 1 (Winter 1997): 90. Indeed, the first guide to drafting dates was written twenty years before the Royal Commission on nationality law. See George Coode, *On Legislative Expression: or, The Language of the Written Law* (Philadelphia: T. and J. W. Johnson, 1848). I thank Simon Stern for calling my attention to this resource.

9. See Dummett and Nicol, *Subjects, Citizens, Aliens*, 26. See Matthew J. Gibney, "Banishment and the Pre-history of Legitimate Expulsion Power," *Citizenship Studies* 24, no. 3 (2020):

287. Key, however, is the fact that banishment was a punishment most often used to dispel poor subjects of the realm, not foreigners qua foreigners.

10. Clive Parry, *British Nationality Law and the History of Naturalisation* (Milano: Giuffrè, 1954), 10.

11. Dummett and Nicol, *Subjects, Citizens, Aliens*, 27.

12. William Ferguson, *Scotland's Relations with England: A Survey to 1707* (Edinburgh: Donald, 1977), 104.

13. Price, "Natural Law," 97. See also Daniel J. Hulsebosch, "The Ancient Constitution and the Expanding Empire: Sir Edward Coke's British Jurisprudence," *Law and History Review* 21, no. 3 (Autumn 2003): 447.

14. Dummett and Nicol, *Subjects, Citizens, Aliens*, 60.

15. Marilyn C. Baseler, *"Asylum for Mankind": America, 1607–1800* (Ithaca, NY: Cornell University Press, 1998), 45.

16. It is easy to miss the radical implications of *Calvin's Case* as set forth by Coke. The case implicitly encouraged subjects from the American colonies and Scotland to immigrate to England to assume their right to hold property therein. See Daniel J. Hulsebosch, "English Liberties outside England: Floors, Doors, Windows, and Ceilings in the Legal Architecture of Empire," in *The Oxford Handbook of English Law and Literature, 1500–1700*, ed. Lorna Hutson (Oxford: Oxford University Press, 2017), 747–71.

17. Hulsebosch, "Ancient Constitution," 465.

18. Hulsebosch, "English Liberties outside England," 750. See also Daragh Grant, "Sir Edward Coke's Infidel: Imperial Anxiety and the Colonial Origins of a 'Strange Extrajudicial Opinion,'" forthcoming in the *Journal of Modern History*. "Even if," Grant suggests, "denization offered a route by which some aliens might become English subjects, the prospect of innumerable infidels joining the ranks of the king's subjects, a prospect that was explicitly raised in the course of *Calvin's Case*, filled Coke with a familiar metropolitan anxiety."

19. David Armitage, *Foundations of Modern International Thought* (Cambridge: Cambridge University Press, 2013), 23.

20. King James assumed the throne with a vision of a more complete union between the kingdoms, one that would merge them into single, enlarged, and unified state. This was a vision that Lord Colville fervently shared and that he was helping to realize when he launched the case seeking to affirm the English landholding rights of his Scottish grandson. The union they sought would be another hundred years off, but the case that was brought forward as part of an effort toward its realization is central to an early understanding of British nationality law.

21. See Price, "Natural Law"; Grant, "Sir Edward Coke's Infidel"; Barbara A. Black, "The Constitution of Empire: The Case for the Colonists," *University of Pennsylvania Law Review* 124 (1976): 1157–211; Hulsebosch, "Ancient Constitution"; Mary Sarah Bilder, *The Transatlantic Constitution: Colonial Legal Culture and the Empire* (Cambridge, MA: Harvard University Press, 2004), 35–40; Paul D. Halliday, *Habeas Corpus: From England to Empire* (Cambridge, MA: Harvard University Press, 2010), 201–8; Christopher L. Tomlins, *Freedom Bound: Law, Labor, and Civic Identity in Colonizing English America, 1580–1865* (New York: Cambridge University Press, 2010), 82–92; Craig Yirush, *Settlers, Liberty, and Empire: The Roots of Early American Political Theory, 1675–1775* (New York: Cambridge University Press, 2011), 34–40; Robert A. Williams, *The American Indian in Western Legal Thought: The Discourses of Conquest* (New York: Oxford University Press, 1990), 199–218; and Gavin Loughton, "Calvin's Case and the Origins of the Rule Governing 'Conquest' in English Law," *Australian Journal of Legal History* 8, no. 2 (2004): 143–80.

22. Herbert Broom, *Constitutional Law Viewed in Relation to Common Law*, 2nd ed. (London: W. Maxwell and Son, 1885), 31.

23. According to Daniel Statt, "On a popular level, the doctrine laid down by *Calvin's Case* seems to have been overpowered, as such legal rules tend to be, by the feeling that the Scots and Irish were simply not Englishmen. Even after the Union with Scotland in 1707 the legal equality of the Scots could not be taken for granted." Statt, *Foreigners and Englishmen: The Controversy over Immigration and Population, 1660-1760* (Newark: University of Delaware Press, 1995), 33.

24. I follow Krishan Kumar's argument that it was not until the nineteenth century that "clear concern with questions of English national identity" was exhibited. Kumar, *The Making of English Identity* (Cambridge: Cambridge University Press, 2003), xi. Also see Kidd, *British Identities before Nationalism*, 5, 10.

25. Price, "Natural Law," 88.

26. Andreas Fahrmeir, *Citizens and Aliens: Foreigners and the Law in Britain and the German States, 1789-1870* (New York: Berghahn Books, 2000), 17. Also see Baseler, "Asylum for Mankind," 52.

27. See Dummett and Nicol, *Subjects, Citizens, Aliens*, 23. Naturalization bills were especially prominent in the medieval period following migrations related to the plague and wars with France and Scotland. During the reign of Edward III, many English subjects, including the king's family, moved abroad for shelter. In 1343, after several of the king's children were born in Belgium, Parliament issued a declaration to make it patently clear that the king's children, even if they were not born on English soil, were still subjects of England with all the basic rights to inherit under common law. See Statute 32d, Henry VIII, c. 16, sec. 9.

28. 25 Edward III, c. 1 (1350).

29. Parry notes that the earliest denization in England on record is for Elyas Daubeny. The parliamentary roll records that in 1295 the king granted Daubeny the right to be heard in royal courts because of his record of service to the Crown. The Calendar of Patent Rolls lists further instances of denization in the fourteenth century. The distinction between denization and naturalization is not clear until as late as Elizabeth I. Parry, *British Nationality Law*, 18.

30. Price, "Natural Law," 116.

31. Arthur J. Slavin, "*Craw v. Ramsey*: New Light on an Old Debate," in *England's Rise to Greatness, 1660-1763*, ed. Stephen B. Baxter (Berkeley: University of California Press, 1983), 32.

32. Quoted in Baseler, "Asylum for Mankind," 45.

33. Slavin, "*Craw v. Ramsey*," 32-33.

34. Coke, *Institutes of the Laws of England*, vol. 1, sec. 198.

35. Coke, vol. 1, sec. 198.

36. Coke, 2 Roll. R. 95.

37. There is some discrepancy over whether the earl's name is Ramsay or Ramsey in the historical record. I follow legal historians James Kettner and Arthur Slavin in using Ramsey.

38. Collingwood v. Pace, Bridgman, 417, 124 English Reports 669 (before 1674).

39. Collingwood v. Pace, Bridgman, 422, 124 English Reports 669 (before 1674).

40. Peter Sahlins, *Unnaturally French: Foreign Citizens in the Old Regime and After* (Ithaca, NY: Cornell University Press, 2004), 67.

41. Crow v. Ramsey [sic], T. Jones, 10, 84 English Reports 1122 (before 1674).

42. Collingwood v. Pace, 1 Keble, 265, 83 English Reports 937 (before 1674).

43. Foster v. Ramsey, 2 Sid, 23, 82 English Reports 1235 (before 1674).

44. Charles Molloy, *De Jure Maritimo et Navali* (London, 1682), 373.

45. Quoted in James H. Kettner, *The Development of American Citizenship, 1608-1870* (Chapel Hill: University of North Carolina Press, 1978), 37.

46. Collingwood v. Pace, 1 Ventris, 413, 86 English Reports 262 (before 1674).

47. Francis Bacon, *Three speeches of the right honorable, sir francis bacon knight, then his majesties sollicitor generall, after lord verulam, viscount saint alban. concerning the post-nati*

naturalization of the scotch in england union of the lawes of the kingdomes of england and scotland (London: printed by Richard Badger, 1641), 25.

48. Clifford Ando, "The Future's Past: Fiction, Biography, and Status in Roman Law," *Acta Classica* 63 (2020): 45.

49. Ando, 48.

50. Ando, 51.

51. Quoted in Kettner, *Development of American Citizenship*, 41.

52. Jeremy Bentham, *The Works of Jeremy Bentham*, ed. J. Bowring (London: Simpkin, Marshall, 1843), 242–43.

53. Giorgio Agamben, *The Time That Remains: A Commentary on the Letter to the Romans*, trans. Patricia Dailey (Stanford, CA: Stanford University Press, 2005), 28.

54. John Baker, *The Collected Papers on English Legal History* (Cambridge: Cambridge University Press, 2013), 82.

55. Craw v. Ramsey, Vaughan, 274, 124 English Reports 1072 (before 1672).

56. Kettner, *Development of American Citizenship*, 37–38.

57. Armitage, *Foundations of Modern International Thought*, 39.

58. Caroline Robbins, "A Note on General Naturalization under the Later Stuarts and a Speech in the House of Commons on the Subject in 1664," *Journal of Modern History* 34, no. 2 (1962): 170.

59. Robbins, 170.

60. *Sundry considerations touching naturalization of aliens whereby the alledged advantages thereby are confuted, and the contrary mischiefs thereof are detected and discovered* (London, 1695), 3.

61. *Sundry considerations*, 5.

62. Cited in Robbins, "Note on General Naturalization," 171.

63. John Locke, *Political Essays*, ed. Mark Goldie (Cambridge: Cambridge University Press, 2004), 325.

64. However, John Vile does include it as a key historical document for national law in early America. See Vile, *American Immigration and Citizenship: A Documentary History* (Lanham, MD: Rowman and Littlefield, 2016), 8. See also Laurence D. Houlgate, "John Locke on Naturalization and Natural Law: Community and Property in the State of Nature," in *Citizenship and Immigration: Borders, Migration and Political Membership in a Global Age*, ed. Ann E. Cudd and Win-chiat Lee (Cham, Switzerland: Springer Nature, 2016), 123–36; Brian Smith, "Hands, Not Lands: John Locke, Immigration, and the 'Great Art of Government,'" *History of Political Thought* 39, no. 3 (2018): 465–90; and J. K. Numao, "Locke on Consent, Membership, and Emigration: A Reconsideration," *European Journal of Political Theory*, online ahead of print, May 29, 2019, https://doi.org/10.1177/1474885119852709.

65. See Dummett and Nicol, *Subjects, Citizens, Aliens*, chap. 3.

66. Armitage, *Foundations of Modern International Thought*, 178.

67. John Locke, *The Two Treatises of Government*, ed. Peter Laslett (Cambridge: Cambridge University Press, 2005), II, sec. 145, 365.

68. Locke, II, sec. 121, 349.

69. Locke, II, sec. 118, 347.

70. John Dunn, *John Locke: A Very Short Introduction* (Oxford: Oxford University Press, 2003), 22.

71. On the later, post-Revolutionary phase, see Mark Goldie, "The Carlyle Lectures 2021: John Locke and Empire," University of Oxford, January 19–February 23, 2021, https://www.history.ox.ac.uk/event/the-carlyle-lectures-2021-john-locke-and-empire.

72. See Roberto Esposito, *Two: The Machine of Political Theology and the Place of Thought* (New York: Fordham University Press, 2015), for an overview of the "superimposition" of

Roman and Christian "logics" of personhood, which "led to further division between fact and law, [and] natural reality and legal reality" (83).

73. Nancy Armstrong, *How Novels Think: The Limits of Individualism from 1719–1900* (New York: Columbia University Press, 2005), 6.

74. Parry, *British Nationality Law*, 103.

75. See Sections 97 and 114 of the Fundamental Constitutions of Carolina, which allow for, respectively, the admission of "jews, heathens and other dissenters" from Christianity and for automatic naturalization in Carolina simply by subscribing publicly to the constitutions.

Chapter 2 · Ideas of Naturalization

1. Raymond Williams, "Ideas of Nature," in *Problems in Materialism and Culture* (London: Verso, 1980), 84.

2. Raymond Williams, *Keywords: A Vocabulary of Culture and Society* (New York: Oxford University Press, 2005).

3. Fredric Jameson, "Of Islands and Trenches: Naturalization and the Production of Utopian Discourse," *Diacritics* 7, no. 2 (1977): 2–21.

4. *Oxford English Dictionary Online*, s.v. "naturalization, n.," December 2021, https://www-oed-com.libproxy.lib.unc.edu/view/Entry/125342?redirectedFrom=naturalization.

5. Daniel Defoe, *Robinson Crusoe*, ed. John Richetti (New York: Penguin Books, 2003), 5.

6. William A. Shaw, *Letters of Denization and Acts of Naturalization for Aliens in England and Ireland, 1701–1800*, ed. William A. Shaw (London: Publications of the Huguenot Society of London, 1923), 1:51.

7. Shaw, 63.

8. Shaw, 67–68.

9. Samuel Johnson, *Johnson on the English Language*, ed. E. L. MacAdam and Gwin J. Kolb (New Haven, CT: Yale University Press, 2005), 31.

10. Samuel Johnson, *The Yale Edition of the Works of Samuel Johnson*, ed. John Middendorf et al. (New Haven, CT: Yale University Press), 85. See Lynda Mugglestone, "Defending the Citadel, Patrolling the Borders," in *Samuel Johnson and the Journey into Words* (Oxford: Oxford University Press, 2015).

11. Defoe, *Crusoe*, 142; *Oxford English Dictionary Online*, s.v. "naturalization, n."

12. John Donne, *The Sermons of John Donne* (Berkeley: University of California Press, 2021), 7:221.

13. Michael de Montaigne, *The Essays of Michael de Montaigne*, trans. Peter Coste (London: printed for W. Miller, 1811), 99.

14. Priscilla Wald, "Naturalization," in *Keywords for American Cultural Studies*, 2007, https://keywords.nyupress.org/american-cultural-studies/essay/naturalization/.

15. Wald.

16. *The History of Naturalization with Some Remarques upon the Effects thereof* (London, 1680).

17. *History of Naturalization*.

18. Lauren Berlant, *The Queen of America Goes to Washington City: Essays on Sex and Citizenship* (Durham, NC: Duke University Press, 1997), 1.

19. Berlant, 192.

20. Berlant, 192.

21. Siobhan B. Somerville, "Notes toward a Queer History of Naturalization," *American Quarterly* 57, no. 3 (2005): 659–75.

22. Somerville, 663.

23. Somerville, 667.

24. Somerville, 668–69.

25. Somerville, 661.
26. Terry Eagleton, *Ideology of the Aesthetic* (Oxford: Basil Blackwell, 1990), 10.
27. Lorraine Daston and Fernando Vidal, *The Moral Authority of Nature* (Chicago: University of Chicago Press, 2004), 2.
28. Michael McKeon, *Theory of the Novel: A Historical Approach* (Baltimore: Johns Hopkins University Press, 2000), 394.
29. Clifford Siskin, *The Historicity of Romantic Discourse* (New York: Oxford University Press, 1988), 142.
30. Laura Brown, *The Ends of Empire: Women and Ideology in Early Eighteenth-Century English Literature* (Ithaca, NY: Cornell University Press, 1993), 35.
31. Joseph Slaughter, *Human Rights, Inc.: The World Novel, Narrative Form, and International Law* (New York: Fordham University Press, 2007), back cover.
32. Roland Barthes, *Mythologies*, trans. Annette Lavers (New York: Noonday, 1991), 130.
33. Jameson, "Of Islands and Trenches," 2.
34. Jonathan Culler, *Structuralist Poetics; Structuralism, Linguistics and the Study of Literature* (New York: Routledge, 2002), 162.
35. Culler, 180.
36. Stephen Best and Sharon Marcus, "Surface Reading: An Introduction," *Representations* 108, no. 1 (2009): 2.
37. Rita Felski, *The Limits of Critique* (Chicago: University of Chicago Press, 2015), 81.
38. Jonathan Culler, "Naturalization in 'Natural' Narratology," *Partial Answers: Journal of Literature and the History of Ideas* 16, no. 2 (June 2018): 246.
39. Culler, "Naturalization in 'Natural' Narratology," 243.
40. Felski, *Limits of Critique*, 81.
41. Thomas Pavel, *The Lives of the Novel: A History* (Princeton, NJ: Princeton University Press, 2015), 7.
42. William Congreve, preface to *Incognita, or Love and duty reconcil'd a novel* (London: printed for Peter Buck, 1692).
43. Henry Fielding, *Joseph Andrews*, ed. Paul A. Scanlon (Peterborough, ON: Broadview, 2001), 42.
44. Richard Hurd, *A Dissertation on the Idea of Universal Poetry* (London: printed for A. Miller, 1766), 21.
45. At the beginning of the eighteenth century, the novel was regarded as a rebellious form that undid traditional precedents. By midcentury, those same traits were viewed as the mechanical and formulaic "manufacture" of the market. McKeon, 239.
46. See generally J. Paul Hunter, *Before Novels: The Cultural Contexts of Eighteenth-Century English Fiction* (New York: Norton, 1990).
47. Guido Mazzoni, *Theory of the Novel*, trans. Zakiya Hanafi (Cambridge, MA: Harvard University Press, 2017), 17.
48. Aristotle, *Poetics* (Oxford: Oxford University Press, 2013), 36.
49. Mazzoni, 111.
50. Samuel Richardson, *Pamela* (Oxford: Oxford University Press, 2008), 5.
51. Stephanie DeGooyer, "'The Eyes of Other People': Adam Smith's Triangular Sympathy and the Sentimental Novel," *ELH* 85, no. 3 (2018): 669–90.
52. In the first year of its publication, *Pamela* generated at least five responses in fiction, most famously Henry Fielding's parody *Shamela*, which appeared within seven weeks of *Pamela*'s expanded second edition. Pamela's claim to convey "nothing but the truth," echoed by Freval in his prefatory "puff" for the novel ("her letters borrow none of [their] Excellencies from the romantic Flights of unnatural Fancy"), was, for commentators such as Fielding, not so incontestable or ready-to-hand (5). Fielding's parody flagrantly exposes Pamela's

proclamations of innocent virtue as the calculated use of "vartue." Framed anew by the fictional editor Parson Oliver, Pamela is defamed as a social upstart who uses a "Misrepresentation of Facts" and "Perversion of Truth" to beguile an unwitting aristocrat into marriage (313). Henry Fielding, *The History of the Adventures of Joseph Andrews and of His Friend Mr. Abraham Adams: And, an Apology for the Life of Mrs. Shamela Andrews* (Oxford: Oxford University Press, 1999). Fielding tries to deface the myth of Pamela's "natural" goodness, locating in her too-pious truth-telling a secret and exploitative desire for upward mobility.

53. Jacques Rancière, *Dissensus: On Politics and Aesthetics* (London: Bloomsbury, 2015), 64.
54. Lynn Hunt, *Inventing Human Rights: A History* (New York: Norton, 2007), 38.
55. Hunt, 39.

Chapter 3 · Law of the Foreign Father

1. Ian Watt, "*Robinson Crusoe* as a Myth," *Essays in Criticism* 1, no. 2 (1951): 117.
2. Walter Scott, *The Miscellaneous Prose Works of Sir Walter Scott* (Paris: Baudry's European Library, 1837), 232; Karl Marx, *Capital: A Critique of Political Economy* (New York: Modern Library, 1906), 88; Leslie Stephen, *Hours in a Library* (London: Smith, Elder, 1892), 44.
3. In twenty-first-century receptions, the conception of Crusoe as a British colonizer has remained dominant. See, e.g., Jiao Dan and Li Rui, "Analyzing 'Other' Construction in *Robinson Crusoe* from Post Colonialism Perspective," *Studies in Linguistics and Literature* 2, no. 3 (2018): 195; Adam Lifshey, "Castaway Colonialism: Daniel Defoe's *Robinson Crusoe* and Álvar Núñez Cabeza de Vaca's Account," in *Specters of Conquest: Indigenous Absence in Transatlantic Literatures* (New York: Fordham University Press, 2010), 62–89; Mike Marais, "Colonialism and the Epistemological Underpinnings of the Early English Novel," *English in Africa* 23, no. 1 (1996): 47–66; Brett C. McInelly, "Expanding Empires, Expanding Selves: Colonialism, the Novel, and *Robinson Crusoe*," *Studies in the Novel* 3, no. 1 (2003): 1–21; Jay Rajiva, "Secrecy, Sacrifice, and God on the Island: Christianity and Colonialism in Coetzee's *Foe* and Defoe's *Robinson Crusoe*," *Twentieth Century Literature* 63, no. 1 (2017): 1–20; Susan Smit-Marais, "Converted Spaces, Contained Places: *Robinson Crusoe*'s Monologic World," *Journal of Literary Studies* 27, no. 1 (2011): 102–14; and Dennis Todd, "*Robinson Crusoe* and Colonialism," in *The Cambridge Companion to "Robinson Crusoe*," ed. John Richetti (Cambridge: Cambridge University Press, 2018), 142–56. McInelly says that, "not surprisingly, contemporary readers commonly regard Defoe's novel as the prototypical colonial novel of the eighteenth century." McInelly, "Expanding Empires, Expanding Selves," 1. In "Converted Spaces, Contained Places," Smit-Marais writes that "Crusoe's relation to space emulates processes of colonization, as illustrated by his appropriation and domestication of the island" (103). Finally, Marais argues in "Colonialism" that "just as the island goes from wilderness to home, so too Crusoe is transformed from castaway to colonist" (55). In 2019, citing James Joyce's description of Crusoe, the author Jamaica Kincaid used the occasion of her introduction to an anniversary edition of *Robinson Crusoe* to write a letter to Crusoe in the voice of Friday: "Dear Mr. Crusoe, Please stay home. There's no need for this ruse of going on a trading journey, in which more often than not the goods you are trading are people like me, Friday." Jamaica Kincaid, introduction to *Robinson Crusoe*, by Daniel Defoe (Brooklyn, NY: Restless Books, 2019), https://books.substack.com/p/diary-a-letter-to-robinson-crusoe.
4. Daniel Defoe, *Robinson Crusoe*, ed. John Richetti (New York: Penguin Books, 2001), 5. Unless otherwise noted, citations refer to this edition.
5. Hence Defoe says in the *Tour*, "Here I saw what I have not observ'd in any other country of England, namely, a pocket of wool." Daniel Defoe, *A Tour Thro' the Whole Island of Great Britain: Divided into Circuits or Journies* (London, 1724), 128.

6. Christopher GoGwilt, for example, briefly mentions the issue of Crusoe's foreign name in his entry on the novel and the nation but does not go further to discuss his father's status in England. See Christopher GoGwilt, "The Novel and the Nation," in *A Companion to the English Novel*, ed. Stephen Arata (Chichester, UK: John Wiley and Sons, 2015), 441.

7. Daniel Defoe, *A True collection of the Writings of the Author of the True-Born Englishman* (London, 1703), 12.

8. "William III, 1698–99: An Act to enable His Majesties naturall borne Subjects to inherit the Estate of their Ancestors either lineall or collaterall notwithstanding their Father or Mother were Aliens," in *Statutes of the Realm*, vol. 7, *1695–1701*, ed. John Raithby (n.p., 1820), 590. The Navigation Acts of the seventeenth century also excluded alien merchants from colonial trade and from importing goods into England. See Thomas C. Barrow, *Trade and Empire: The British Customs Service in Colonial America, 1660–1775* (Cambridge, MA: Harvard University Press, 1967).

9. By 1758, the jurist Emer de Vattel, taking up the matter of the children of foreign-born fathers, would write in *The Law of Nations*: "If he [the father] has fixed his abode in a foreign country, he is become a member of another society, at least as a perpetual inhabitant; and his children will be members of it also." Emer de Vattel, *The Law of Nations, or the Principles of the Law of Nature, Applied to the Conduct and Affairs of Nations and Sovereigns*, ed. Joseph Chitty (Cambridge: Cambridge University Press, 2011), 102.

10. Many merchants did not pursue the legal opportunity of naturalization, and those who did waited until it served some advantage to their trade. If Crusoe's father did establish a family before seeking legal redress for restrictions placed on foreigners, then, as Kettner explains, only an act of naturalization could retroactively enable him to alter his status before he pursued such an act: "The parliamentary act operated retrospectively to the birth of the party, enabled him to inherit as well as to take lands by descent, purchase, or devise." Only naturalization had this retroactive ability; denization, which was the prerogative of the king, continued to acknowledge a foreigner's birth. James H. Kettner, *The Development of American Citizenship, 1608–1870* (Chapel Hill: University of North Carolina Press, 1978), 33.

11. Defoe, *Robinson Crusoe*, 6.

12. This chapter contributes to what might be called the "global turn" of novel studies, joining scholars who focus on *Robinson Crusoe*'s immense spatial geography and substantiate Defoe as a writer of global rather than national fiction. Ala Alryyes, for example, tracks the spatial design of the novel in "Defoe's *Robinson Crusoe*: 'Maps,' Natural Law, and the Enemy," *Eighteenth-Century Life* 44, no. 3 (2020): 51–74. Srinivas Aravamudan examines the novel's "multiple transnational, oceanic, and global settings for England" (60) in "Defoe, Commerce, and Empire," in *The Cambridge Companion to Daniel Defoe*, ed. John Richetti (Cambridge: Cambridge University Press, 2008), 45–63. See also chap. 2 of Margaret Cohen, *The Novel and the Sea* (Princeton, NJ: Princeton University Press, 2010); and chap. 5 of Ning Ma, *The Age of Silver: The Rise of the Novel East and West* (New York: Oxford University Press, 2017).

13. John Locke, *The Two Treatises of Government*, ed. Peter Laslett (Cambridge: Cambridge University Press, 2005), II, sec. 119, 347.

14. John Donne, *Devotions Upon Emergent Occasions*, ed. John Sparrow (Cambridge: Cambridge University Press, 1923), 98.

15. Daniel Defoe, *The Novels and Miscellaneous Works of Daniel Defoe*, ed. Walter Scott (London: Bell and Daldy, 1868), 234.

16. Patrick Parrinder, *Nation and Novel: The English Novel from Its Origins to the Present Day* (Oxford: Oxford University Press, 2006), 66.

17. Defoe, *Captain Singleton*, 6.

18. An Act for Naturalizing Foreign Protestants, 7 & 8 Anne c. 5 (1708–9).

19. William Petty, *The Economic Writings of Sir William Petty: Together with the Observations upon the Bills of Mortality, More Probably by Captain John Graunt* (Cambridge, UK: University Press, 1899), 1:266.

20. There are conflicting accounts of how many Palatines entered. Some historians argue fifteen thousand, others thirteen thousand or even fifty thousand. See Philip Otterness, *Becoming German: The 1709 Palatine Migration to New York* (Ithaca, NY: Cornell University Press, 2004), 8.

21. Joseph Addison, *Spectator*, July 30, 1711, quoted in Otterness, 61.

22. Margarit Schulte Beerbuhl, *The Forgotten Majority: German Merchants in London, Naturalization, and Global Trade, 1660–1815*, Studies in British and Imperial History, vol. 3 (New York: Berghahn Books, 2014), 20.

23. Jonathan Swift, *Examiner*, January 4, 1710.

24. Daniel Defoe, *Review*, June 23, 1709.

25. Defoe.

26. For a fascinating reading of why Defoe returned to his project to settle the Palatines later in life, see Dave Alff, *The Wreckage of Intentions: Projects in British Culture* (Philadelphia: University of Pennsylvania Press, 2017), 166–77. Alff argues that Defoe may have returned to the New Forest project "to press failed plans in the service of narrative" and to "convert its imaginary debris into a resource of literary invention (176). A similar maneuver could be argued for the incorporation of details about naturalization in *Robinson Crusoe*, yet Defoe's return to naturalization in *Robinson Crusoe* does more to prove what had indeed transpired, rather than what failed: England's attempt to legally secure residence for foreigners.

27. Daniel Defoe, *Lex Talionis, Or, An Enquiry into the Most Proper Ways to Prevent the Persecution of the Protestants in France* (London, 1698), 24.

28. See Alff, *Wreckage of Intentions*, 168–69; and, generally, Vittoria Di Palma, *Wasteland: A History* (New Haven, CT: Yale University Press, 2014).

29. See Daniel Statt, *Foreigners and Englishmen: The Controversy over Immigration and Population, 1660–1760* (Newark: University of Delaware Press, 1995), 154–63.

30. *Canary-Birds Naturalized in Utopia. A Canto. Dulce est paternum solum* (London, 1709), 2.

31. Stuart Schwarz notes that 60 percent of sugar planters in colonial Brazil were immigrants, but he only mentions immigrants from Portugal: "The Portuguese-born merchant who acquired a mill and who himself (or whose son) married the daughter of a Brazilian planter family was common phenomenon." There is no mention of immigration of merchants from England. Schwarz, "Plantations and Peripheries," in *Colonial Brazil*, ed. Leslie Bethell (Cambridge: Cambridge University Press, 1987), 89.

32. In Brazil, Defoe effectively globalizes the effects of the English Aliens Act. The practice seems to have been entirely fictionalized on Defoe's end. The reason can only be that he wanted to underline this point: in Brazil, as in England, foreigners will not settle their wealth in a country without the ability to do so in law. I have not uncovered any historical evidence that suggests that Portuguese law demanded or allowed for the naturalization of free settlers in Portugal's vassal states. Historically, foreigners were not allowed in Brazil until 1808. See C. R. Cameron, "Colonization of Immigrants in Brazil," *Monthly Labor Review* 33, no. 3 (October 1931): 36. According to Portuguese law, then, Crusoe would have been in Brazil illegally, and any property he had would have been held under the same conditions.

33. Peter Hulme, *Colonial Encounters: Europe and the Native Caribbean, 1492–1797* (London: Routledge, 1986), 181.

34. Ian Watt, *The Rise of the Novel: Studies in Defoe, Richardson and Fielding* (Berkeley: University of California Press, 2000), 64.

35. Étienne Balibar, "The Nation Form: History and Ideology," in *Race, Nation, Class: Ambiguous Identities*, by Étienne Balibar and Immanuel Wallerstein (New York: Verso, 1991), 96.

36. Balibar, 95.
37. Balibar, 95.
38. My gratitude to Katherine Stein for pointing me to this passage.
39. Aristotle, *Poetics* (Oxford: Oxford University Press, 2013), 36.
40. Linda Colley, *Britons: Forging the Nation, 1707–1837* (New Haven, CT: Yale University Press, 1992), 28.
41. Stuart Sim has linked the two in "Bunyan and the Early Novel: The Life and Death of Mr Badman," in *The Cambridge Companion to John Bunyan*, ed. Anne Dunan-Page (Cambridge: Cambridge University Press, 2010), 95–106. Patricia Meyer Spacks opens her book on the experimental nature of the early novel with a discussion of Bunyan: "The devices Bunyan used for divine allegory would resurface in the eighteenth-century novel, where they won readers for less clearly defined purposes." Spacks, *Novel Beginnings: Experiments in Eighteenth-Century English Fiction* (New Haven, CT: Yale University Press, 2006), 16.
42. G. A. Starr, *Defoe and Spiritual Autobiography* (Princeton, NJ: Princeton University Press, 1965), 87–88.
43. Michael McKeon, *Theory of the Novel: A Historical Approach* (Baltimore: Johns Hopkins University Press, 2000), 318.
44. McKeon, 320.
45. The fear was not unfounded, however. Of the 6,500 refugees who reached London from Germany in 1709, one-third were Catholic. See William O'Reilly, "Strangers Come to Devour the Land: Changing Views of Foreign Merchants in Early Eighteenth-Century England," *Journal of Early Modern History* 21, no. 3 (2017): 175.
46. See O'Reilly, 163.
47. *An Humble Address to the Honorable House of Commons on behalf of the Trades of England against Naturalizing Aliens* (London, 1699). Defoe was outspoken about occasional conformity and has been criticized for vehemently opposing it but then also strongly opposing the bill that sought to prevent it.
48. See Colley, *Britons*, 11–54.
49. *Examiner*, January 25, 1710.
50. Charles Gildon, *The life and strange surprizing adventures of Mr. D—— de F* (London: printed for J. Roberts, 1719), viii.
51. Gildon, 5.
52. Gildon, x.
53. Jonathan Swift, *Gulliver's Travels* (London: Jones, 1826), 93. Swift satirizes the readiness of the Dutch to undertake the test. A Dutch trader claims he is "not a Christian but a Dutchman" by having Gulliver refuse to take the test, despite claiming to be Dutch himself. The Emperor of Japan begins to "doubt that [he] was a real Hollander but suspected [he] might be a Christian" (93).
54. James Joyce, "'Daniel Defoe,' Edited and Translated from the Italian Manuscripts by Joseph Prescott," *Buffalo Studies* 1 (1964): 24–25.
55. Edward Said, *Culture and Imperialism* (New York: Vintage Books, 1994), xii.
56. Said, xii.
57. Said, 51.
58. Said, xii.
59. Ma, *Age of Silver*, 13.
60. Ma, 164, 145.
61. Ma, 145.
62. *Oxford English Dictionary*, s.v. "colony, n.," December 2021, https://www-oed-com.libproxy.lib.unc.edu/view/Entry/36547?rskey=XokNOy&result=1&isAdvanced=false.
63. Christopher Hill, "Robinson Crusoe," *History Workshop* 10, no. 1 (1980): 12.

64. Hulme, *Colonial Encounters*, 199.

65. Defoe, *The Farther Adventures of Robinson Crusoe*, ed. W. R. Owens (London: Pickering and Chatto, 2008), 125.

66. Aravamudan, "Defoe, Commerce, and Empire," 52.

67. Daniel Defoe, *A Plan of the English Commerce*, ed. John McVeagh, in *Political and Economic Writings of Daniel Defoe*, ed. W. R. Owens and P. N. Furbank (London: Pickering and Chatto, 2000), 7:121, 327.

68. Daniel Defoe, *A New Voyage Round the World*, in *The Novels and Miscellaneous Works of Daniel De Foe: With Prefaces and Notes, Including Those Attributed to Sir Walter Scott* (London: G. Bell and Sons, 1856), 6:458.

69. Hulme, *Colonial Encounters*, 181.

70. Daniel Defoe, *An Essay on the South-Sea Trade*, ed. John McVeagh, in *Political and Economic Writings*, 7:50–51.

71. Defoe, 45.

72. Defoe, *Plan of the English Commerce*, 303.

73. See Todd, "*Robinson Crusoe* and Colonialism."

74. Gildon, *Life and strange surprizing adventures*, viii.

75. Marcus Vinicius de Freitas, in one of the only scholarly articles to address Crusoe's plantation, argues that Brazil's role in the novel is to "reinforce the widespread myth of Brazil as a paradise, a land of opportunity, a country of equitable social relations" (454), and that "having a character participate in the Brazilian sugarcane industry was Defoe's effective strategy to present a meditation on economics and society centered upon the idea of the self-made man" (455). There is no mention of Crusoe's naturalization. De Freitas, "The Image of Brazil in *Robinson Crusoe*," *Portuguese Literary and Cultural Studies* 4/5 (2000): 453–59.

76. Locke, *Two Treatises of Government*, 347.

77. Locke, 347.

78. See Brian Smith, "Hands, Not Lands: John Locke, Immigration, and the 'Great Art of Government,'" *History of Political Thought* 39, no. 3 (2018): 470; and David Resnick, "John Locke and the Problem of Naturalization," *Review of Politics* 49, no. 3 (1987): 369.

79. John Locke, "For a General Naturalization," in *Political Essays*, ed. Mark Goldie (Cambridge: Cambridge University Press, 2004), 325.

80. David Armitage, *Foundations of Modern International Thought* (Cambridge: Cambridge University Press, 2013), 88.

Chapter 4 · Open-Door Domestic Fiction

1. Tobias Smollett, *The Adventures of Ferdinand Count Fathom* (Oxford: Oxford University Press, 1990), 46.

2. *A Letter from A Gentleman to his Friend, Concerning the Naturalization of the Jews* ([London], 1753).

3. Ian Watt, *The Rise of the Novel: Studies in Defoe, Richardson and Fielding* (Berkeley: University of California Press, 2000), 135–36; Nancy Armstrong, *Desire and Domestic Fiction: A Political History of the Novel* (New York: Oxford University Press, 1987); Margaret Anne Doody, *The True Story of the Novel* (New Brunswick, NJ: Rutgers University Press, 1996), though she disagrees; Aravamudan disagrees as well but upholds the idea of the domestic novelists. Franco Moretti, *Atlas of the European Novel, 1800–1900* (London: Verso, 1998); Edward Said, *Culture and Imperialism* (New York: Vintage Books, 1994); Srinivas Aravamudan, *Enlightenment Orientalism: Resisting the Rise of the Novel* (Chicago: University of Chicago Press, 2012). For a summary of the nationalizing thesis, see Carolyn Berman, *Creole Crossings: Domestic Fiction and the Reform of Colonial Slavery* (Ithaca, NY: Cornell University Press, 2018), 18–19.

4. Guido Mazzoni, *Theory of the Novel*, trans. Zakiya Hanafi (Cambridge, MA: Harvard University Press, 2017), 140.
5. Aravamudan, *Enlightenment Orientalism*, 20.
6. Aravamudan, 20.
7. Aravamudan, 4.
8. Moretti, *Atlas of the European Novel*, 17. Joseph Slaughter, in a fascinating essay on the formal and historical relationship between human rights law and the bildungsroman, argues that the novel creates a narrator in the same way the nation-state shapes its citizens. Slaughter, "Enabling Fictions and Novel Subjects: The 'Bildungsroman' and International Human Rights Law," *PMLA* 121, no. 5 (2006): 1405–23.
9. Margaret Doody agrees: "The 'domestic novel' in the eighteenth and even the nineteenth centuries is a vortex of energies, strong lines radiating outward from the home center and drawing foreign elements to it. The walls of the 'home' are very porous; only sillies like Mr. Woodhouse think that they can shut off the world and keep an unbroken and static family circle." Doody, *True Story of the Novel*, 278.
10. Aravamudan, in *Enlightenment Orientalism*, for instance, argues that domestic fictions "embrac[ed] history and the local and then [drew] boundaries around the national to expel the foreign and the transcultural" (6) and positions the Oriental tale as an alternative genre to the domestic novel, one that offers "new scholarly forms of cosmopolitanism and comparativism that can avoid the worst excesses of the national literature paradigm" (7). I agree with Aravamudan about the need for new scholarly forms but otherwise resist the interpretation that prose fiction is as domestic in orientation as we have been led to think.
11. For a tandem claim, in relation to the professed dominance of the marriage plot in less canonical and domestic eighteenth-century fiction, see Melissa M. Adams Campbell, *New World Courtships: Transatlantic Alternatives to Companionate Marriage* (Hanover, NH: Dartmouth College Press, 2015). Campbell argues that "comparative marriage plots," such as in the novels *The Female American* (1767), *The History of Emily Montague* (1769), *Secret History; or, The Horrors of St. Domingo* (1808), and *The Woman of Colour* (1808), "offer an alternative vision of what marriage meant in the eighteenth and early nineteenth centuries and how it served as a point of encounter between different, diverse cultures" (2).
12. Michael McKeon, *The Secret History of Domesticity: Public, Private, and the Division of Knowledge* (Baltimore: Johns Hopkins University Press, 2005), 326.
13. Samuel Richardson, *Clarissa; or the History of a Young Lady* (London: Penguin Books, 2004), 25.
14. With the exception of an expensive edition available by mail and published by the University of Otago, Richardson's *Sir Charles Grandison* is currently out of print.
15. Samuel Richardson, *The History of Sir Charles Grandison*, ed. Joselyn Harris (London: Oxford University Press, 1972), 1:xxvi.
16. As Bonnie Latimer argues, "It is hard to imagine that mere weeks after the Act's repeal, the story of the conversion and convenient death of an Iberian Jewish gentleman would not have struck a chord. By the end of this 'tolerant' novel, Merceda has been restored to his expected position as a cultural bogey with which to frighten the unrepentant, returned to his place in the Collect's morally irredeemable quartet of infidel heretic, Turk, and Jew." Latimer, "Samuel Richardson and the 'Jew Bill' of 1753: A New Political Context for Sir Charles Grandison," *Review of English Studies* 66, no. 275 (June 2015): 538.
17. "It must not be expected," he wrote to the writer Elizabeth Carter, "that the Clamours raised about the Jews Act, will subside until the next Elections are over. The foolish, the absurd Cry, will then be stilled. But as the Jews get no great Matter by this Act, methinks I would wish them to declare, that seeing it is likely to excite popular Prejudices against them . . . they will humbly petition the Legislature, in the next Session, to repeal it." Richardson's

rejection of the bill had less to do with an intolerance toward Jews, as was the case with the general criticism, than it did with the increased intolerance that the act produced in the public.

18. Francis Bacon, *Three speeches of the right honorable, sir francis bacon knight, then his majesties sollicitor generall, after lord verulam, viscount saint alban. concerning the post-nati naturalization of the scotch in england union of the lawes of the kingdomes of england and scotland* (London: printed by Richard Badger, 1641), 25.

19. Several recent articles have underlined the geographical and religious debates in the novel. See Lisa O'Connell, "Sir Charles Grandison, Natural Law and the Fictionalised English Gentleman," *Intellectual History Review* 23, no. 3 (2013): 349–63; Teri Doerksen, "Sir Charles Grandison: The Anglican Family and the Admirable Roman Catholic," *Eighteenth-Century Fiction* 15 (2003): 539–58; Patricia Brückmann, "'Men, Women and Poles': Samuel Richardson and the Romance of a Stuart Princess," *Eighteenth-Century Life* 27 (2003): 31–52; and Patrick Mello, "'Piety and Popishness': Tolerance and the Epistolary Reaction to Richardson's *Sir Charles Grandison*," *Eighteenth-Century Fiction* 25 (2013): 511.

20. For discussions of Richardson's sympathetic representation of Catholicism in *Grandison*, see S. K. Marks, *Sir Charles Grandison: The Compleat Conduct Book* (Lewisburg, PA: Bucknell University Press, 1986), 59; Margaret Anne Doody, *A Natural Passion: A Study of the Novels of Samuel Richardson* (Oxford: Clarendon, 1974); and Doerksen, "Sir Charles Grandison."

21. Richardson, *Grandison*, appendix.

22. Richardson, "Concluding Note by Author," in *Grandison*, 464–65.

23. David Armitage, *Foundations of Modern International Thought* (Cambridge: Cambridge University Press, 2013), 70. See also Christopher Warren, *Literature and the Law of Nations, 1580–1680* (Oxford: Oxford University Press, 2015). As Warren argues, Christian readers of the early modern period would have understood the law of nations as referencing a fallen, less permanent state of relations between men for meanings of national law and law between nations (98).

24. Richardson, "Concluding Note by Author," 465.

25. O'Connell, "Sir Charles Grandison," 362.

26. Quoted in Warren, *Literature*, 116.

27. Laurence Sterne, *A Sentimental Journey and Continuation of the Bramine's Journal with Related Texts*, ed. Melvyn New and W. G. Day (Indianapolis: Hackett, 2006), 97.

28. Robert Markley, for example, makes the case that sentimental feelings are the bourgeois's compensation for the aristocratic status he lacks in his person. Robert Markley, "Sentimentality as Performance: Shaftesbury, Sterne, and the Theatrics of Virtue," in *The New Eighteenth Century: Theory, Politics, English Literature*, ed. Felicity Nussbaum and Laura Brown (New York: Methuen, 1987), 210–30. John Mullan argues that sentimentalism is a privatizing discourse that makes men of feeling into elite men of feeling in *Sentiment and Sociability: The Language of Feeling in the Eighteenth Century* (Oxford: Clarendon, 1998). In *Trouble with Strangers*, Terry Eagleton offers an updated take on the narcissistic tendencies of sentimentalism. *Trouble with Strangers: A Study of Ethics* (Malden, MA: Wiley-Blackwell, 2009), 8.

29. Eagleton, for example, squares Sterne off as a profiteer of sentiment ("sentimentalists like Steele and Sterne are self-conscious consumers of tender feelings, chewing the cud of their own congenial emotions") but then guiltily adds a footnote where he admits, "Sterne, however, is an ambiguous case, as a satirist of sentimentalism as well as a probable champion of it." Eagleton, *Trouble with Strangers*, 25.

30. One primary objection to this point may be that the droits d'aubaine, though costly for the family of the deceased, or for the spirit that wants to retain its image of a loved one, does not have any bearing on Yorick before he travels to France, and even there it only affects

his property at death. It might be argued, then, that as long as he is alive, Yorick does remain a free subject while in France. As I suggest via the work of Peter Sahlins, however, the droits d'aubaine was a law that served the purposed of demarcating strangers from citizens; it was an identifying law more than a feudal tax. Moreover, as I demonstrate, Yorick is an "unwary passenger" driven to posit ideals of charity and humanity as a way of overriding the rights that accrue only to members of specific kingdoms.

31. See generally Mullan, *Sentiment and Sociability*.

32. Judith Frank argues that Yorick's performance of sentimentality amounts to a disciplinary performance of a "safe" self. Yorick can act the part of suffering without really suffering in the same way that he can allege to be Yorick the gravedigger without occupying the lowly status of a laborer. But Frank does not speculate on the possibility that Yorick's privileged position as an English gentleman could not cross with him into France. The only way that Frank can justify her argument that Yorick parodies suffering in order to become its connoisseur is by assuming that Yorick is *naturally* separate from the pathetic people whose suffering he attempts to make his own. But the droits d'aubaine is designed to arrest Yorick's gentlemanly status, reducing him, in law, to the status of a stranger, thus making what seems a parody of marginalization an actual expression of it. See Frank, *Common Ground: Eighteenth-Century English Satiric Fiction and the Poor* (Stanford, CA: Stanford University Press, 1997), 66.

33. Peter Sahlins, *Unnaturally French: Foreign Citizens in the Old Regime and After* (Ithaca, NY: Cornell University Press, 2004), 32.

34. See Mark Salter, *Rights of Passage: The Passport in International Relations* (Boulder, CO: Lynne Rienner, 2003).

35. See Frank H. Ellis, *Sentimental Comedy: Theory and Practice* (Cambridge: Cambridge University Press, 1991), 7.

36. Frances Burney, *Journals and Letters*, ed. Peter Sabor et al. (New York: Penguin, 2001), 451.

37. Burney, 452.

38. Salter, *Rights of Passage*, 12–13.

39. See Clive Emsley, *British Society and the French War, 1793–1815* (London: Macmillan, 1979), 20–21.

40. Daniel Trilling, "'Cruel, Paranoid, Failing': Inside the Home Office," *Guardian*, May 13, 2021.

41. Burney, *Journals and Letters*, 452.

42. Quoted in Margaret Anne Doody, introduction to *The Wanderer; or, Female Difficulties*, by Frances Burney, ed. Margaret Anne Doody, Robert Mack, and Peter Sabor (Oxford: Oxford University Press, 2001), 5.

43. Leanne Maunu argues, for example, that "Burney calls attention to the artificial and culturally constructed nature of nationalism. . . . The randomness of one's birthplace and peer circle, Burney points out, influences our attachments and dislikes, which ultimately influence our understanding of other nations and people." Maunu, *Women Writing the Nation: National Identity, Female Community, and the British-French Connection, 1770–1820* (Lewisburg, PA: Bucknell University Press, 2007), 216.

44. Doody, introduction, 4.

45. See Catherine Frank, "Wandering Narratives and Wavering Conclusions: Irreconciliation in Frances Burney's *The Wanderer* and Walter Scott's *Waverley*," *European Romantic Review* 12, no. 4 (2001): 429–56. Also see Carmel Murphy, "'The Stormy Sea of Politics': The French Revolution and Frances Burney's *The Wanderer*," *Women's Writing: The Elizabethan to Victorian Period* 22, no. 4 (2015): 485–504. For a reading of the opening passage of the novel as a border crossing, see Mitchell Gauvin, "Is Arrival Still Possible? Frances Burney's *The Wanderer* and the New Cartography in the Long Eighteenth Century," *Oxford Research in English*, no. 11 (2020): 23–42.

46. Frances Burney, *The Wanderer; or, Female Difficulties* (Oxford: Oxford University Press, 1991), 873.

47. Tara Czechowski, "'Black, Patched and Pennyless': Race and Crime in Burney's *The Wanderer*," *Eighteenth-Century Fiction* 25, no. 4 (2013): 677–700.

48. Roxann Wheeler, *The Complexion of Race: Categories of Difference in Eighteenth-Century British Culture* (Philadelphia: University of Pennsylvania Press, 2000); Felicity Nussbaum, *The Limits of the Human: Fictions of Anomaly, Race, and Gender in the Long Eighteenth Century* (Cambridge: Cambridge University Press, 2003); Nicholas Hudson, "From 'Nation' to 'Race': The Origin of Racial Classification in Eighteenth-Century Thought," *Eighteenth-Century Studies* 29, no. 3 (Spring 1996): 247–64; Jürgen Osterhammel, *Unfabling the East: the Enlightenment's Encounter with Asia*, trans. Robert Savage (Princeton, NJ: Princeton University Press, 2018).

49. Czechowski, "'Black, Patched and Pennyless,'" 689.

50. *Sundry considerations touching naturalization of aliens whereby the alledged advantages thereby are confuted, and the contrary mischiefs thereof are detected and discovered* (London, 1695), 3.

51. Granville Sharpe, *Extract from a representation of the injustice and dangerous tendency of tolerating slavery, or admitting the least claim of private property in the persons of men in England* (London, 1771), 5.

52. See Peter Fryer, *Staying Power: The History of Black People in Britain* (London: Pluto, 1984).

Chapter 5 · Unnatural-Born Subjects

1. Tacitus, *The Works of Tacitus: In Four Volumes* (London, 1737), 24.

2. Erich Auerbach, *Mimesis: The Representation of Reality in Western Literature* (Princeton, NJ: Princeton University Press, 2013), 39.

3. Tacitus, *Works of Tacitus*, 24.

4. Auerbach, *Mimesis*, 27.

5. Jacques Rancière, *The Names of History*, trans. Hassan Melehy (Minneapolis: University of Minnesota Press, 1994), 28.

6. Rancière, 26.

7. Rancière, 29.

8. Maria Edgeworth, *Harrington*, ed. Susan Manly (Peterborough, ON: Broadview, 2004), 87.

9. Maria Edgeworth to Rachel Mordecai, August 4, 1816, in *The Education of the Heart: The Correspondence of Rachel Mordecai Lazarus and Maria Edgeworth*, ed. Edgar E. MacDonald (Chapel Hill: University of North Carolina Press, 1977), 8.

10. [John Toland], *Reasons for Naturalizing the Jews in Great Britain and Ireland, on the same Foot with Other Nations, Containing Also, A Defense of the Jews against All Vulgar Prejudices in All Countries* (1714), reprinted in *Pamphlets Relating to the Jews in England during Seventeenth and Eighteenth Centuries*, ed. P. Radin (San Francisco: California State Library, 1939), 50.

11. See Susan Manly, introduction to Edgeworth, *Harrington*, 35.

12. Richard Lowell Edgeworth to Maria Edgeworth, August 4, 1816, in *Education of the Heart*, 8.

13. Lynn Hunt, *Inventing Human Rights* (New York: Norton, 2007), 32. Novels, in Hunt's influential reading, effect physically charged relations between reader and book—the kind imagined (and ultimately shown to be ineffective) in Laurence Sterne's *Sentimental Journey*. Through new kinds of reading experiences, new political ideas about human rights were able to emerge; readers imagining the pain of others created the notion of a community made up of benevolent individuals.

14. James Shapiro, *The Making of the National Poet: Shakespeare, Adaptation, and Authorship, 1660–1769* (Oxford: Clarendon, 1992), 78.
15. Rachel Mordecai to Maria Edgeworth, in *Education of the Heart*, 16.
16. Maria Edgeworth to Rachel Mordecai, in *Education of the Heart*, 8.
17. Rachel Mordecai to Maria Edgeworth, in *Education of the Heart*, 16.
18. Manly, introduction, 53.
19. Catherine Gallagher, *Nobody's Story: The Vanishing Acts of Women Writers in the Marketplace, 1670–1820* (Berkeley: University of California Press, 1995), 311.
20. See generally John B. Roney and Martin I. Klauber, *The Identity of Geneva: The Christian Commonwealth, 1564–1864* (Westport, CT: Greenwood, 1998).
21. Mary Shelley, *Frankenstein*, ed. Paul Hunter (New York: Norton, 2012), 41.
22. On May 17, 1816, Shelley wrote in her journal, "There are two roads to Geneva; one by Nion, in the Swiss territory, where the mountain route is shorter and comparatively easy at that time of the year, when the road is for several leagues covered with snow of an enormous depth; the other road lay through Gex, and was too circuitous and dangerous to be attempted at so late an hour in the day. Our passport, however, was for Gex, and we were told that we could not change its destination; but all these police laws, so severe in themselves, are to be softened by bribery, and this difficulty was at length overcome." Mary Shelley, *The Life and Letters of Mary Wollstonecraft Shelley*, ed. Mrs. Julian Marshall (London: Richard Bentley and Son, 1889), 1:132.
23. In *The Secret History of Domesticity*, Michael McKeon works with a distinction between public and private narration methods that I will use provisionally here: epistolary form offers access to the "secret" and private life of a writer, whereas third-person narration is a public method of passing commentary or judgment. In many ways, however, McKeon notes that third-person narration can provide even more private knowledge than the first-person "I" since an outside narrator can always convey ulterior and interior motives that are unavailable to an epistolary speaker. I am here interested in an epistolary method that does not profess to offer unadorned private or firsthand information, a method that does not use writing in the third person or in free indirect style, a method that is simply indirect, with the first-person pronoun delivered by another speaker in a narrative form akin to biography. Michael McKeon, *The Secret History of Domesticity: Public, Private, and the Division of Knowledge* (Baltimore: Johns Hopkins University Press, 2005).
24. This is the hand that also erases part of the dates and writes, "*Walton, in continuation.*" Anne Mellor discerns that the initials of Walton's addressee must be M. W. S., Mary W. Shelley's own. See Mellor, *Mary Shelley: Her Life, Her Fiction, Her Monsters* (New York: Methuen, 1988), 54.
25. Plutarchan biography was a familiar enough form for Mary Shelley. Between 1832 and 1839, Shelley wrote the biographies of many notable Italian, Spanish, Portuguese, and French men and a few women for Dionysius Lardner's *Lives of the Most Eminent Literary and Scientific Men*, itself a collection modeled on Plutarch's *Lives* in response to growing middle-class demand for self-education. "It would seem from the evidence of the *Cyclopaedia Lives*," Greg Kucich rightly argues, "that the project of revisioning history helped give a maturing Mary Shelley the courage, steadiness, and self-worth to carry on her own political interventions, in however mediated a form, through even the darkest of times. Kucich, "Mary Shelley's *Lives* and the Reengendering of History," in *Mary Shelley in Her Times*, ed. Betty T Bennett and Stuart Curran (Baltimore: Johns Hopkins University Press, 2000), 212–13. Kucich situates biography as a somewhat compromised form ("however mediated") for political activism in Shelley's later writing. I suggest that Shelley was interested in the form of biography in her younger years, and that it is precisely the mediated form of biography that can help account for the vexing narratology, and the politics associated with it, of her first novelistic effort.

26. For a fuller explication of the linkage between Romanticism and autobiography, see Candace Lang, "Autobiography in the Aftermath of Romanticism," *Diacritics* 12 (1982): 2–16.

27. Jean-Jacques Rousseau, *Confessions* (Oxford: Oxford University Press, 2000), 5.

28. Tim Duff, *Plutarch's Lives: Exploring Virtue and Vice* (Oxford: Clarendon, 1999), 262.

29. Thomas McLaughlin, "Figurative Language," in *Critical Terms for Literary Study*, ed. Frank Lentricchia and Thomas McLaughlin (Chicago: University of Chicago Press, 1990), 83.

30. Barbara Johnson argues that Victor Frankenstein's project to create a man "like himself" demonstrates the failure of generic norms to provide an adequate form for the complexity of individual existence, particularly for female writers: "The tale is designed to reinforce the resemblance between teller and listener so that somehow transgression can be eliminated. Yet the desire for resemblance, the desire to create a being like oneself—which is the autobiographical desire par excellence—is also the central transgression in Mary Shelley's novel." Johnson, "My Monster/Myself," *Diacritics* 12 (1982): 1–10.

31. "Shelley," says Spivak, "had attempted to come to terms with the making of the colonial subject. Sympathetic, yet monstrous, clandestinely reared on sacred and profane histories of salvation and empire, shunned by the civilization that produced his subjectivity, the creature's destructive rage propels him out of the novel into an indefinite future." Gayatri Spivak, "Intervention: Thinking Academic Freedom in Gendered Postcoloniality," in *Postcolonial Intellectuals in Europe*, ed. Sandra Ponzanesi and Adriano Habed (London: Rowman and Littlefield, 2018), xxix.

32. Hannah Arendt, *The Origins of Totalitarianism* (San Diego: Harvest, 1968), 67.

33. Susan Lanser, "The Novel Body Politic," in *A Companion to the Eighteenth-Century English Novel and Culture*, ed. Paula R. Backscheider and Catherine Ingrassia (Hoboken, NJ: Wiley-Blackwell, 2009), 485–86.

34. Peter Brooks, "'Godlike Science/Unhallowed Arts': Language, Nature, and Monstrosity," in *The Endurance of "Frankenstein": Essays on Mary Shelley's Novel*, ed. George Levine and U. C. Knoepflmacher (Berkeley: University of California Press, 1979), 205.

35. Spivak, "Intervention," xxxi.

Coda

1. Hannah Arendt, *The Origins of Totalitarianism* (San Diego: Harvest, 1968), 267.

2. Arendt, 284.

3. Stefan Zweig, *The World of Yesterday* (New York: Viking, 1943), 436. In a chapter entitled "Europe before the War," John Maynard Keynes describes prewar mobility as a condition in which the individual "could secure forthwith, if he wished it, cheap and comfortable means of transit to any country or climate without passport or other formality." Keynes, *The Economic Consequences of Peace* (New York: Macmillan, 1920), 11.

4. My essay "The Right to Leave," in *Lapham's Quarterly*, discusses the fight between the American colonies and the British monarchy over the issue of perpetual allegiance at length.

5. See generally Atossa Araxia Abrahamian, *The Cosmopolites: The Coming of the Global Citizen* (New York: Columbia Global Reports, 2015).

6. Immigration, Asylum and Nationality Act 2006 (c. 13), sec. 56.

7. C. J. McKinney, "How Many People Have Been Stripped of Their British Citizenship?," Free Movement, January 10, 2022, https://www.freemovement.org.uk/how-many-people-have-been-stripped-of-their-british-citizenship-home-office-deprivation/.

INDEX

Act of Settlement (1701), 8
Acts of Union (1706, 1707), 18–19
Adventures of Ferdinand Count Fathom, The (Smollett), 12–13, 113–15, 117, 119, 121, 136, 147
Aesop: "The Ass and the Lapdog," 159
affirmative reading, 172–73
Africa, 13, 23, 94, 106, 135
Aliens Act (1698), 28, 87, 90, 92, 94, 134, 188n32
Aliens Act (1793), 134
Aliens Restriction Act (1914), 1
allegiance: artificial, 54, 56; doctrine of, 41, 54; dual, 48, 50, 114; feudal, 15, 41, 53, 60, 91, 122; national, 3, 12, 17, 20, 59, 69, 94, 114–19, 130, 138, 146; natural, 34–36, 43–47, 53, 58–61, 69, 109; naturalized, 40, 44, 54, 66, 125, 133; paranational, 34, 134, 141; perpetual, 2, 10, 14, 20, 29, 35–37, 48, 57–58, 63, 110, 121; transnational, 130; voluntary, 34–35, 40, 56, 60, 91
anagnorisis (Aristotle concept), 97
Anderson, Benedict, 16, 18, 134, 139, 177–78n49, 178n55. *See also* imagined community
Ando, Clifford, 49–50
Anglicanism. *See* Church of England; Protestantism
anti-Semitism, 5, 146, 148, 150–52, 167. *See also* Jewish people
Arabian Nights, 156
Aravamudan, Srinivas, 19, 106, 116–17, 191n10
Arendt, Hannah, 1–3, 34, 163, 169–70
Aristotle, 77, 97–98
Armitage, David, 56–57, 110
Armstrong, Nancy, 18, 59, 178n58
assimilation, 11, 34, 50, 60, 71, 74, 77, 80, 91, 146
Auerbach, Erich, 12, 145
Austen, Jane, 73, 178n55

Bacon, Francis, 38, 40, 49, 120–21, 123, 125
Balibar, Étienne, 17, 96–97
Barthes, Roland, 63, 73–74
Batailhey, Joseph, 66–67
Behn, Aphra, 13. *See also Oroonoko*
Bentham, Jeremy, 20, 50
Berlant, Lauren, 63, 70–72
bildungsroman, 73, 191n8
Black people: Burney on, 119, 136, 138–39; and English subjecthood, 5, 138, 171. *See also* slavery

Blackstone, William, 35
borders (territorial), 20–22, 33, 133–34, 173
Brazil, 94–95, 106, 108, 188n31–32, 190n75
Bremen, Germany, 66, 85–86, 92–93
Bridgman, Orlando, 47–48
British Nationality and Status of Aliens Act (1914), 1, 33
Brooke, Henry: *Fool of Quality*, 81
Broom, Herbert, 40
Brown, Charles Brockden: *Wieland, or the Transformation*, 156
Bunyan, John: *Pilgrim's Progress*, 98–99, 189n41
Burney, Frances: *Cecilia*, 133; diary of, 133–34; *Evelina*, 133; prose fiction of, 12, 19, 28, 119, 141, 193n43. *See also Wanderer, The*
Burton, Robert, 132

Calais, France, 125–27, 137
Calvin, John, 155
Calvin's Case (1608): and English subjecthood, 8, 10, 47, 53, 72, 123, 181n16, 182n23; and naturalization, 54, 58, 69, 114, 120; overview of case, 40–44; precedent in, 180n8; and property inheritance, 27, 44–46
Canary-Birds Naturalized in Utopia (Anon.), 93, 94
capitalism, 70, 73–74, 111, 170, 171
Carter, Elizabeth, 191–92n17
Case of the Post-nati. *See Calvin's Case* (1608)
Catholicism: in England, 55, 149, 189n45; in France, 55, 149; in Geneva, 155; naturalization of, 34, 42, 59, 88, 95, 101, 102; in *Robinson Crusoe*, 3, 13, 68, 88, 95, 98–104, 108, 110–11, 137, 140; in *Sir Charles Grandison*, 13, 80, 121–22
Charles II (England), 4
Child, Josiah, 54, 92
China, 19, 105
Chinese Exclusion Act (1882), 33
Church of England, 55, 90, 101, 103. *See also* Protestantism
citizenship: in ancient Rome, 49–51, 56, 105; in English colonies, 138; in France, 47, 128, 134; in Geneva, 155; Locke on, 56, 89, 114; and naturalization, 1, 29, 34, 63–64, 70–72; revoking of, 2, 170–71; in the United States, 6, 8, 40, 70–71, 170

Clarendon Code, 101
Clarissa (Richardson), 119, 156
climate catastrophe, 171
Cockburn, Sir Alexander, 35. See also Royal Commission (1868)
Coke, Sir Edward, 12, 35–36, 40–47, 53, 58, 123, 125, 180n8, 181n16, 181n18. See also *Calvin's Case* (1608)
Coleridge, Samuel Taylor: "Rime of the Ancient Mariner," 166
Colley, Linda, 16, 98–99
colonialism: in *Frankenstein*, 162, 196n31; and nationality, 19, 26, 34; in novels, 13; in *Robinson Crusoe*, 85, 104–8, 110, 186n3; in the United States, 23, 26, 89
Columbus, Christopher, 107
Colville, James, 39–40, 46. See also *Calvin's Case* (1608)
Congreve, William, 76
Corporation Act (1661), 101
Cowell, John, 40
Craig, Thomas, 38
Craw v. Ramsey, 45, 48, 52–53. See also Ramsey, John
Crusoe, Robinson. See *Robinson Crusoe*
Culler, Jonathan, 63, 75, 146; "Naturalization and Convention," 74
cultural theory, 11, 63, 70, 72–76
Czechowski, Tara, 138

D'Arblay, Alexandre, 133
Daubeny, Elyas, 182n29
Defoe, Daniel: *Captain Singleton*, 90; *Colonel Jack*, 89; and colonialism, 104–8, 116; "Essay on the South Sea Trade, An," 107; *Farther Adventures of Robinson Crusoe, The*, 95, 106, 108; *Lex Talionis*, 92; *Memoirs of a Cavalier*, 90; *Moll Flanders*, 89, 178n55; on nationality, 96–98, 109, 112, 117–18; on naturalization, 6, 54, 58, 77, 87–96, 101, 108, 110–11, 150, 188n26, 189n47; *New Voyage Round the World, A*, 107; *Plan of the English Commerce, A*, 106–7; *Tour thro' the Whole Island of Britain*, 92; "True-Born Englishman, The," 14, 86, 177n39. See also *Robinson Crusoe*; *Roxana*
denationalization, 22, 105, 170–71
De natis ultra mare (1350), 42
denaturalization, 1, 11, 29, 49, 62, 74–75, 169
denizenship, 8, 43, 49, 68, 181n18, 182n29

deportation, 1, 33, 130, 176n22
de Vattel, Emer, 35, 187n9
domestication (Culler concept), 75
domestic fiction, 28, 116–19, 124, 191n9–10. See also individual titles
domesticity, 21–22, 118, 139
domestic realism, 28, 116
Donne, John, 68, 89
Doody, Margaret, 21, 191n9
Dover, UK, 125–27
Dunkirk, France, 133–34, 140
Dunn, John, 58

Eagleton, Terry, 72, 80, 126, 192n29
Edgeworth, Maria, 12, 29, 147–54, 167; *Castle Rackrent*, 148; "Good Aunt, The," 148; "Prussian Vase, The," 148. See also *Harrington*
Edict of Nantes, 2, 55, 58, 90
Edward III (England), 182n27
Elizabeth I (England), 37, 182n29
Engels, Friedrich, 11, 73
England: Catholicism in, 55, 149, 189n45; early naturalization in, 3–8; and France, 37, 98, 132–33, 182n27; naturalization petitions in, 66–67; Protestantism in, 8, 23, 34, 55, 58, 60, 67, 88–90, 149; Scots' status in, 8, 36–47, 60, 80, 114, 120, 122, 181n16, 182n23; versus Britain, 18–19. See also individual laws and cases; Union of the Crowns (1603)
Enlightenment era, 15, 19, 29, 35, 170, 172
epistolary novels, 13, 29, 79, 81, 112, 118–20, 124, 147, 156, 195n23. See also individual titles
Examiner, 92, 102
Exchequer Chamber, 46–47

Fathom, Ferdinand. See *Adventures of Ferdinand Count Fathom, The*
Felski, Rita, 75
Female American, The (Anon.), 13
fiction, definition of, 50–51
Fielding, Henry, 76, 80; *Shamela*, 185–86n52
Finch, Heneage, 48
First World War, 1, 169
Flanders, 13, 87, 113–14
Foreign Protestants Naturalization Act (1709). See Naturalization of Foreign Protestants Act (1709)
Foster, J., 45
Foster v. Ramsey, 46, 48

Foxe, John: *Book of Martyrs*, 98–99
France: Burney in, 133–34; droits d'aubaine in, 127, 128, 192–93n30, 193n32; and England, 37, 98, 132–33, 182n27; naturalization in, 47–48; in *A Sentimental Journey*, 119, 125–30, 132, 140, 192–93n30, 193n32; in *Sir Charles Grandison*, 123–25; in *The Wanderer*, 12–13. *See also* Huguenots
Frank, Judith, 193n32
Frankenstein; or, The Modern Prometheus (Shelley): colonialism in, 162, 196n31; Creature's unnatural birth in, 13, 72, 147; linguistic naturalization in, 155, 157–64, 166; narrative naturalization in, 29, 162, 167, 172; narrative structure of, 147, 156–57, 164–67; Victor's naturalization in Geneva, 14, 29, 154–56
Freitas, Marcus Vinicius de, 190n75
French Revolution, 20, 134, 137
Freud, Sigmund, 73, 75
Freval, Jean Baptiste de, 78, 185n52
Fuller, Lon, 9

Gallagher, Catherine, 116, 153
General Naturalization Act (1709). *See* Naturalization of Foreign Protestants Act (1709)
Geneva, Switzerland, 29, 147, 154–56, 195n22
Germany, 1, 66, 87, 91–92, 96, 114. *See also* Palatines
Gibney, Matthew, 176n22
Gildon, Charles: "An Epistle to . . . ," 103; *Life and Strange Surprizing Adventures . . . , The*, 102; on *Robinson Crusoe*, 87, 108
Godwin, William, 155; *Caleb Williams*, 156
Goldsmith, Oliver: *Traveller, The*, 14; *Vicar of Wakefield*, 81
Goldsmith, Stewarton Lewis: *Female Revolutionary Plutarch*, 156
gothic novels, 13, 112, 140, 156. *See also* individual titles
Grandison, Sir Charles. *See History of Sir Charles Grandison, The*
Granville, Juliet. *See Wanderer, The*
Great Britain. *See* England; Scotland; Wales
Griffith, Elizabeth, 76

Haiti, 137
Harrington (Edgeworth), 12, 146–54, 160, 164
Hegel, Georg, 73, 76
hermeneutics of suspicion (Riceour concept), 75

heterosexuality, 70–71
Hill, Christopher, 106
History of Sir Charles Grandison, The (Richardson), 13, 80, 117, 119–25, 129, 137, 140, 153, 156, 191n16
Hobart, Henry, 40
Hobbes, Thomas, 56–57
Holland, 3, 13, 55, 58, 69, 77, 113–14
Homer, 114, 123
Huguenots, 2–5, 7, 14, 42, 55, 89–91, 115
Hume, David: on contiguity, 179n71; *Enquiry concerning Human Understanding, An*, 24–25; *Treatise on Human Nature, A*, 24
Hunt, Lynn, 81–82, 150, 153, 194n13
Hurd, Richard, 76

imagined community (Anderson concept), 16, 177–78n49, 178n55
Immigration, Asylum and Nationality Act (2006), 170
immigration law. *See* individual cases
Indigenous peoples, 23, 59, 171
individualism, 15, 21, 26–27, 56–59, 96–98, 109, 116–18, 140–41
intimacy (Lowe concept), 26
Ireland, 5, 8, 13, 18, 37, 52–53, 93, 137, 182n23
Italy, 104, 117, 121–25

Jamaica, 13
Jameson, Frederic, 62–63, 73–74
James VI (Scotland and I of England), 37–38, 40–45, 181n20
Japan, 19, 103, 105
Jefferson, Thomas, 125
Jewish Naturalization Act (1753), 5, 12, 29, 115, 120, 125, 138, 147–51, 171, 191n16–17
Jewish people (in fiction), 115, 120, 148–50, 152–53, 191n16. *See also* anti-Semitism; Jewish Naturalization Act (1753)
John (King of England), 10, 37
Johnson, Barbara, 162, 196n30
Johnson, Dr. Samuel, 7–8, 11, 67–68
Johnson, Samuel, 7, 56, 132
Johnson-Reed Immigration Act (1924), 33
Joyce, James, 85, 104, 107–8, 186n3; *Ulysses*, 74

Kant, Immanuel, 35
Kettner, James, 53
Keynes, John Maynard, 169, 196n3

Keywords: A Vocabulary of Culture and Society (Williams), 27, 62–63
Knight, Sir John, 6, 101
Knight the Younger, Sir John, 55

Lanser, Susan, 163
legal fictions: in ancient Rome, 49, 51; definition of, 9–11; of nationality, 18, 22, 45–46; naturalization as, 26, 35–37, 52, 56, 61, 63, 65, 146, 169, 171
legal naturalization. *See individual cases and laws*
linguistic naturalization, 67–68, 98
literature. *See* novels
Locke, John: on allegiance, 12, 27, 35, 54, 123, 125, 170; *Essay concerning Human Understanding*, 59; "For a General Naturalization," 56; on individualism, 57–59, 88, 109; on naturalization, 4, 6, 10, 37, 56, 57–60, 109–10, 114, 137; *Two Treatises on Government*, 27, 57–58, 109
London, UK, 5, 37, 39, 55, 66, 89, 138
Louis XIV (France), 2, 55, 90, 101
Lowe, Lisa, 26

Ma, Ning, 19, 105
Marin, Louis: *Utopiques: Jeux d'espaces*, 62
Marvel, Andrew, 54
Marx, Karl, 73, 75, 85, 95
Marxism, 27, 62, 73
Maynard, John, 48, 49, 52
Mazzoni, Guido, 17, 76–77, 81–82
McKeon, Michael, 72–73, 99–102, 116, 118, 195n23
methodological nationalism, 19
metonymy, 160, 162–63
Moll Flanders (Defoe), 89, 178n55
Molloy, Charles, 48
Montaigne, Michel de, 68–69
Mordecai, Rachel, 148, 150–53
More, Thomas: *Utopia*, 93
Moretti, Franco, 15, 18, 116–17, 134, 178n55
Mullan, John, 128, 192n28
myths, 73–74

Napoleon, 133–34
narrative naturalization, 29, 81, 146–47, 157–58, 162, 167, 174
nationality, development of, 15–23, 26, 63, 170–73. *See also* paranationality
nationality law. *See individual laws*
nativism, 23, 98, 105, 113

naturalization: definition of, 62–63; etymology of word, 11, 64–65, 71–72; modern meanings of, 63, 91, 172–73; scholarship on, 15–16, 21. *See also* linguistic naturalization; narrative naturalization; racialized naturalization; universal naturalization
Naturalization Act (1790, US), 71
naturalization imaginary, 34–35, 47
naturalization laws. *See individual laws*
Naturalization of Foreign Protestants Act (1709), 3–6, 55, 59, 70, 90–91, 93, 101, 134, 138, 149
Nietzsche, Friedrich, 75
North, Roger, 101
novels: early critiques of, 76–77, 185n45; English canon of, 19, 28, 104–5, 117–18, 172; rise of, 17–19, 115–16, 178n55. *See also individual genres; individual titles*

Odyssey, The, 97
Orientalism, 191n10. *See also* Aravamudan, Srinivas; Said, Edward
Oroonoko (Behn), 13, 73
Oxford English Dictionary, 20, 64, 68, 105–6

Palatines, 5, 14, 28, 58, 91–95, 108, 110, 138, 188n20
Pamela: or, Virtue Rewarded (Richardson), 64, 77–81, 119–20, 124, 140, 156, 178n55, 185–86n52
Papists Act (1778), 149–50
paranationality: definition of, 20–23, 34, 115; and fiction, 28, 113, 117–19, 127, 141; Locke on, 27, 54–61; in *Robinson Crusoe*, 88, 95–96, 111, 115; in *Sir Charles Grandison*, 122, 124; in *The Wanderer*, 134, 139
Paris, France, 125, 129–30, 133
Parkinson, John, 39
Parkinson, William, 39
Parry, Clive, 59, 182n29
Pavel, Thomas, 76
Percennius, 145–47, 157, 165
Petty, William, 54, 56, 91
Philip II (France), 10, 37
picaresque novels, 28, 102, 116, 140
Plutarch: *Parallel Lives*, 147, 156–57, 164, 195n25
Poor Laws (UK), 7
Portugal, 3, 88, 90, 94–95, 99, 106–8, 111, 170, 188n31–32
postcolonialism, 85, 104–5, 115
poststructuralism, 27, 162

Protestant Gordon Riots (1780), 149–50
Protestantism: in England, 8, 23, 34, 55, 58, 60, 67, 88–90, 149; in *Fernand Count Fathom*, 115; in *Robinson Crusoe*, 85, 88, 98–104; in *Sir Charles Grandison*, 121–22. *See also* Church of England; Huguenots; Naturalization of Foreign Protestants Act (1709); Palatines
Pushkin, Alexander: *Eugene Onegin*, 77

race: in early novels, 13, 23; and naturalization, 5–6, 55, 60, 138–40, 171; in *The Wanderer*, 135–38
racialized naturalization, 5–6, 138, 147, 171
Raleigh, Sir Walter, 107
Ramsey, George, 46, 49
Ramsey, John, 10, 27, 45–56, 58–59, 69, 72, 120, 122, 151. *See also Craw v. Ramsey*; *Foster v. Ramsey*
Ramsey, John II, 45–47
Ramsey, Nicholas, 45–46, 52
Ramsey, Patrick, 45–46, 52
Ramsey, Robert, 45–46
Rancière, Jacques, 80–82, 145–46, 166
Reagan, Ronald, 70–71
Reasons for Naturalizing the Jews in Great Britain and Ireland (Toland), 149
refugees, 1–3, 88, 91, 171. *See also* Huguenots; Palatines
religions. *See* Catholicism; Protestantism
reproduction, 63, 71–72
reverse apostrophe, 158
Riceour, Paul, 74–75
Richardson, Samuel, 12, 19, 28, 77–80, 119–25, 141, 150, 191–92n17. *See also Clarissa*; *History of Sir Charles Grandison, The*; *Pamela*
Riddell, Chris, 67
Robert Calvin's Case. See Calvin's Case (1608)
Robinson Crusoe (Defoe): Catholicism in, 3, 13, 68, 88, 95, 98–104, 108, 110–11, 137, 140; colonialism in, 85, 104–8, 110, 186n3; Crusoe's father's naturalization, 13, 66–68, 85–87, 91–92, 94, 109, 131, 154; Crusoe's naturalization, 13, 73, 82, 89, 97–98, 111, 136, 170, 188n26; as an English novel, 19, 67, 85, 104–5, 111, 115, 187n12; paranationality in, 88, 95–96, 111, 115; Protestantism in, 85, 88, 98–104; slavery in, 28, 68, 82, 88, 93, 104, 106, 108, 170
romance novels, 28, 78–79, 115–16, 122, 136, 140–41
Rome (ancient), 49–51, 55, 105. *See also* Plutarch; Tacitus

Rousseau, Jean-Jacques: *Confessions*, 154, 157; *Julie*, 81
Roxana, the Fortunate Mistress (Defoe), 3, 12, 89
Royal Commission (1868), 35–36

Sahlin, Peter, 128
Said, Edward, 104–5, 108, 116
Schlegel, Friedrich, 76
Scotland: antenati and postnati, 38–39, 42–43, 45–46, 52, 72; and English subjecthood, 8, 36–47, 60, 80, 114, 120, 122, 181n16, 182n23; French people in, 64; in novels, 13, 77; property rights in, 7–8, 40. *See also Calvin's Case* (1608); Union of the Crowns (1603)
Scott, Walter, 13, 85, 156; *Guy Mannering*, 77
Second World War, 163
Sentimental Journey through France and Italy, A (Sterne), 12, 82, 117, 125–33, 135, 138, 140, 159–60, 192–93n30, 194n13
sentimental novels, 13, 81–82, 118, 125–30, 132, 192n29, 193n32. *See also individual titles*
Seven Years' War, 133
Shakespeare, William: *Hamlet*, 126, 129–32, 159–60; *Merchant of Venice*, 147–48, 151–52; *Othello*, 114
Sharpe, Granville, 5, 138
Shelley, Mary, 12, 19, 27, 147, 155–56, 167, 195n22, 195n25. *See also Frankenstein*
Shelley, Percy, 156
Sierra Leone Resettlement Scheme, 5, 138
Slaughter, Joseph, 73, 191n8
slavery: abolition of, 138; in America, 5, 26; in ancient Rome, 49–51; in novels, 13, 77; in *Robinson Crusoe*, 28, 68, 82, 88, 93, 104, 106, 108, 170; in *The Wanderer*, 119, 136–37, 139
Smith, Charlotte: *Celestina*, 13
Smollett, Tobias, 12, 19, 28, 82, 115, 118, 125, 141. *See also Adventures of Ferdinand Count Fathom, The*
Somerville, Siobhan, 71–72
Sophia of Hanover, 8
Spain, 19, 105–7, 110, 115, 123, 148
Spivak, Gayatri, 162, 166, 196n31
Srinivasan, Ragini, 22
Sterne, Laurence, 12, 19, 28, 125–26, 129, 150, 192n29; *Tristram Shandy*, 130. *See also Sentimental Journey through France and Italy, A*
subject formation, 8–9, 14–15, 18, 22–24, 34–36, 64–65, 91, 147, 172

Sussman, Charlotte, 23
Swift, Jonathan, 6, 92, 102, 176n18, 189n53; *Gulliver's Travels*, 103
Switzerland, 29, 154–55
synkrisis, 157

Tacitus: *Annals*, 145–47, 157, 165
Test Acts (1673), 101
Thirty Years' War, 92
Toland, John, 149
transnationality, 20–21, 98, 115, 117–18, 121–24, 130, 173
travel narratives, 116, 125, 127
Trumpener, Katie: *Bardic Nationalism*, 177n36
Tucker, Josiah, 12

Union of the Crowns (1603), 8, 18, 36–39, 44–45, 114, 120
United Irishmen uprising (1798), 149
United Kingdom, 1, 18, 171. *See also* England; Ireland; Scotland; Wales
United States: borders in, 33; citizenship in, 6, 8, 40, 70–71, 170; and England, 35, 93, 107; Indigenous peoples in, 23; naturalization in, 1, 5–6, 55, 72, 89; revolution in, 5, 20, 137, 170–71; slavery in, 5, 26

universal naturalization, 4–5, 55, 122, 138
US Department of Homeland Security, 119

Vaughan, John, 50, 52–53

Wald, Priscilla, 69
Wales, 13, 18, 177n36
Wanderer; or Female Difficulties, The (Burney), 13, 117, 133–40, 152, 165, 171
Watt, Ian, 15, 59, 68, 85, 96, 116, 176n26
Wentworth, John, 66
Wentworth, Thomas, 66
West Indies, 13, 135, 137
William III, 86
William of Orange, 8
Williams, Raymond: "Ideas of Nature," 62; *Keywords: A Vocabulary of Culture and Society*, 27, 62–63
Woman of Colour, The (Anon.), 13, 191n11
Woolf, Virginia: *Mrs. Dalloway*, 77
Wordsworth, William, 62

Yorick. See *Sentimental Journey through France and Italy, A*
York, UK, 66, 85–86

Zweig, Stefan, 169

www.ingramcontent.com/pod-product-compliance
Lightning Source LLC
Chambersburg PA
CBHW022019220426
43663CB00007B/1138